Framing the Net

The Internet and Human Rights

Rikke Frank Jørgensen
The Danish Institute for Human Rights

Edward Elgar
Cheltenham, UK • Northampton, MA, USA

Published by
Edward Elgar Publishing Limited
The Lypiatts
15 Lansdown Road
Cheltenham
Glos GL50 2JA
UK

Edward Elgar Publishing, Inc.
William Pratt House
9 Dewey Court
Northampton
Massachusetts 01060
USA

A catalogue record for this book
is available from the British Library

Library of Congress Control Number: 2013935045

This book is available electronically in the ElgarOnline.com Law Subject Collection, E-ISBN 978 1 78254 080 9

MIX
Paper from
responsible sources
FSC® C013056
FSC
www.fsc.org

ISBN 978 1 78254 079 3

Printed and bound in Great Britain by T.J. International Ltd, Padstow

Contents

Preface vii
List of abbreviations xi

Introduction 1

PART I HUMAN RIGHTS IN THE INTERNET ERA

1. Theorizing the internet era 17
2. Revisiting public and private 25
3. Human rights 33

PART II FRAMING THE NET

4. The internet as infrastructure 65
5. The internet as public sphere 81
6. The internet as a medium 107
7. The internet as culture 122

PART III ICT AND SOCIAL CHANGE

8. ICT as a tool for empowerment in Uganda 147
9. Wikipedia as a platform for community life and collaboration 181
10. Conclusion 216

Appendix A: Summary of internet metaphors 224
Appendix B: List of interviewees (Uganda) 225
Appendix C: List of interviewees (Wikipedia) 227
Bibliography 228
Glossary 257
Index 259

Preface

My engagement with internet politics and activism started in the mid-1990s. In 1995 Denmark had launched its first Ministry for Research and Information Technology, and I was fortunate to join a group of enthusiastic people working on the first Danish 'information society' strategy. At that time people in the ministry were still debating whether the internet was a passing phenomenon, thus whether it made sense to strategize on its societal implications. In the report that laid the framework for the information society policy, the Dybkjær–Christensen report from 1994, the internet is not mentioned once. In the following years, however, policy issues related to the internet continued to emerge, including issues such as privacy and security, digital signatures, electronic commerce, design and accessibility, digital divides, use of computers in primary schools, digital libraries, use of electronic health records, online public services, and so forth.

In 2000 human rights issues related to the internet had started to surface in Danish debate, and some friends and I founded Digital Rights, a small grass-roots organization concerned with human rights protection on the internet. Over the next ten years Digital Rights engaged in advocacy related to, among other things, workplace surveillance, anti-terrorism legislation, data retention, internet filters at public libraries, and self-regulation by internet service providers. In the beginning this was mainly at national level, but in 2002 we took part in the formation of European Digital Rights (EDRI), which has now grown into a 30-plus network of organizations from across Europe involved in internet-related standard-setting and advocacy from a human rights perspective.

Parallel to this work at grass-roots level, I started to work for the Danish Institute for Human Rights (DIHR) in 2001. The institute was well renowned in the human rights community, but with limited focus on information and communication technology (ICT) issues. In 2002, however, the first United Nations World Summit on the Information Society (WSIS) was announced, and with this both DIHR's and my own involvement in the international ICT policy field took off. WSIS comprised two summits. The first was held in Geneva in December 2003 and the second in Tunis in November 2005, with numerous preparatory meetings in between. The WSIS process brought together a variety of non-governmental organizations (NGOs), academics, companies, and state representatives to negotiate and adopt a 'Declaration of Principles' and 'Plan of Action' for the information society. The summit was the first attempt by the United Nations to address the linkage between development and global communication policy, with resolution 56/183 as the formal mandate (United Nations General Assembly 31 January 2002).

In the WSIS process it was frequently stressed that ICT, and in particular the internet, holds great potential for advancing human rights, not least in the developing world. One of the political commitments that emerged from WSIS was that governments agreed on promoting this potential, and declared human rights the baseline for ICT policy (World Summit on the Information Society 2003). Furthermore, it was stressed that civil society should play a key role in the development of the information society. The WSIS negotiations gave rise to several controversies related to the development of the information society, especially concerning US control over the internet, financing digital divides, and promoting and protecting human rights online (Drake and Jørgensen 2006: 36). The summit was also controversial with regard to civil society participation. While civil society was formally included in the process, participation was de facto restricted by lack of the financial means that participation required, resulting in a geographic and gender-based imbalance. Also, since civil society had no voting rights, its role was limited to that of observer with the right to submit written contributions and with some restricted speaking rights.[1]

During the WSIS process I carried out two different roles: one as human rights adviser to the Danish governmental delegation, the second as co-coordinator of civil society's Human Rights Caucus together with Meryem Marzouki, head of the French NGO 'Imaginons un Réseau Internet Solidaire' (IRIS). The Danish government, together with Germany and a few other countries, had included representation from civil society or national human rights institutions in their delegation, which provided a unique opportunity for more informal discussions on controversial issues with government officials.

Two issues were of particular importance to the Human Rights Caucus during the process: first, to have states endorse a commitment to the Universal Declaration of Human Rights in the WSIS Declaration of Principles, and second, to apply human rights standards as the baseline in specific policy areas. Some of the contentious policy issues included, in no particular order, privatized law enforcement, content regulation, online censorship, imprisonment of internet journalists, privacy and data

[1] For an analysis of civil society participation in the WSIS process see Servaes et al. (2006) and Dutton and Peltu (2010).

protection, cyber security, file sharing, access to knowledge, and intellectual property rights.[2]

While participating in these policy debates, both at national and international level, I frequently noticed how various actors frame the internet differently when approaching it as a subject for policy making. Some address it as a new, though different, medium and refer to media law when debating regulation of the internet. Others approach it primarily as a global infrastructure that needs to be secured and maintained. Some approach it as a public sphere to which everyone should have access, while others emphasize the specific social norms and values that exist online. The different framings typically relate to different aspects of internet use, as well as competing and often vaguely defined claims related to the internet as a public and private realm. Inspired by this experience, I set out to examine how various framings of the internet shape specific human rights issues. The analysis is carried out in the broad context of the way human rights are translated and applied in the internet era in academic literature, in the international community's policy discourse, and at local level.

The book is based on my PhD dissertation, which I conducted at the Institute for Communication, Business and ICT at Roskilde University and as a PhD fellow at the Danish Institute for Human Right. It is, however, substantively revised, taking into account developments that have occurred since I defended the thesis in January 2012.

I am grateful for all the brilliant and engaged people from all over the world I have met throughout my work in this field, many of whom have become friends. While it is impossible to name everyone, I want to mention Meryem Marzouki, Karen Banks, Anriette Esterhuysen, Dorothy Okello, Sharon Hom, Diana Bronson, Deborah Hurley, Marc Rotenberg, Stephanie Perrin, Jane Johnsen, Ralf Bendrath, Markus Beckedahl, Heike Jensen, Jeanette Hofmann, Frédéric Dubois, Michel Lambert, Gus Hosein, David Banisar, Simon Davis, Ian Brown, Joris von Hoboken, Sjoera Nas, Andreas Krisch, Urs Gasser, Fernando Bermejo, Ryan O'Toole, Tanja Krabbe, Tomas Kønigsfeldt, Per Helge Sørensen, Anders Kjærulff, Birgitte Kofod Olsen, Wolfgang Benedek, Matthias Ketterman, Lee Hibbard, Lisa Horner, Dixie Hawtin, Milton Müller, Wolfgang Kleinwachter, William Drake, Avri Dora, Tomas Tufte, and Jens Hoff. A special note of thanks goes to the people from Uganda and Wikipedia who agreed to participate in my case studies and provided valuable insights. I also wish to thank my

---

[2] *Human Rights in the Global Information Society* (Jørgensen 2006) was created on the back of WSIS. Each chapter addresses the challenges and opportunities a particular human right faces in the internet era.

dear colleagues and friends at the Danish Institute for Human Rights, who have provided an inspiring and fun working base for the past 12 years.

A heartfelt thanks goes to my family and friends who have supported me each in their own way, and especially to my parents who continue to provide me with invaluable support.

I dedicate this book to my sons Oscar and Anton, with love and gratitude.

Abbreviations

A2K	Access to Knowledge
ACLU	American Civil Liberties Union
ACTA	Anti-Counterfeiting Trade Agreement
AoIR	Association of Internet Researchers
APC	Association for Progressive Communications
BROSDI	Busoga Rural Open Source and Development Initiative
CC	Creative Commons
CEEWA-U	Council for Economic Empowerment for Women of Africa, Uganda Chapter
CoE	Council of Europe
CRIS	Communication Rights in the Information Society
CSCW	computer-supported cooperative work
CSISAC	Civil Society Information Society Advisory Committee
DNS	Domain Name System
DOC	(US) Department of Commerce
DPA	Data Protection Agency
EAAI	Enhancing Access to Agricultural Information
EASSI	East African Sub-regional Support Initiative for the Advancement of Women
EC	The European Commission
ECHR	The European Convention on Human Rights
ECtHR	The European Court of Human Rights
EDRI	European Digital Rights
EFF	Electronic Frontier Foundation
EPIC	Electronic Privacy Information Center
EU	The European Union
FOSS	Free and Open Source Software
GAC	Governmental Advisory Committee
GFDL	GNU Free Documentation License
GNI	Global Network Initiative
gTLD	generic top level domain names
HIVOS	The Humanist Institute for Development Cooperation
IANA	Internet Assigned Numbers Authority
ICANN	The Internet Corporation for Assigned Names and Numbers

ICCPR	International Covenant on Civil and Political Rights
ICESCR	International Covenant on Economic, Social and Cultural Rights
ICT	Information and communication technology
IGF	The Internet Governance Forum
IP	Internet Protocol/intellectual property
ISIS	Women's International Cross Cultural Exchange
ISP	Internet service provider
ITU	International Telecommunication Union
KIC	Kubera Information Centre
MoU	Memorandum of Understanding
NGO	Non-governmental organization
NSI	Network Solutions
NHRI	National Human Rights Institution
NPOV	Neutral point of view
NWICO	New world information and communication order
OA	Open access
OAS	The Organization of American States
OECD	Organization for Economic Co-operation and Development
ONI	Open Net Initiative
OSCE	Organization for Security and Co-operation in Europe
PI	Privacy International
RFC	Request for comments
STS	Science and technology studies
TCP/IP	Transmission Control Protocol/Internet Protocol
UDHR	The Universal Declaration of Human Rights
UNESCO	United Nations Educational, Scientific and Cultural Organization
UN	United Nations
UNDP	United Nations Development Programme
WOUGNET	The Women of Uganda Network
WIPO	The World Intellectual Property Organization
WSIS	The World Summit on the Information Society

Introduction

> So as technology hurtles forward, we must think back to that legacy [Universal Declaration of Human Rights]. We need to synchronize our technological progress with our principles … Today, we find an urgent need to protect these freedoms on the digital frontiers of the 21st century.
>
> (Clinton 2010)

THE INTERNET AND HUMAN RIGHTS

The human rights implications of internet use have been subject to debate since the mid-1990s, yet recently the agenda has taken on a new momentum.[1] Over the past couple of years civil society, academics, policy makers and companies practically compete to highlight the role of the internet as a tool for social change with policy implications in a number of spheres.

At the beginning of 2011 the uprisings in North Africa and the Middle East gave rise to the term 'Facebook revolution', indicating the role that social media played as a resource to organize and distribute information amongst the individuals and groups opposing the regime.[2] During the uprisings various restrictions were imposed on internet access in several countries, and subsequently the former Egyptian president and two of his officials were fined US$90m for cutting internet and mobile phone communications (UPI 28 May 2011). At a gathering in Copenhagen in May 2011 a number of the participating bloggers, activists, writers, and so on, shared their stories and debated the role of the internet in the revolution.[3] At that meeting several of the speakers stressed that while the revolution

[1] By the internet I am referring to a global information and communication system that is linked together via the TCP/IP protocol (Federal Networking Council Resolution 1995).

[2] See, for example, the coverage in *The Guardian* (Naughton 23 January 2011). Also, the Iranian revolt in 2009 was spoken of as something that would not have happened without Twitter (Morozov 2011: 2–3).

[3] Conference on Cyber Activism, 9 May 2011, in Copenhagen. Arranged by Kvinfo Information, available at: http://forside.kvinfo.dk/nyhed/arabiske-kvinder-online-og-i-front, retrieved 12 October 2012. The meeting was covered in the Danish newspaper *Weekendavisen* (Rifbjerg 13 May 2011).

did not start in cyberspace, social media did provide an important platform for sharing information and mobilizing voices. As a consequence, internet freedom is now being debated as part of the new Egyptian Constitution.[4]

At policy level, the link between the internet and human rights has recently been on the agenda at several high-level meetings. At the 17th session of the United Nations (UN) Human Rights Council in June 2011, the UN for the first time debated a report specifically focused on the internet and the right to freedom of expression. The report produced by the UN Special Rapporteur on the promotion and protection of the right to freedom of opinion and expression addresses the opportunities and challenges that the internet poses to the right to freedom of expression (La Rue 2011). The report stresses that the internet has become an indispensable tool for realizing a range of human rights, combating inequality, and accelerating development and human progress. In consequence, ensuring universal access to the internet should be a priority for all states (La Rue 2011: para. 85). The report also emphasizes that censorship measures should never be delegated to private entities, and that intermediaries should not be held liable for refusing to take action that infringes individuals' human rights (La Rue 2011: para. 75).[5] Subsequently the Swedish Minister of Foreign Affairs, on behalf of 41 states, supported the report and stressed that 'For us, one principle is very basic: The same rights that people have offline – freedom of expression, including the freedom to seek information, freedom of assembly and association, amongst others – must also be protected online' (Bildt 10 June 2011).

More or less at the same time, the internet was addressed in the Deauville Declaration: Internet, as an outcome of the G8 meeting in Paris.[6] The Declaration stresses that the leaders commit to 'encourage the use of the Internet as a tool to advance human rights and democratic participation throughout the world' (Article 13). It also iterates that the principles of openness, transparency and freedom of the internet have been key to its development and success, and must, together with non-discrimination and fair competition, continue to be an essential force behind its development (Article 9).[7] As part of the G8 meeting, the German Minister of Foreign

---

[4] Speech by Lina Attalah, 9 May 2011, at the Conference on Cyber Activism in Copenhagen.

[5] The report was prepared in consultation with a number of organizations, including civil society networks such as the Association for Progressive Communications (APC) and European Digital Rights (EDRI). See http://www.edri.org/edrigram/number9.11/un-report-online-censorship, retrieved 12 October 2012.

[6] The Declaration is available at: http://www.g8.utoronto.ca/summit/2011deauville/2011-internet-en.html, retrieved 12 October 2012.

[7] The Declaration has been criticized by civil society groups for not recognizing the protection of human rights as core principles above all others, rather than

Affairs spoke at length about freedoms in cyberspace, stressing that free access to the internet is a human right, and that freedom of expression and freedom of association are only protected in the twenty-first century if these rights are also valid in cyberspace.[8]

Most recently the UN Human Rights Council has by consensus adopted a resolution on the promotion, protection and enjoyment of human rights on the internet. Presented by Sweden, the resolution affirms that 'the same rights people have offline must also be protected online' (United Nations Human Rights Committee 5 July 2012).

The above examples highlight how policy makers increasingly embrace the notion of internet freedoms, and stress that these are essential to an internet based on human rights standards.[9] At the same time, however, just as many attempts to increase control of the internet may be found, including in democratic countries. One example is the proposal of a virtual Schengen border around EU countries, in order to strengthen control over dissemination of information to and from European Union (EU) member states.[10] The proposal suggests that European cyberspace should have 'virtual access points' and that internet service providers would block illicit content at these border points on the basis of an EU blacklist. Similar to physical roadblocks, access points are suggested in order to strengthen regional control over the flow of information into the EU region. The European Commission (EC) has refuted the assertion that the virtual Schengen border represents official EU policy,[11] yet the security of European cyberspace is an ongoing policy issue within the EU.

On a similar note, scholars have claimed the 'Rise of a Cybered Westphalian Age' pointing to national and regional border-making in cyberspace:

---

including them in a framework to be balanced with the protection of intellectual property. See, for example, the ARTICLE 19 response available at: http://www.article19.org/resources.php/resource/1774/en/g8-the-deauville-declaration-on-internet-fails-to-recognise-importance-of-human-rights-including-freedom-of-expression, retrieved 12 October 2012.

[8] The speech was printed in the German newspaper *Frankfurter Rundschau* (Westerwelle 27 May 2011).

[9] The notion of internet freedom has been contested for the cyber-utopianism and internet-centrism often associated with its use (Morozov 2011: 318).

[10] See, for example, the coverage in EDRI-Gram 9.9, 4 May 2011, available at: http://www.edri.org/edrigram/number9.9/virtual-schengen-border, retrieved 12 October 2012.

[11] In response to a question raised by Christian Engström, member of the European Parliament for Piratpartiet, Sweden, Commissioner Cecilia Malmström replied that the notion of a virtual EU border appeared in a presentation by a national delegate (Hungary) and was not to be interpreted as EU policy as such (European Commission 20 June 2011).

> From the Chinese intent to create their own controlled internal Internet, to increasingly controlled access to the Internet in less-democratic states, to the rise of Internet filters and rules in Western democracies, states are establishing the bounds of their sovereign control in the virtual world in the name of security and economic sustainability.
>
> (Demchak et al. 2011: 32)

As a recent example of expanding national control in cyberspace, the Iranian government has announced the first phase of a national internet, also referred to as 'Our Own Internet', while blocking access to Google and Gmail.[12] Moreover, in order to prevent and react to 'cyber warfare' (attacks on a country's digital infrastructure by another country) the USA and the EU have strengthened the military grip on the internet via the US Cyber Command (USCYBERCOM) and the European Network and Information Security Agency (ENISA) respectively.[13]

What may at a first glance look like increased support for internet freedoms is thus countered by at least as many examples of increased control of the internet.[14] This is indicative of competing interests such as freedom versus control, but also indicates essentially different perspectives toward the internet. The debate on internet freedom is focused on the internet as a democratic space closely linked to human rights and social change. Participants in this discourse may easily agree upon the importance of internet policies that are respectful of human rights, and repeatedly condemn attempts to unduly restrict those freedoms – for example at the UN Human Rights Council. The debate on cyber security, by contrast, refers to the internet as a critical national infrastructure that needs to be secured and controlled in order to protect vital interests of society. Participants in this discourse are not ignorant of human rights, yet their primary concern lies with infrastructure protection, and with potential attacks on the stability of the internet, as addressed, for example, at the Military Cyber Security conference in Washington.[15]

This book argues that different framings of the internet highlight specific human rights issues. The book proposes four metaphors around which to organize our debate on human rights challenges in the internet era.

---

12 See the coverage by Reuters available at: http://www.reuters.com/article/2012/09/23/net-us-iran-internet-national-idUSBRE88M0AO20120923, retrieved 17 October 2012.

13 See http://www.enisa.europa.eu/ and http://www.defense.gov/home/features/2010/0410_cybersec/, retrieved 12 October 2012.

14 See MacKinnon (2012) for a wide list of examples of increased control over the internet.

15 See http://www.militarycybersecurity.com/, retrieved 12 October 2012.

The themes are infrastructure, public sphere, medium, and culture. The infrastructure dimension focuses on the internet as a global resource that enables communication; the public sphere dimension highlights the internet as a public space; the media dimension draws attention to the internet as a new media platform; whereas the cultural dimension focuses on the internet's social norms and practices. The themes are not seen as exclusive; on the contrary, they coexist in policy as well as in scholarly debate. Each of them, however, highlights specific features of the internet and is associated with certain human rights challenges.

BOOK OUTLINE

The book consists of three main parts and a concluding chapter.

The first part outlines and critically examines the field of human rights in the information society. This comprises a brief introduction to the notion of an information society and to some of the scholars who have made contributions in this field, in particular scholars such as Castells and Luhmann. Next, the public and private distinction is explored, as well as how it relates to the themes of infrastructure, public sphere, medium and culture, respectively. The examination of public and private is included since internet policy challenges in many instances relate to various aspects of the internet as public and private. Finally, the human rights framework is presented, including an analysis of how human rights have intersected with ICT in four different spheres: civil society; the intergovernmental sphere; the business domain; and the research sphere.

In the second part the four suggested metaphors are outlined and debated. The metaphors are presented on the back of associated research themes and human rights issues related to that particular framing. The infrastructure metaphor focuses on the internet as a universal and non-discriminatory resource; the public sphere metaphor on the new modalities for public and political life; the medium metaphor on the democratization of broadcasting and publishing; and the culture metaphor on the potential for a more participatory culture.

While the book's first two parts develop an analytical framework, the third, empirically oriented, part explores concrete spaces of internet-related social interaction, tracing the discursive, metaphoric frames that guide the involved actors' articulation of their agency. In particular, two empirical case studies (women's use of ICT in Uganda and the German Wikipedia community) are used to explore the implications of the actors' framing of these phenomena primarily in terms of the internet as public sphere and the internet as culture. Both cases address the means by which local groups deploy ICT for social change,[16] while being essentially different on most parameters. The women's groups are situated in a developing country and seek to empower local women via use of conventional media as well as the internet, whereas Wikipedia is an online community of internet-savvy users with the declared goal of enhancing the public domain of knowledge in all languages of the world.

The concluding chapter will discuss the current state of affairs with regard to human rights protection in the internet era, present some cross-cutting perspectives, and suggest areas for future research.

INTERNET METAPHORS

The notion of metaphors is inspired by the work of Krippendorff (1993) and Lakoff and Johnson (1980). In *Metaphors We Live By*, Lakoff and Johnson argue that the use of metaphors is pervasive in everyday life, in language, thought and action, and that our conceptual system is essentially metaphorical in nature. The essence of metaphors is to provide associational frameworks, enabling us to understand and experience one kind of thing in terms of another (Lakoff and Johnson 1980: 5). However, a metaphor is not merely the words used to talk about something – for example 'time is money', 'love is a journey', 'internet explorer' – but also the underlying logic or approach for addressing the issue. As stressed by Krippendorff, metaphors (1) carry explanatory structures from a familiar domain of experiences into an other domain in need of understanding and restructuring, (2) require seeing some structural similarities between these two domains, (3) have entailments for the target domain they thereby organize far beyond any initial structural similarity, and (4) organize their user's perceptions and, when acted upon, can create the realities experienced (Krippendorff 1993: 2–3). The notion of framing has both sociological and psychological foundations, but generally addresses the construction of meaning, for example via metaphors, exemplars, catchphrases, depictions, and visual images (Borah 2011: 249). By framing the internet as infrastructure, public sphere, medium and culture, respectively, the idea is to illuminate different associational frameworks from the target domain, and how these relate to specific human rights issues.

Several scholars have used metaphors to capture various features of the internet. In the internet's early days Stefik (1996) suggested four metaphors

---

[16] Social change refers to a societal transition towards greater conformity with human rights standards.

for thinking about the emerging 'information infrastructure', namely digital library (keeper of knowledge), electronic mail (communicator), electronic marketplace (trader), and digital worlds (adventurer) (Stefik 1996: xx). Kurbalija, who has been closely involved in WSIS, speaks of internet analogies such as telephony, post, television, library, photocopier, highway, high seas, and of 'baskets' of internet governance policy issues. These baskets relate to the infrastructure of the internet; the use of the internet; issues with wider impact such as intellectual property rights; and issues related to the developmental aspects of the internet (Kurbalija 2010: 22–7). The cyberspace and market of ideas metaphors are addressed, amongst others, by Gandy and Farral in their examination of cases related to enforcement of property law in cyberspace.[17] The authors argue that technically cyberspace is not a metaphor, but merely a merger of the two words *cybernetics* and *space*:

> To say that the Internet is a 'library' or a 'town square' are metaphorical constructions that involve key entailments of a source domain (library, town square) that the receiver of the message can then map on to the target domain (the Internet). In the case of cyberspace, the entailments of this source domain, other than that it is some form of space, do not emerge from common experience.
>
> (Gandy and Farral 2010)

The marketplace of ideas metaphor was widely used in policy making and judgments especially related to free speech cases, long before the advent of the internet.[18] As pointed out by the authors, there is disagreement in the legal literature as to the specific role of metaphors, for instance the extent to which the use of metaphors constrains the thinking of the court or not (Gandy and Farral 2010: 351). As a final example, Andrade investigates how metaphors such as 'giant brains', 'information highways', 'metaverse', 'cyberspace' and 'ambient intelligence' contribute to the social acceptance and implementation of technology. Drawing on Flichy's analysis of how the utopian vision of the internet was shaped (Flichy 2007), the author argues that commonly accepted metaphors are used to create a societal identification with the technology available (Norberto Gomes de Andrade 2010: 43).[19]

---

17 See also Patry (2009) on metaphors used in the 'copyright war'.

18 The metaphor was first used by Justice Holmes in his dissenting opinion in the 1919 case *Abrams* v. *United States*, available at: http://www.law.cornell.edu/supct/html/historics/USSC_CR_0250_0616_ZD.html, retrieved 12 October 2012.

19 Other examples of a metaphorical approach to the internet include Blavin and Cohen (2002) and Ratzan (2000).

The four metaphors used to structure the analysis of this book are inspired by two sources in particular. First by a broad review of internet-related literature covering communication and media studies, political science, and cultural studies. Secondly by a review of internet- and human rights-related policy discourses at the WSIS (2003–2005), at the IGF (2007 and 2009), within the EU, and at Council of Europe level. As part of this exercise, policy themes were mapped according to the human rights issues they highlighted, as illustrated in Table I.1.

As previously stressed, many competing internet-related metaphors exist; however, the four metaphors proposed here all show up in policy controversies related to social change/human rights. To give an example, the cyberspace metaphor entails no obvious connection to any specific human rights issues, whereas many human rights-related controversies relate to the public sphere metaphor (for example, access to participate in democratic life, violations of internet freedoms, participation of civil society, and so on). Obviously no one metaphor covers the multiple dimensions of the internet; however, each of them addresses specific features of the target domain, as further explained below.

The first metaphor, infrastructure, was used to characterize the internet from early on. As stressed by Stefik, the internet was originally called the 'national information infrastructure' in the USA and subsequently referred to as 'the information super highway' (Stefik 1996: xviii). When the internet (as the target domain) is referred to as an infrastructure (the source domain), it highlights that it is the basis for something else: an underlying resource in line with highways, railways or the postal system. At WSIS and the Internet Governance Forum (IGF) the infrastructure metaphor shows up in the policy debates related to, for example, the operation of the internet, that is specific themes and controversies related to coordinating and governing the internet's critical resources. As such, the infrastructure metaphor is closely related to the technology that carries the internet and that consists of various technical resources. Like other infrastructures, the internet's technical layer was constructed at a certain point in time, and is now operated and maintained on an ongoing basis.[20] In terms of social change (human rights potential), the metaphor highlights the universal and non-discriminatory characteristics of the internet's technical layer.

The second metaphor, public sphere, is reflected in a policy and scholarly debate that addresses the internet as a space for democratic participation,

---

[20] The responsibility for a number of tasks related to the daily management of the internet is vested with the US-based Internet Corporation for Assigned Names and Numbers (ICANN) on contract with the US government. The mandate and operation of ICANN was a controversial issue at WSIS, and led to the inception

Table I.1 Mapping themes at the IGF in Sharm El Sheikh (2009)

Thematic cluster*	Policy challenge	Human rights issues (not exhaustive)	Proposed metaphor
Access and diversity	How to ensure an internet for all	Access to participate online Non-discrimination Access to knowledge	Public sphere Culture
Security, openness and privacy	How to find the right balance between openness and control on the internet	Internet security Protection of online freedoms Protection of specific audiences	Infrastructure Public sphere Medium
Managing critical internet resources	How to operate and manage the internet as a global resource	HR protection in relation to a global resource	Infrastructure
Internet governance in the light of the WSIS principles	How to ensure a people-centred and inclusive development of the information society	Rights-based approach to internet policy and regulation	Cross-cutting

Note: * See the Chairman's summary (Internet Governance Forum 2009).

including themes such as access, freedoms, and resources to participate. The metaphor highlights the internet's features as a public sphere and the new modalities for democratic life enabled by the internet. Moreover, it raises policy issues related to how resources necessary for communication are made available, and to whom. Themes of access, freedoms, and resources to participate were high on the WSIS agenda and have been equally prominent on the IGF agenda.[21] With regard to social change, the public sphere metaphor points to the internet's potential for revitalizing democratic life, and in providing new mechanisms and tools for civil society groups.

---

of the Internet Governance Forum (IGF) as a global platform to discuss a broad range of issues pertaining to internet governance.

[21] IGF is organized as an annual four-day meeting with a mixture of plenary debates, workshops, exhibitions, and so on. The themes are recurring topics from the WSIS process such as access, openness, security, capacity building, and critical internet resources. See http://www.intgovforum.org/cms/, retrieved 12 October 2012.

The third metaphor, medium, shows up in discourses that address the internet as a new medium comparable to (though different from) conventional media. The specific affordances of 'new media' have been addressed in numerous publications from media and communication scholars. Commonly raised questions within this line of research include how the internet differs from previous media, its effect on the media ecosystem, and its ability to provide a structural alternative to current media powers. In the policy arena, a great amount of European internet policy speaks to the internet as a medium, which is reflected in commonly used notions such as harmful content, positive online content, media literary, protection of youth audiences, internet archiving and so forth. In other words, these notions would not be obvious from a public sphere perspective, which speaks of public discourse and democratic participation, rather than content and audiences. Neither would they describe the internet as a global resource, which is the focus of the infrastructure metaphor. With regard to social change the medium metaphor points to the internet as an open and participatory medium that democratizes access to publishing and broadcasting.

Finally, the culture metaphor shows up in literature and policy debates concerned with the social life that unfolds online and is reflected in notions such as cyberculture and cybercommunities. A large body of literature explores the internet from the perspective of social practices, focusing on the various examples of online communities, their entailed norms and values, collaborative practices, identity formation, means of self-regulation, and so forth. At policy level, a cultural take on the internet is presented among others by advocates of the free culture movement (Lessig 2004), who point to the practices of openness and sharing that occur online and argue that these practices conflict with conventional property rights regimes. The policy debates on these issues is ongoing at both UN and European level. In relation to social change, the culture metaphor highlights the potential of a more participatory culture.

CASE STUDIES

Two qualitative case studies are included in the book, addressing women's use of ICT in Uganda and the German Wikipedia. The studies are used to explore how local groups deploy and perceive communication technology as a resource for their respective courses, as well as to examine the involved actors' framing of their social practices in terms of the public sphere and the culture metaphors.

The case study research indicates an exploration of a phenomenon within its context, using a variety of data sources (Baxter and Jack 2008:

544). The case study represents 'a phenomenon of some sort occurring in a bounded context' (Huberman and Miles 1994: 440). Case study research requires a close cooperation between the researcher and the participants, while encouraging the participants to share their views on the subject matter, for example via interview.

In the Uganda case study, the unit of analysis is the Women of Uganda Network (WOUGNET) and some of their partners, whereas the second study has the German Wikipedia community as the unit of analysis. In both cases qualitative interviews, field notes, observations, informal conversations, and analysis of various written material were used to provide a thick description of the case.[22] In order to strengthen the validity of the case studies, the data material was examined for patterns and recurring arguments; multiple sources of evidence were included where possible; and key actors were asked to review the draft analysis. In order to ensure data reliability, the data collection was documented via recording and transcribing interviews, as well as by field notes (Yin 2009: 41).

The two case studies are essentially different in scope and context. Whereas the German Wikipedia study represents a loosely coupled community of individuals anchored in a virtual platform, the women's groups in Uganda share a physical base for action and deploy a mixture of conventional media and the internet. In addition, the women's groups are situated in a developing country characterized by poverty and limited access to the internet, while the German Wikipedia community represents well-connected users in a Western country.

The choice of the Uganda case study to explore how the actors involved frame their social practices in terms of the public sphere metaphor, and the German Wikipedia to examine the culture metaphor, does not imply that the German Wikipedia could not have been examined from a public sphere perspective, and likewise the Uganda case from a cultural perspective. It does imply, however, that public sphere themes related to participation in public and political life resonate with the way the women's groups describe themselves and their mission. The same is true for themes related to online cultures, for example norms of openness and sharing, which have been associated with collaborative platforms such as Wikipedia by scholars and practitioners alike. The concluding chapter will illustrate how either case study might be approached from the perspective of infrastructure, public sphere, medium and culture, respectively.

---

[22] The term 'thick description' refers to the method used by the anthropologist when he/she distils a description of a phenomenon from a complex set of practices (Geertz 1973: 382).

Data collection and analysis

The qualitative data collection and analysis focused on how the actors involved experience, perceive, and explain their practices. The selection of interviewees followed a general approach of prioritizing people who where recommended as being engaged, open, knowledgeable or in some other way important in relation to the unit of analysis. The interviews were conducted in a semi-structured form using a thematic interview guide reflecting core issues associated with the public sphere and culture metaphor. The semi-structured format allowed for improvization and to track themes that appeared during the interview, including issues that were not part of the interview guide. Similarly there were themes that were relevant in some contexts but not in others, and that were therefore omitted in some interviews.

The data for the Uganda case study was collected during a field visit in the autumn of 2007, with some updates made in 2011 on the level of internet penetration in the country and with recent examples of online censorship. During the field visit 28 interviews were conducted with WOUGNET staff, the women involved in the rural access project in Apac, and a number of people working with or in relation to WOUGNET in Kampala. I also engaged in a number of more informal conversations.[23] The majority of the 28 interviews were conducted with women and men engaged in WOUGNET, or member or partner organizations, rather than end users. As the main focus was on how local groups worked with and reflected on ICT as a resource for social change, the study prioritized people who represented a broad set of experiences with ICT at civil society level, rather than end users. I did meet with a group of local farmers in Apac, however; as the women only spoke the local language, Luo, the conversation had to be facilitated by an interpreter, and it was difficult to obtain very detailed answers.

The data collection for the Wikipedia case study was based on the large amount of text that the site in itself represents, and on seven qualitative interviews with people from the Berlin Wikipedia community, as well as a member of the Wikipedia Advisory Board, conducted in 2007 and 2009. The interviewees were recruited with a view to ensuring awareness of community norms and active participation in Wikipedia. The interviewees were identified by asking around in the community, and contacting people who were recommended as being engaged and knowledgeable Wikipedians. All

---

[23] Please refer to Appendix B for an anonymous list of interviewed people/groups.

of those interviewed are experienced Wikipedia editors and several of them have been active in Wikipedia policy spaces, nationally as well as internationally. As such, the interviewees represent people who have been active in Wikipedia more or less since the beginning, and several of the interviewees have held positions of trust within the community.[24]

The data analysis was conducted by a combination of meaning condensation/coding and narrative structuring, employing a theme-based approach (Thagaard 2004: 158–63). As part of the analysis, theme-related points from the interview scripts were identified, and relevant examples and arguments collected. In order to retain some level of privacy on the part of those interviewed, while qualifying the findings to the widest extent possible, they are identified by affiliation but not by name.

---

[24] Please refer to Appendix C for an anonymous list of interviewed people/groups.

PART I

Human rights in the internet era

The first part of the book will outline and critically examine the field of human rights in the internet era and by doing so seek to answer two interrelated questions: first, what is implied by notions such as an 'information society' and a 'networked society'?, and second, how do these societal characteristics influence the protection of human rights?

1. Theorizing the internet era

1. THE NOTION OF AN INFORMATION SOCIETY

The term 'information society' dates back to the 1960s[1] and is a contested notion with competing interpretations.[2] In a political context the term was revitalized by the American and European project to privatize and liberalize the telecom sector globally in the mid-1990s. In 1994 US Vice President Al Gore announced the creation of 'The Global Information Infrastructure', which was echoed at the European level in a number of white papers and reports (the most well known being the Report of the Bangemann High Level Expert Group from 1994). In Japan and Singapore similar initiatives took off.[3] The official rhetoric for speaking about the many political, economic, scientific, and social changes related to globalization and communication technology soon became the information society.[4] In a political context the concept of the information society was grounded in a narrative that stressed broadband access for all (households, schools and universities, public administration, and so on) as a way to provide for economic

---

[1] One of the first scholars to introduce the concept information society was Fritz Machlup in *The Production and Distribution of Knowledge in the United States* from 1962. However, the concept became widely known with Daniel Bells's *The Coming of Post-Industrial Society* from 1973 (Crawford 1983). In the late 1990s 'knowledge society' emerged as an alternative notion in some academic circles and was applied by, for example, the United Nations Educational, Scientific and Cultural Organization (UNESCO) (Burch 2005: 54).

[2] Information society theories are often divided into two philosophical positions. The first group frame it as a new emerging society – for example Bell, Lyotard and Castells – whereas the second group stress the historical continuity from previous structures – for example Habermas, Giddens and Garnham (Finnemann 2005: 126–7; Webster 2006: 6). For a critical discussion of the concept and vision of an information society see, for example, Lyon (1988: Chapter 1); Finnemann (2005: Chapter 3); Webster (2006: Chapter 2); Mansell (2009).

[3] The Singapore government launched *A Vision of an Intelligent Island* in 1993. In Japan *Reforms Towards the Intellectually Creative Society of the Twenty-first Century* was launched in 1994 (Qvortrup 2003: 163–4).

[4] The information society as a European policy theme is described in Ó Siochrú (2004).

growth. The challenge was thus to overcome social and organizational constraints in order to realize the many inherent possibilities in the new technologies (Qvortrup 2003: 164).[5]

One of the scholars who have elaborated on the implications of an information society is the Spanish sociologist Manuel Castells, who speaks to the transformation in the distribution of power with information as the key factor.[6] Castells stresses networks as the defining characteristic and dominant social structure of the information age, with the internet as the technical backbone (Castells 2001: 5). The current societal changes are formed by a globalized flow of information and by informational capitalism as something distinctively different from earlier forms of market society (Castells 1996). The term informational capitalism implies that generation, processing, and transmission of information are the fundamental source of productivity and power. Castells's theory has been criticized for placing too much emphasis on the informational dimension of current societies, thereby underestimating long-established forms of inequality as well as the role that information has always played in society (Garnham 2004/1998: 168–79). Hence elements of the information society can be seen in all societies in the history of mankind. However, the current information society differs in one important aspect, namely by connecting all countries to the same globally distributed communicative infrastructure: the internet (Finnemann 2005: 53).

2. REDISTRIBUTION OF POWER

One of Castells's key points addresses the organization of new forms of time and space: referred to as 'timeless time' and the 'space of flows'. Space is presented as the material support of time-sharing social practices, thus the space of places is the predominant space of experience, of everyday life, and of social and political control. Time is the biological rhythm turning present into past, while awaiting future. In contrast to biological time, the network society is seeking to compress time and to eliminate the traditional sequencing of time into one hypertext (timeless time). Space of flows is used to describe societal functions based on exchanges between

---

[5] When internet access started to be more widespread, especially in the USA and Europe, it was followed by a period with great commercial expectations of new online business models, called the dot.com period. The dot.com period reached its peak with a NASDAQ index at 5048.62 on 10 March 2000. Soon afterwards the bubble burst and the majority of the new online businesses closed down (Thorhauge and Bjerge 2004).

[6] Power is defined as the relational capacity that enables a social actor to influence asymmetrically the decisions of other social actor(s) in ways that favour the empowered actor's will, interests, and values (Castells 2009: 10).

electronic circuits rather than physical encounters. In the network society the logic of timeless time and space of flows is increasingly seen as the fundamental form of social domination (Castells 1997: 145–7). The increasing penetration of the space of flows by 'expressions of experience' by civil society actors is mentioned as a counter-tendency (Castells 2009).[7]

In addition, 'access' and 'recognition' are central notions in Castells's theory and in theories concerned with power more generally as indicators for measuring power, that is who is included/excluded, who is recognized/not recognized. It follows that power in the network society is related to access to the means of communication such as the internet (Hoff et al. 2006: 20). This further implies new powers assigned to those who may define or implement barriers to internet access. With regard to recognition this is related to the construction of identity, hence the need to comply with the information society's imperative of 'being online' (Castells 1996: 9). As pointed to by Hoff (2004: 38–40), the notion of access includes not only the established political structures (parliament, local council, and so on) but also increasingly new 'constituencies' of political power. These new constituencies may be a private entity, or they may be in the realm of civil society. To have access to power is thus to have access to the de facto political authorities in any given context. Further, to gain recognition is to be able to put issues on the political agenda (to influence the mobilization of bias) and to gain acceptance for these (Hoff 2004: 40).

Scholars inspired by Castells have emphasized a transformation from classical models of democracy to network models, where the state is decentred and political arenas occur across society. This implies a shift in focus from 'government to governance', as well as broader access to agenda setting by different actors both at national and international level (Hoff et al. 2006: 18–25). An example of this is the internet's potential to enable political and social networks and to mobilize civil society across borders (Florini 2000; Deibert 2002; Keane 2003; Donk et al. 2004). It also includes discourses on how the internet may strengthen civil society's ability to participate in political processes, to interact with those in power, and to gain a resource base for self-autonomy (Burch 2002; Donk et al. 2004; Earl and Kimport 2011).[8]

---

[7] In *Communication Power*, Castells elaborates how media have provided civil society with new means of local action and global connection (Castells 2009). The key affordances of activism in the internet age are also addressed in *Digitally Enabled Social Change* by Earl and Kimport (2011).

[8] Stalder has argued that human rights may serve as cultural codes that can travel across networks and help reinvent local democracy. 'A renewal of fundamental rights could serve as a starting point for this project to reinvent democracy in

3. MODERNITY AND COMPLEXITY

Another scholar with a grand theory of modern society is the German sociologist Niklas Luhmann.[9] Luhmann emphasizes the hypercomplex character of modern society and the focus on communication as a means to reduce complexity at individual, organizational, and societal level. In this account of modern society notions of space and territory are replaced with notions of communicative borders, which is interesting since the internet represents a communicative system rather than a space-bound territory.[10]

Luhmann's analysis of modernity is in many ways in line with that of Habermas and Giddens with an emphasis on increased complexity, functional differentiation, and contingency as a tendency and premise in modern society and life. The increasing number of functionally differentiated subsystems – such as economics, justice, politics, art, science – represent society's way of handling an increasing level of social complexity. Accordingly, complexity reduction is seen as the core mechanism whereby social systems differentiate into subsystems, each specialized in handling specific types of complexity (legal issues, economic issues, policy issues, love issues, and so on). However, whereas most modernists keep the rational subject as the point of departure for analysing processes of complexity and contingency, Luhmann suggests a level of abstraction in which subjects are replaced by living systems that produce life, and psychic and social systems that produce meaning. Social systems are further divided into society, organizations, and interactions (Luhmann 1986: 173).

4. SOCIAL SYSTEMS

Social systems are described as systems of communication, defined by a boundary between the system and its environment. Communication within a given social system, such as an organization, operates by a selection process that selects a limited amount of the information available, thereby

---

the space of places, using the space of flows to expand the range of cultural expression, rather than diminishing it' (Stalder 2005: 69).

[9] Luhmann has written extensively on a variety of subjects, including law, economy, politics, religion, mass media, and communication. Until his death in 1998, he had an ongoing dispute with Jürgen Habermas, concerning among other things Habermas's ideal of communicative rationality vis-à-vis Luhmann's system approach to sociology.

[10] For a critique of Luhmann's work see, for example, Viskovatoff (1999) and Mathur (2005).

constantly reducing complexity. Each system has a distinctive identity – the border between system and environment, which is constantly reproduced in its communicative process according to what information is selected as meaningful and what is not. If a system fails to maintain its identity, it ceases to exist as a system and dissolves. Social systems are autopoietically closed since they use and rely on resources from their environment, while not allowing those resources to become part of the operation of the systems.[11] As communication does not think, and thoughts do not talk, they belong to different autopoietic systems. These closed systems, however, interact through interpenetration/communicative coupling, which is the concept used when systems make their complexity available for one another, without becoming one and the same system. The environment can also irritate the system when it is produced as information within the system. Differentiating between psychic and social systems is in Luhmann's universe what makes societies able to observe themselves, which is the closest the theory gets to a concept of rationality. Rationality is thus related to the ability to reflect on the difference between system and environment.

5. THE ROLE OF COMMUNICATION

Two alternative views of communication have influenced modern media theory: one being the 'transmission view', the other the 'ritual view'. According to the transmission view, media are transmitting information from a sender to a receiver, with an assumed correspondence between reality and its mediated representation. This perspective has dominated Western media theory since Shannon and Weaver (1949) presented their communication model in the 1930s. The theoretical presumption is a common world that can be communicated via a common code system. In contrast, the main focus of the ritual view is the construct of a common world. The media are not primarily seen as transmitters but rather as dramatists building public stages of narratives, thereby reducing complexity to simple societal schemata. The common world is not transmitted but rather

[11] Luhmann is inspired by the Chilean biologist Maturana's definition of autopoietic systems as 'systems that are defined as unities, as networks of productions of components, that recursively, through their interactions, generate and realize the network that produces them and constitute, in the space in which they exist, the boundaries of the network as components that participate in the realization of the network' (Maturana cited in Luhmann 1986: 174). Luhmann transfers the concept of autopoietic (literally: self-creation) from the work of Maturana and Varelas on cognitive biology and makes it a core concept in his theory of social systems.

created in a network of actors and audiences (Carey 1989 referenced in Qvortrup 2003: 125–6).

Luhmann's communication model emphasizes communication as a selection of meaning/understanding made by the social system itself, rather than something being transmitted. The communication process is described as a three-phased selection process consisting of selection of information, selection of form, and selection of understanding. A fourth element outside the communication process itself is the reaction, thus whether the system chooses to act on the basis of the communication (Luhmann 1992: 253). Through the process of communication the social system is 'irritated' and develops its inner complexity, which again makes it more capable of handling complexity in its environment. With regard to the media these are categorized as dissemination and effect media, respectively. The first category is media in the more conventional sense (print, radio, television). These media are means for irritating society by making communicative choices on the basis of their own criteria, thereby 'keeping society on its toes' (Luhmann 2000: 22). By comparison, the function of effect media is to reduce the potential communicative couplings. This is achieved by providing the social system with 'interpretation codes' according to which communication is selected. These are described as binary codes indicating the difference, which guide how information is selected, processed, and understood within each system, for example love/not love, true/false, economic gains/losses, legal/illegal.

6. THE INTERNET AS A HYPERCOMPLEX STRUCTURAL MATCH

Qvortrup is one of the scholars who has applied Luhmann's theory to the internet, arguing that there are certain qualities of the internet, a 'structural match', that relate it to the characteristics of modern societies (Qvortrup 2003: 166).[12] Current societies are confronting an immense complexity because so many social actions have become communicatively

[12] A similar line of argument is found in Rasmussen (2003). Drawing on Luhmann's theory, Rasmussen argues that the technical model of the internet (packet-switching and distributed routing) point towards central characteristics of modern societies, and the way distributed and contingent communication reproduce these societies (Rasmussen 2003: 462–3). There is thus some compatibility between the development of the internet and the transformation of the societies in which it operates; hence the internet suggests a distributed society based on an ability to handle risk rather than central control (Rasmussen 2003: 62).

assessable, and the response or stabilizing factor to deal with this social complexity is communication-based processes of coordination. In this 'polycentric society', information and communication technologies such as the internet are seen as socially shaped technologies formed by the need for decentred processes of mutual observation and coordination among sub-centres (Qvortrup 2003: 4–5). From this perspective, the differentiation of the current and emerging society is primarily based on processes of inclusion and exclusion, shaped by the ability to manage complexity, rather than classes determined by the ownership of means of production. Further, it is based on a different mechanism of structuration compared to earlier societies, namely informed decisions rather than *ex ante* given principles (Qvortrup 2003: 10–11). The internet provides for an unseen number of structural couplings, thus an opportunity to relate to an indefinite number of communications, while also providing for mechanisms to select only a few of these communications. It is a dissemination medium and an effect medium combined in one communicative structure. 'Maybe this is the real revolutionary effect of the internet: that it copies the structure of society into the medium, providing the internet with an extraordinary social complexity-management potential compared with any other medium' (Qvortrup 2003: 174).

Particular structural qualities of the hypercomplex society have thus been transformed into the structure of the internet, particularly the potential for managing complexity. The internet is not, however, an autopoietic system in the Luhmann sense since it does not create its own elements in a closed process. It consists of countless interaction systems, which are established and dissolved on an ongoing basis, rather than a stable social system (Qvortrup 2003: 176). The internet resembles a global society composed of millions of interactions, while at the same time providing for spontaneous self-organization, rather than being organized in advance.[13]

In summary, Castells and Luhmann offer two different perspectives on the information society located within a theoretical narrative of modernity. Both scholars emphasize the evolution of increasingly complex societies, and the importance of communication as a constituting factor within these societies. Yet their theories also differ in several aspects. Whereas Castells stresses the evolution from nation states to a global network society, Luhmann's theory addresses modern society as differentiated functional

---

[13] Internet protocols such as URI, HTTP, and HTML are used as examples of how this self-organization is facilitated at the technical level by providing for text/file exchange and links. 'The WWW has the capability of allowing its users to change its own capabilities' (Andersen quoted in Qvortrup 2003: 181).

subsystems, which are by nature global and not addressed in relation to the nation state. Whereas Castells stresses the power of networks, Luhmann has no cross-cutting theme of power, except as a code of communication within the political subsystem. As such Luhmann's theory is at a very different level of abstraction, and not easy to compare with Castells's theory, or most other theories for that matter. However, despite its level of abstraction, the concept of social systems and of communication has been a source of inspiration for this book, including how it relates to various characteristics of the internet. Similarly with Castells's debate on transformation of power in the networked society, which has inspired in particular the elaboration of the role of the internet in relation to public participation (public sphere metaphor).

2. Revisiting public and private

> If you want to keep something private, that's the hard part. And so in addition to collapsing to this dichotomy of public and private, we've also go[t] this world where keeping things private is a costly, expensive activity. And making things public is effortless and cheap.
>
> (Shirky quoted in BigThink 6 July 2010)

One of the characteristics of the internet era is the way it changes the modalities for public and private life. Public life is increasingly recorded, trackable, shareable, and utilized as a commodity to generate income. Private life, by contrast, requires a special effort, which is an option that one has to activate. Moreover, policy controversies related to internet regulation in many cases concern conflicting interests related to various internet domains and activities as public in relation to private. This is the case, for example, in controversies where ownership rights conflict with online practices of sharing information. In order to understand the human rights implications of these dynamics, the public/private distinction is next explored, including how it relates to the internet metaphors presented in the second part of this book.

1. INTRODUCING PUBLIC AND PRIVATE

'Public' and 'Private' have served as meta-categories in Western academic discourse, legal practice, and policy debates since classical antiquity (Weintraub 1997: xi). The distinction may be used to describe a boundary between the private world of intimacy and the public world of sociability, or the public (visible, open for all) character of processes as opposed to private processes (closed, limited entry), or particular interests (economic or individual) as different from general (public) interest.

Often the public/private notions are used in an implicit way without clarifying their exact meaning, thus opening up the possibility of a blurred landscape of assumptions and implications. As the notions ascribe the meaning as being one element in a paired opposition, it is important to know what is being contrasted against in any given context. 'Debates about how to cut up the social world between public and private are rarely innocent analytical exercises, since they often carry powerful normative implications – but quite disparate normative implications, depending on context and perspective'

(Weintraub 1997: 3). The public/private dichotomy has been subject to intense critique, including whether the distinction is in fact meaningful.[1] It has also been suggested that rather than a paired opposition, public and private is better described along a continuum (Sveningsson 2009: 74). Others have stressed the need for a third category, 'the social' (Arendt 1958: 38), or a 'third place' (Oldenburg 1989: 20). Critical legal scholars have argued that the public/private distinction has lost its capacity to capture plausibly features of reality and specify differences that are consistent and relevant for legal decision making (Kennedy quoted in Turkel 1992: 219).

In the legal field the distinction between public and private law has been a priori categories, with pre-eminence over other distinctions, since the neo-Kantian philosophy of law (Radbruch quoted in Bobbio 1989: 2). In legal language, the notions are defined independently of each other, though public is stronger in the sense that private may be defined as not-public, but seldom the other way around. Whereas public law regulates relationships between those in power and those governed, private law regulates relationships between equals.[2] Public law is the only legitimate foundation for the state since, first, the bonds that unite the state to its citizens are permanent and irrevocable, whereas contractual bonds can be revoked, and second, the state can in exceptional circumstances demand the sacrifice of life from its citizens, which is contractually speaking not an option (Bobbio 1989: 7). The proponents for the primacy of private and public law respectively are generally linked to the right and left side of the political spectrum albeit with some nuances.[3]

In the following sections the public/private distinction is addressed as different domains of society characterized by different interests, and as the status of any particular kind of activity or information.[4]

---

1 See, for example, Benn and Gaus (1983); Bobbio (1989); Turkel (1992); Weintraub (1997); Gal (2002).

2 Bobbio stress that there are exemptions to this, such as the regulation of the family, that belong to the realm of private law, but that historically do not constitute a regulation between equals (Bobbio 1989: 4–5).

3 'Indeed the two processes – the publicization of the private and the privatization of the public – are not incompatible and in fact interpenetrate each other. The first reflects the process of the subordination of private interests to collective interests represented by a state which increasingly surrounds and invades civil society; the second represents the revenge of private interests through the formation of large organized groups which make use of the public apparatus in order to achieve their own aims' (Bobbio 1989: 17).

4 The distinction is inspired by Weintraub's two images of public and private: (1) what is hidden or withdrawn versus what is open, revealed, or accessible; (2) what is individual, or pertains only to an individual, versus what is collective, or affects the interests of a collectivity of individuals (Weintraub 1997: 5).

2. PUBLIC AND PRIVATE AS DIFFERENT DOMAINS OF SOCIETY

At least four public and private distinctions operate under the surface of current scholarly as well as political debate, representing different theoretical roots (Weintraub 1997: xiii). The four types differ in their focus on social realms, and physical/social spaces, but are all related to 'the domain dimension of public and private'.

(1) A liberal-economic model that defines the public as the state administration and the private as the market economy.
(2) A republican model, which focuses on the public realm related to the political community, distinct from the state and the market economy.
(3) A sociability model that distinguishes between the private sphere and a public sociability, with a focus on the physical spaces facilitating this sociability.
(4) A feminist model, which starts in the domestic sphere and contrasts this with publicness defined largely as the economy of wage-earners.

The Liberal-economic Model

In the liberal-economic model, public and private refers to a distinction between the 'public sector' and the 'private sector' with representatives such as Hobbes and Bentham on the one hand, and Locke and Smith on the other (Weintraub 1997: 9). This refers to a distinction between governmental (public) and non-governmental (private market), and the underlying assumptions are linked to neoclassical economics, with a focus on individuals pursuing their self-interests more or less efficiently. The framework is especially occupied with questions of regulation and, therefore, questions relating to which activities should be left to the market and which should be subject to governmental intervention, often called the 'public policy' debate.

As discussed in the second part of this book, the human rights issues related to the framing of the internet as infrastructure concern the demarcation line between the state and the private sector. This relates in particular to the operation and governance of the internet as a global resource. The analysis addresses, among other things, the functions performed by the Internet Corporation for Assigned Names and Numbers (ICANN) and the role they play with regard to human rights protection.

The Republican Model

In the republican model the 'public' refers to the political community, drawing on notions such as citizenship and participation in decision making (Weintraub 1997: 10). The public is understood as a realm in which public debate and deliberations take place, directly or indirectly influencing the distribution of wealth and public services within a society. The republican model is thus occupied with the conditions and modalities for conducting political life.

Political philosophers who have developed this realm of the public include Tocqueville (1955/1856), Arendt (1958), and Habermas (1989). Habermas's ideal model of the public sphere represents one of the most well-known attempts to theorize this understanding of the public. Habermas divides society into a private realm of lifeworld relations (the family), a private realm of system relations (market economy), a public realm of system relations (the state), and a public realm of lifeworld relations (the public sphere).[5] In consequence, public and private refer to a distinction between practices governed by orientation toward universal values, that is the state and the public sphere, and those governed by particularistic values, that is the family and the market (Barnett 2003: 55).

When framing the internet as a public sphere, attention is directed towards the new modalities for public participation. This entails a democratic potential, but also points to critical dimensions, such as barriers to access and violations of online freedoms. In the physical world, access to spaces such as public plazas, parks, streets, and so on is 'freely available', whereas access to the virtual public sphere is provided for by companies, on commercial terms. Likewise companies play a key role as enablers of public life, for example by facilitating information searches in the public domain. These characteristics of the virtual public sphere raise a number of human rights challenges, as discussed in relation to the public sphere metaphor.

The two models (liberal-economic and republican) rest on different conceptual cuts between state, market, and the public sphere, yet they both refer to public as something related to politics (state or citizenship) in contrast to the following perspective, which relates public to sociability in a more general sense.

---

[5] In Habermas's later work, he increasingly speaks of spaces between public and private and how civil society groups play a key role in bringing private concerns into the public sphere (Habermas 1996).

The Sociability Model

In the sociability model, the public is linked to the public domain, whereas the private represents the domestic realm. The public domain lies in the public spaces of streets, parks, neighbourhoods, and cafes, and its ability to encourage public life is closely related to how these zones facilitate the flow of everyday movement and activity. Scholars from this tradition represent the public as a diverse complex of encounters (Jacobs 1961; Ariès 1962; Sennett and Zola 1976; Elias 1982/1939; Oldenburg 1989). The notion of public is thus linked to sociability, which may be both intentional and non-intentional, and to the spatial organization of social life. The sociability model is concerned with the intercourse of individuals and groups as part of modern coexistence and life, rather than self-interest or collective action.

> Public spaces have many purposes in social life. They allow people to make sense of the social norms that regulate society, they let people learn to express themselves and learn from the reactions of others, and they let people make certain acts or expressions 'real' by having witnesses acknowledge them.
>
> (in boyd 2007: 2)

On the internet, online communities and social network sites represent new forms of sociability. These spaces are public in the sense that they are open to everyone, but private in the sense that members may have expectations of privacy that differ from physical public spaces (Sveningsson 2009). Sveningsson suggests that the various online spaces may be categorized according to their placement on a private–public continuum, as public, semi-public, semi-private, and private environments. A 'public environment' is one that is open and available for everyone, and that does not require any form of registration or membership. Examples of this category would be open chat rooms or web pages. A 'semi-public environment' is one that in principle allows access for anyone, but requires membership or registration. Most web communities or social network sites would be situated in this category. A 'semi-private environment' is one that has restricted access, thus besides membership and registration it is restricted by formal requirements such as belonging to the organization that created the environment. Intranets are typical examples of domains in this category. A 'private online environment' is one that is unavailable by default, and where access is restricted to the creator of the content and their invited guests. Examples belonging in this category would be private rooms within chat rooms (Sveningsson 2009: 75). The human rights implications of the new forms of sociability enabled by the internet are explored in relation to the culture metaphor.

The fourth and final perspective starts in the domestic sphere, with origins in feminist scholarship.

The Feminist Model

The distinction between public and private has been a central theme in feminist scholarship (Rosaldo and Lamphere 1974; Benhabib and Cornell 1987; Fraser 1997). Feminist scholars have emphasized the way the public and private distinction is gender-linked, with the private sphere being disproportionately the sphere of women, while the public sphere has been dominated by men.[6] The private sphere of the family is thus presented in opposition to societies' economic and political activities, as discussed by Fraser, for example, who addresses the practices whereby private issues get accepted as public topics (Fraser 1997). The feminist argument of a public/private gender division is often backed by three main points. First, much social and political theory has ignored the domestic sphere or treated it as trivial; second, the public/private distinction is linked to ideologies that assign men and women to different spheres of social life; and, thirdly, classifying the family as private may shield domination and abuse from political scrutiny or legal redress (Weintraub 1997: 28–9). The feminist model thus treats the family as the theoretical point of departure, and has less focus on defining the roles and boundaries of the public.

With regard to the internet, some of the issues addressed in relation to the public sphere metaphor concern the way the internet may renegotiate the domestic in relation to the public sphere, thus providing new opportunities for participation in public life. One of the particular characteristics of a virtual public sphere is the possibility of being public while at home, that is accessing the internet from home. Related to this is the possibility of transforming private issues into matters of public concern. In the Uganda study, these characteristics were central to the local groups seeking to empower women and to counter gender-based discrimination, as addressed in the third part of this book.

Following these conceptual takes on public and private as different domains of society, the categories are now used to examine the 'status of any particular kind of activity or information' as public in contrast to private.

---

[6] 'The dichotomy between the private and the public is central to almost two centuries of feminist writing and political struggle; it is, ultimately, what the feminist movement is about' (Pateman quoted in Weintraub 1997: 27).

3. PUBLIC AND PRIVATE AS A STATUS ASCRIBED TO ACTIVITIES OR INFORMATION

Public as Open

One of the commonly used distinctions is between the public (open for all) character of activities or information as opposed to an activity or information with restricted access. In line with this, Thompson defines public as 'what is visible or observable, what is performed in front of spectators, what is open for all or many to see or hear about. What is private, then, by contrast, is what is hidden from view, what is said or done in privacy or secrecy or among a restricted group of people' (Thompson 1995: 123). This distinction is used, for instance, with regard to public documents versus private documents, public meetings versus private meetings, or public actions versus private actions.[7]

A related type of distinction is suggested by Gavison (1983), who proposes the following three dimensions. First, a dimension related to 'availability/being known', thus the more available and known a piece of information is, the more public it seems, and vice versa. Second, a dimension linked to 'access': the more accessible an activity or information is, the more public it is, and the more closed it appears, the more private. Third, a dimension related to the interest concerned, that is the more a given conduct affects the interest of others, the stronger the call for public accountability, in contrast to activities or information that are relevant only to the person in question. In addition to these dimensions, Gavison distinguishes between the descriptive and normative status of a given activity or information, emphasizing that something is public, or ought to be public, according to existing norms or to the moral merits of the situation. For example, if something is claimed to be of public interest, it may mean that the public is in fact interested in the matter, or that the matter is of public interest according to an existing norm, or that the public ought to have an interest in its dimensions (Gavison 1983: 114–15).

According to Luhmann's theory, public and private represent two different systems guided by different interpretation codes. If an issue or person is found to have 'public interest', it thus means that it is viewed in a specific manner: by the eye of the public. It is a particular way by which society observes itself (Qvortrup 2003: 156). Whether something is deemed

---

[7] In relation to individual behaviour, scholars such as Goffman distinguish between front stage (public face) and backstage action (private face) (Wolfe 1997: 184).

Table 2.1 Summary of the public and private models

Model	Public	Private
Liberal	State administration	Market
Republican	Political community	Family, market
Sociability	Public life	Domestic
Feminist	Economic and political activity	Family
Public-as-open	Open for all	Restricted access or availability

public or not is something that the public system decides on an ongoing, self-regulatory basis. Following from this, public interest is an observation principle that sets and transgresses boundaries between private and public. When issues are interpreted as 'public', the issue is generalized and interpreted according to general public principles. This implies a shift in topic from private criterion to public concern, thus a shift in interpretation code from a private code to a moral code (Qvortrup 2003: 160).

The human rights issues addressed in the medium metaphor concern, among others, the way the internet challenges the status of a given activity or piece of information as public in relation to private. One of the characteristics of the internet is that it not only enables individual publishing and broadcasting, but also enables recording of personal information and social activity for a variety of purposes. The practice of archiving 'internet editions', for example, raises issues of how to distinguish between published text and 'social life', where individuals have no expectation of lifelong recording. These and other human rights issues related to the internet as a medium are examined in the second part of this book. The public and private models are summarized in Table 2.1.

3. Human rights

The field of human rights standards has developed since the mid-1990s and represents a large body of international law, institutions, and groups that work to protect and promote human rights at local, regional, and international level. It also includes various research agendas related to human rights mechanisms and standards; the history and philosophy of human rights; human rights and globalization; human rights and security; and so forth. In this chapter, the basics of the human rights regime are introduced. This includes a closer look at some of the rights that have received particular attention in the internet era, as well as an examination of the way human rights have intersected with ICT in four different spheres: civil society, the intergovernmental sphere, the business domain, and the research sphere.

1. HUMAN RIGHTS BASICS

The institutionalization of international human rights standards has constituted one of the major normative shifts in world politics since the Second World War. In December 1948 the UN General Assembly approved the Universal Declaration of Human Rights (UDHR) by a vote of 48 to 0, with eight abstentions. Later referred to by then UN Secretary General U Thant as the 'Magna Carta of Mankind' (Korey 1998: 43) the UDHR comprised 30 articles dealing with two broad categories of human rights: civil and political rights; and economic, social, and cultural rights. The General Assembly subsequently decided that the two categories would be detailed in separate treaty instruments – the International Covenant on Civil and Political Rights (ICCPR) and the International Covenant on Economic, Social and Cultural Rights (ICESCR), both agreed by the General Assembly in December 1966. Together, the UDHR, ICCPR, and ICESCR constitute the International Bill of Human Rights, which is the overarching framework for global human rights today.[1]

[1] The UDHR was drafted and approved in a short period of just two years. In contrast, negotiations over the two legal instruments lasted for over a decade before concluding in 1966. The process of national ratification, which delivered a binding commitment by the states, has taken much longer and is still incomplete.

Civil and political rights are often referred to as first-generation rights because they were recognized at the national level in a number of eighteenth- and nineteenth-century constitutions, whereas economic, social, and cultural rights were generally developed in national constitutions and international instruments in the post-Second World War era. As such, the former are more deeply embedded in multiple legal systems and traditions. Moreover, political and civil rights have often been described as 'negative' rights in that they proscribe state interference with individual freedoms, whereas economic, social, and cultural rights have been described as 'positive' rights that require states to create the conditions in which individuals can enjoy a certain quality of life, or to provide certain goods or services to that end. In operational terms, though, the distinction is not so clear-cut.[2] Habermas has argued that the catalogue of human rights is closely related to the liberal model of the public sphere and entails five broad categories of rights. The first three categories represent the basic negative liberties, membership rights, and due process rights that together guarantee individual freedom of choice and autonomy. The fourth group entails the rights of political participation that guarantee public autonomy, whereas the fifth group represents social-welfare rights which are necessary since the exercise of the other rights depends on certain social and material conditions being met (Habermas 1996: xxvii).

Human rights are historically formulated in response to concrete experiences of human suffering, most notably revulsion against fascist atrocities during the Second World War that played a catalytic role in expanding the scope and domain of human rights to be elaborated and enshrined in binding international agreements. In addition, they traditionally concern the relationship between state and individual, thus protecting the individual against the arbitrary use of power by the state. The 'horizontal effect', however, is part of this relationship, implying that state obligations include a positive obligation to protect the individual against a private party by legislation and/or preventive measures or by investigating violations.[3]

While the International Bill of Human Rights provides the overarching foundation, the global human rights system also comprises a range of other instruments. Four additional core treaties are the Convention on the

---

The ICCPR and ICESCR build directly on the UDHR, reinforcing through codification the strength of its injunctions (Drake and Jørgensen 2006: 13).

[2] For a discussion on the complexity of this distinction, see for example Koch (2005: 81–103).

[3] Legal scholars speak of 'Drittwirkung' (effect by third party), which is used to stress that contracting states that have ratified human right treaties must protect individuals' human rights in the realm of private parties as well. See van Dijk and van Hoof (Dijk et al. 2006: 29).

Elimination of All Forms of Racial Discrimination (1965); the Convention on the Elimination of All Forms of Discrimination Against Women (1979); the Convention Against Torture and Other Cruel, Inhuman or Degrading Treatment or Punishment (1984); and the Convention on the Rights of the Child (1989). In addition, there are many other instruments dealing with the interpretation and application of rights in particular areas or contexts. These take a variety of legal forms, ranging from 'hard law' covenants and conventions to 'soft law' declarations, guidelines, and recommendations.[4] The global governance of human rights is substantively and architecturally very complex. Human rights is a deeply institutionalized field involving, at the global level, the UN Human Rights Council,[5] a multitude of monitoring mechanisms, General Comments on specific rights (providing authoritative guidance on how to interpret the right in question), Special Rapporteurs, and so on – working in a dense policy space to elaborate and interpret internationally agreed rights, build capacity, and promote compliance. The UN-based human rights system is supplemented by regional human rights mechanisms that vary widely in constitution and effectiveness. The European regime is more 'legalized' than the international regime, and is based on the European Convention on Human Rights (ECHR), which was agreed upon by the Council of Europe in 1950. It includes a European Court of Human Rights to which unresolved cases may be presented for binding rulings. The Council of Europe has also adopted a series of additional human rights instruments. In parallel, within the European Union (EU), the European Court of Justice and other EU institutions have been progressively expanding the scope and strength of human rights protections and have reinforced the ECHR's influence. The most recent example is the Charter of Fundamental Rights of the European Union 2007, which is included in the Treaty of Lisbon.[6]

The inter-American regime is also institutionally well developed, and shares broad commonalities with the European system. The Charter of

---

[4] While many of the instruments amplify rights previously established in the International Bill of Human Rights, there are also additions. These sets of rights are often described as 'third-generation' rights. Leading examples include the rights invoked in the UN General Assembly's 1984 Declaration on the Right of Peoples to Peace and the 1986 Declaration on the Right to Development. The aspirational principles of these declarations have been affirmed in subsequent political statements or soft law, but they have not been embodied in binding treaties (Drake and Jørgensen 2006: 21–2).

[5] The Human Rights Council is a successor to the Human Rights Commission, which was replaced in 2006.

[6] The Treaty of Lisbon came into force on 1 December 2009. The treaty is available at: http://europa.eu/lisbon_treaty/index_en.htm, retrieved 10 July 2012.

the Organization of American States (OAS), signed in 1948, lists human rights as one of the Organization's guiding principles. In 1959 the OAS created an expert Inter-American Commission on Human Rights, which later acquired the ability to receive complaints from individuals. The American Convention on Human Rights, which was agreed in 1969 and came into force in 1978, created an Inter-American Court of Human Rights that can issue nominally binding rulings. Regional regimes elsewhere are less developed and operate under far more constraining conditions. The African Charter of Human Rights and Peoples' Rights, adopted in 1981, is supposed to extend protections not only to individuals but to collectives as well. It also contains an expansive menu of third-generation rights, including the rights to a healthy environment, development, and peace, and has bolder provisions on economic, social, and cultural rights than its equivalents in Europe and the Americas. The Charter also created an African Commission on Human and Peoples' Rights and established an African Court on Human and Peoples' Rights, which came into being in January 2004. Similarly, the League of Arab States adopted an Arab Charter on Human Rights in 1994, and there is an Arab League Human Rights Committee. In contrast, Asia still lacks a regional human rights regime and, given the cultural and political diversity of China, India, and Japan, among others in the region, this is not likely to happen any time soon. Finally, complementing the international and regional regimes and associated organizations are a variety of national mechanisms. These include national human rights institutions (NHRIs), which increasingly interact and cooperate on promoting human rights compliance and national capacity building. The NHRIs operate under a mandate established by the UN Paris Principles that were adopted by the UN General Assembly in 1993.[7]

In summary, the international community has made significant progress in establishing human rights standards and mechanisms for the ongoing monitoring of progress toward their realization. This is not to suggest that human rights are not consistently violated all around the world, often on a massive scale. However, the existence of a global framework for human rights provides mechanisms through which political and legal pressure can be applied to compel states toward greater conformity. Moreover, since the millennium development agencies have increasingly adopted a

---

[7] For information on the role and mandate of NHRIs, please refer to the NHRI platform provided by the Office of the High Commissioner for Human Rights, available at: http://www.ohchr.org/en/countries/nhri/pages/nhrimain.aspx, retrieved 15 August 2012.

human rights-based approach in relation to development projects (Filmer-Wilson 2005).[8]

2. HUMAN RIGHTS RELATED TO PRIVATE AND PUBLIC LIFE

While practically every human right is influenced by the internet era, some rights have received particular attention since the core of the right is influenced by the use of technology in a significant way. In some cases ICT may strengthen the means of enjoying the right, or on the contrary, technology may weaken the protection afforded to the individual. This is true, in particular, for rights related to public and political life, and to privacy. Whereas there is an established right to privacy, there is not a right to public life as such. However, a number of human rights support the individual's rights to participate in public and political life. This includes the right to freedom of expression and freedom of information, the rights of peaceful assembly and association, the right to take part in the conduct of public affairs, and the right to privacy. All of these rights are part of the UDHR and the ICCPR.[9]

The Right to Privacy

The right to privacy was stipulated in UDHR Article 12 and ICCPR Article 17 long before technology was part of everyday life.[10] As with most human rights, the right was formulated in response to a concrete historical experience with human suffering (Winston 2007: 287), in this instance as a response to the British authorities' use of general warrants (writ of assistance) to conduct broad searches of colonists, which eventually triggered the American Revolution and led to the US Fourth Amendment (Snyder

---

[8] According to the definition used by the Office of the High Commissioner for Human Rights, a rights-based approach is a conceptual framework for the process of developing policies that is normatively based upon international human rights standards and operationally directed to promoting and protecting human rights (Office of the United Nations High Commissioner For Human Rights 2006: 22).

[9] Other human rights could have been added to the list; however, the above-mentioned rights represent rights and freedoms that are often debated in relation to the internet era.

[10] The right to privacy is today part of numerous international and regional human rights treaties and conventions. For an overview see, for example, Jacobsen (2008: Chapter 11 part b).

2007: 1).[11] The right to privacy protects the integrity of the individual and his or her home, family, and correspondence.[12]

A common denominator for the different areas of privacy is *access control*: 'something is private when I am in a position to and have a right to control access to it – whether to data, to a home, to decisions or to ways of acting' (Rössler 2007: 26). Rössler divides the notion of privacy into three exhaustive categories: informational privacy (control over what others know about us); decisional privacy (control over private decisions and actions); and local privacy (control over a physical space). From the late 1980s the widespread use of ICTs led to intensification in socio-technical practices of capturing, storing, and exchanging personal information, not least in North America and Europe. In 1995 the EU Directive on Data Protection (95/46/EC) was adopted,[13] and in consequence new data protection acts were enacted in a number of European countries.[14]

The right to privacy builds on the presumption that a zone of autonomy around the individual is central to individual freedom and self-determination: 'In order to behave in a self-determined fashion, we must in general believe and be able to presume that we are not being observed, eavesdropped on, deceived about what data is collected and shared with others, or about the presence of others, and about what those present know about us' (Rössler 2007: 29).

The underlying assumption of privacy as something that has a value in itself, and the emphasis on a private realm in which the individual can be left alone increasingly seems to contradict online social practices

---

[11] The US Fourth Amendment guards against unreasonable searches and seizures, and has its roots in British legal theory. According to William Pitt in 1763, 'The poorest man may in his cottage bid defiance to all the force of the Crown. It may be frail; its roof may shake; the wind may blow through it; the storms may enter; the rain may enter – but the King of England cannot enter; all his forces dare not cross the threshold of the ruined tenement', cited in Hosein (2006: 123).

[12] The right to privacy as stipulated in the ICCPR: '1. No one shall be subjected to arbitrary or unlawful interference with his privacy, family, home or correspondence, nor to unlawful attacks on his honour and reputation. 2. Everyone has the right to the protection of the law against such interference or attacks.' ICCPR, Article 17.

[13] The EU Directive on Data Protection has been in a process of revision since 2010. See the Communication from the European Commission on *A Comprehensive Approach on Personal Data Protection in the European Union*, 4 November 2010, available at: http://ec.europa.eu/justice/news/consulting_public/0006/com_2010_609_en.pdf, retrieved 10 August 2012.

[14] The first data protection law was passed in Sweden in 1973. See Blume et al. (2001) for an overview of data protection in the Nordic countries (Denmark, Finland, Norway, and Sweden).

characterized by self-exposure and sharing of a broad range of personal information. In response, scholars have argued that one should deconstruct the entire notion of privacy and rather shift focus to accountability (Brin 1998). Others have argued for a revised concept of privacy, and suggested the notion of contextual integrity as a normative framework built on the premise that different contexts carry different informational norms. Contextual integrity is an attempt to shift a 'one-size-fits-all' privacy concept to an approach that places emphasis on the situational systems of social rules governing information flows (Nissenbaum 2007: 39).

The right to privacy builds on both a 'domain' and 'informational dimension' of public and private. The protection of a person's body, family, home, and correspondence is related to specific private domains, whereas the informational aspect of privacy is related to specific types of information. Further, individuals have a right to privacy not only in the private domain but also when acting in the public space: 'The right to privacy may not only be invoked in private relationships at home, but may also be perceived as a kind of private sphere which is inherent in the individual person and which accompanies the person when moving about' (Rehof 1999: 258). Restrictions on surveillance of individual behaviour in public spaces, for example, reflect how privacy protection extends beyond the private, domestic realm, and accompanies the person when moving about in the public realm.[15] The right to privacy is frequently iterated as a precondition for a free and open society, including for the right to freedom of expression.[16]

As with other human rights, the protection of the right to privacy relies on national measures such as data protection law and data protection authorities. Besides, there is the challenge of enforcement toward private companies. In EU countries the Directive on Data Protection covers both public institutions and private companies, but many countries still lack data protection law covering the public and/or private sector.

The Right to Freedom of Expression

The right to freedom of expression is stipulated in UDHR Article 19 and ICCPR Article 19 and is present in all major international instruments protecting human rights.[17] The European Court of Human Rights

---

[15] Other examples include privacy protection in the workplace, for instance restrictions on employers' right to monitor their employees' phone conversations and email communication.

[16] See, for example, La Rue (2011) and Scheinin (2009).

[17] Sweden–Finland was one of the first countries to give legal protection to freedom of expression in the eighteenth century (Kortteinen et al. 1999: 393).

has described freedom of expression as one of the essential foundations of a democratic society, one of the basic conditions for its progress and for the development of every man (*Handyside* v. *The United Kingdom*, 7 December 1976: Paragraph 23). The right to freedom of expression protects the individual's right to freely form and express opinions, and to seek information.[18]

Freedom of expression is a typical 'first-generation' right with individual emphasis. The point of departure is the liberty of the individual to be protected from arbitrary restrictions when participating in public debate. One of the shortcomings often emphasized in relation to freedom of expression is the lack of emphasis on the structures and conditions that shape the public sphere in which communication take place (Kortteinen et al. 1999: 395). Restrictions on freedom of expression do not necessarily take the form of censorship, but can also be structured as self-censorship, institutional and/or social constraints, or merely a lack of access to communication: 'The regulation of the structures of communication will actually have more impact on communication than direct measures with regard to some specific contents of expression. The most revolutionizing recent change in these structures has taken place as a result of the tremendous advances in information technology' (Kortteinen et al. 1999: 396).

Another aspect of the right to freedom of expression is freedom of information, or 'the right to know', as it is often called. Freedom of information prohibits a state from restricting a person from receiving information that others wish or may be willing to impart to him (Kortteinen et al. 1999: 413). The right to freedom of information has been applied in cases related to broadcasting and the flow of information into a country, and is increasingly used in relation to laws that give individuals or organizations a legal right to demand information on how the government is acting in their name (Banisar 2006: 73). In relation to the latter, the recent General Comment on ICCPR Article 19 embraces a right of access to information held by public bodies (United Nations Human Rights Comittee 12 September 2011).

---

[18] The right to freedom of expression as stipulated in the ICCPR: '1. Everyone shall have the right to hold opinions without interference. 2. Everyone shall have the right to freedom of expression; this right shall include freedom to seek, receive and impart information and ideas of all kinds, regardless of frontiers, either orally, in writing or in print, in the form of art, or through any other media of his choice. 3. The exercise of the rights provided for in paragraph 2 of this article carries with it special duties and responsibilities. It may therefore be subject to certain restrictions, but these shall only be such as are provided by law and are necessary: (a) For respect of the rights or reputations of others; (b) For the protection of national security or of public order (*ordre public*), or of public health or morals.' ICCPR, Article 19.

Freedom of information is related to the citizen's right to participate in the conduct of public affairs, stressing that the public is only able to participate if they have information about the activities of the government.[19]

The Right of Peaceful Assembly and Freedom of Association

Another human right related to public life is the right of peaceful assembly and freedom of association stipulated in UDHR Article 20 and ICCPR Articles 21 and 22.[20] The right of peaceful assembly and freedom of association protects the individual's right to meet and demonstrate publicly, and to freely choose which organizations to belong to, including forming and joining trade unions.[21] These rights are closely linked to the right to freedom of expression, and are often presented as the core premise for an active civil society and for any participatory democratic processes (Scheinin 1999: 417). The right to associate freely in political organizations or meetings is thus essential to organize and 'express the will of the people'. It is also linked to the right to privacy, since the ability to freely meet and discuss politics or other societal issues requires that the integrity of the communication be protected.

As illustrated by the quote below, ICT may leverage many aspects of human rights work, not least by providing new platforms where groups may assemble and associate:

> E-mail and the internet are not merely additional channels or spaces extending the boundaries of freedom of association and assembly into cyberspace.

---

[19] See the 2011 global overview of Freedom of Information legislation provided by Banisar at: http://www.right2info.org/resources/publications/foi-map-by-david-banisar/view, retrieved 2 May 2013.

[20] The right of peaceful assembly as stipulated in the ICCPR: 'The right of peaceful assembly shall be recognized. No restrictions may be placed on the exercise of this right other than those imposed in conformity with the law and which are necessary in a democratic society in the interests of national security or public safety, public order (*ordre public*), the protection of public health or morals or the protection of the rights and freedoms of others.' ICCPR, Article 21.The right to freedom of association as stipulated in ICCPR: '1. Everyone shall have the right to freedom of association with others, including the right to form and join trade unions for the protection of his interests. 2. No restrictions may be placed on the exercise of this right other than those which are prescribed by law and which are necessary in a democratic society in the interests of national security or public safety, public order (*ordre public*), the protection of public health or morals or the protection of the rights and freedoms of others.' ICCPR, Article 22.

[21] The right to form and join trade unions is also included as a separate issue in rights related to work such as Article 8 in the ICESCR.

> They allow forms of association and assembly that were previously not possible, going beyond mere virtual equivalents of physical association and assembly to a new integration of information, communication, expression, association, and assembly, enabled by ICTs, that are sometimes referred to as 'online communities'.
>
> (Lewis 2006: 159)

The May 2011 appointment of a UN Special Rapporteur on the rights to freedom of peaceful assembly and of association provides an opportunity within the UN system to elaborate in more detail on how the internet era enables and challenges these rights.[22]

The Right to Take Part in the Conduct of Public Affairs

A final right to be mentioned is the right to take part in the conduct of public affairs, which is stipulated in UDHR Article 21 and ICCPR Article 25. The right pronounces the idea of the equal and inalienable rights of the individual in relation to his or her state, and sets minimum requirements for the democratic system of the state.[23] These minimum requirements imply that the authority of the government must be based on the will of the electors and must entail a system of democratic participation whereby every citizen has equal rights to participate (Rosas 1999: 431). The right to take part in the conduct of public affairs does not explicitly mention democracy. In its General Comment on Article 25, the Human Rights Committee has stressed that the conduct of public affairs is a broad concept that 'covers all aspects of public administration, and the formulation and implementation of policy at international, national, regional and local levels' (United Nations 1997: 50). According to this interpretation, the right to participation includes not only formal governmental structures, but also various semi-public and semi-private institutions, and more generally all decision-making of public interest (Rosas 1999: 450). As with the previous rights mentioned above, the right to take part in the conduct of public affairs is closely linked to a number of rights, not least freedom of expression and

---

[22] The link between freedom of peaceful assembly and of association and the internet is addressed in Comninos (June 2011), including a rich amount of empirical examples from around the world.

[23] 'Every citizen shall have the right and the opportunity, without any of the distinctions mentioned in article 2 and without unreasonable restrictions: (a) To take part in the conduct of public affairs, directly or through freely chosen representatives; (b) To vote and to be elected at genuine periodic elections which shall be by universal and equal suffrage and shall be held by secret ballot, guaranteeing the free expression of the will of the electors; (c) To have access, on general terms of equality, to public service in his country.' ICCPR, Article 25.

freedom of information, the right to privacy, and the right of peaceful assembly and freedom of association.[24]

Recalling the public/private models, the above civil and political rights and freedoms may be related to several of these models, yet they are most closely related to the republican model as facilitators for public political life, for example publicly expressing critical opinions, seeking information about public affairs, organizing civil society, participating in the democratic life of the community, and protecting the privacy of communication. Further, the rights to privacy and to freedom of information have an informational dimension, since they address the public versus private character of any given type of information.

In the following section the influence of the human rights system within different spheres are explored, starting with civil society.

3. HUMAN RIGHTS AND ICT POLICY

A Civil Society Perspective

Civil society groups have embraced the link between human rights and communication technology since the mid 1970s, and have done so in a variety of ways. Media, journalist groups, and academics were among the first to address communication policies from a human rights/social justice perspective. From 1975 to 1985 the call for a New World Information and Communication Order was raised at the United Nations Educational, Scientific and Cultural Organization (UNESCO) by the Non-Aligned Movement of UN countries, together with a group of civil society organizations and academics. The campaign for a New World Information and Communication Order (NWICO) concerned the dominance of Western media and news content combined with a growing concentration in media production and ownership, thereby making it difficult for less developed countries to take part in the global sphere of communication. The debate eventually became so controversial that the UK and the USA, as well as Singapore, withdrew from UNESCO.[25] Following the NWICO

[24] Klein has addressed the specific challenges which the right to political participation raises in the context of global communication, for instance whether the information society is a society in its own right with its own political institutions, such as ICANN, separate from existing national governments (Klein 2006: 186).

[25] In short, the USA and others saw the NWICO as a means for non-democratic states to restrict freedom of expression, especially media freedom, while the other side claimed that media should be under stricter state control, and that media concentration should be limited in order to allow for a more pluralistic flow of information (Drake and Jørgensen 2006: 29).

controversy, more civil society groups became involved and continued to rephrase and pursue the issue of inequality in access to communications, with the Communication Rights in the Information Society (CRIS) campaign as a recent example.[26]

Another link between human rights and communication technology has been the leverage of the internet to empower human rights activists.[27] There are numerous illustrations of how the internet has helped human rights activists to report on violations, to campaign across borders and to mobilize support to strengthen their case, with the Arab Spring as a recent example.[28] Groups such as Human Rights Watch, Reporters sans Frontières, Amnesty International, International Freedom of Expression Exchange (IFEX), and ARTICLE 19 have, to varying degrees, documented and reported on internet usage by human rights groups and independent journalists since the mid-1990s. Various resources have also been developed to secure communication for human rights activists handling sensitive information.[29]

A related but different type of activity is the campaigning by various groups to protect human rights standards *on* the internet. North American and European organizations have since the 1990s focused on specific human rights challenges within an online environment, especially in relation to the right to privacy and the right to freedom of expression.[30] The initial North American/European focus on internet rights has today turned into an increasingly large number of groups from all parts of the world, which to a varying degree focus on protecting human rights standards online.[31] Issues of concern include anti-terror legislation, data retention, use of biometrics, workplace surveillance, and internet censorship, including filtering

---

[26] See http://www.waccglobal.org/en/20024-communication-rights-in-the-information-society/666-Communication-Rights-in-the-Information-Society-The-CRIS-campaign.html, retrieved 4 July 2012.

[27] See, for example, Hick et al. (2000) and Mackinnon (2012: 21–8).

[28] For research on the internet's role in the Arab Spring see, for example, *Cyberorient*, Online Journal of the Virtual Middle East 6(1) 2012. Available at: http://www.cyberorient.net/, retrieved 10 October 2012.

[29] See, for example *Digital Security and Privacy for Human Rights Defenders* (Vitaliev 2007).

[30] Examples include groups such as Electronic Frontier Foundation (US-based), American Civil Liberties Union (US-based), Privacy International (UK-based), ARTICLE 19 (UK-based).

[31] Examples include groups such European Digital Rights (Europe-wide network), the Association for Progressive Communications (global network), Internet Rights and Principles Coalition (global coalition formed as part of the IGF process).

and blocking in various forms.[32] Up until now, the majority of these groups have not positioned themselves as human rights organizations in the way that they systematically refer to international human rights treaties and declarations in their advocacy work. Though most of them refer to human rights as an overall normative framework, and often reference specific rights, they typically do not deploy the whole human rights apparatus, including the connected mechanisms of monitoring, state reporting, and human rights courts.[33] Some of the North American groups litigate and challenge the state on new legislation,[34] but the majority remain more advocacy-oriented.[35]

The Association for Progressive Communications (APC) is an example of an organization that increasingly frames its themes and policy agenda with reference to the broader human rights framework.[36] APC was also closely involved with the internet-related debate at the UN Human Rights Council in 2012.[37] APC's human rights framing of technology issues may have a broader impact, since research has found APC to be one of the most well-connected and influential civil society networks concerned with ICT policies (Mueller 2010: 93).

The human rights focus was also reflected at the WSIS process where two distinct human rights controversies took place within the civil society

---

32 See, for example, the numerous national contributors to the annual report on Human Rights and Privacy by Privacy International and the Electronic Privacy Information Center (2010), as well as the global survey on internet filtering produced by the OpenNet Initiative (Deibert et al. 2008). Another source is Herdict, a user-driven platform that collects reports about inaccessible websites covering any type of Web blockage. See www.herdict.org, retrieved 10 December 2012.

33 UK-based ARTICLE 19 is one of the organizations that appear more substantively anchored in the human rights framework.

34 The Electronic Frontier Foundation (EFF) and The American Civil Liberties Union (ACLU), in particular, have been involved in some landmark court cases regarding online freedom of expression. One of the better-known cases concerns the Communication Decency Act, which the US Supreme Court struck down in *Reno et al.* v. *American Civil Liberties Union et al.*, 26 June 1997). EFF has also been leading lawsuits against AT&T, the US government, and Bush and Obama administration officials to stop warrant-less wiretapping. For more information see http://www.eff.org/nsa/faq, retrieved 10 July 2012.

35 The relationship between conventional human rights organizations and organizations concerned with internet rights is addressed in Souter (March 2012).

36 See, for example, the APC campaign Internet Rights are Human Rights, available at: http://www.apc.org/en/projects/internet-rights-are-human-rights, retrieved 30 October 2012; APC and Hivos (2011); and Liddicoat (March 2012).

37 See *A Year in the Life of the Internet at the United Nations*, by Liddicoat (APC), available at: https://www.apc.org/en/news/internet-and-un-human-rights-council-good-bad-and, retrieved 30 October 2012.

arena. The first concerned the idea of a right to communicate, promoted as a new human right by the CRIS campaign.[38] Different rationales were expressed in support of such a right, which reiterated the above-mentioned concerns of media becoming increasingly homogenized and commercialized, and of minority, dissenting, or local voices being excluded from decision-making processes due to a lack of information and a lack of access to the means of communication.

The claim for a right to communicate was challenged by the Human Rights Caucus,[39] and the organization ARTICLE 19 in particular. The groups argued that a broadly defined right to communicate might undermine long-established media freedoms, and claimed that the concerns raised by the CRIS campaign could be met under the existing regime of rights. It was stressed that the right to freedom of expression is recognized to include the right to diverse, pluralistic media and equitable access to the means of communication, as well as access to the media. Rather than suggest a new broadly defined right, enforcement of these provisions may provide for democratization of media and communication and address the concerns of the CRIS campaign. The debate was largely resolved by the end of the first WSIS when most groups agreed that the claim for rights to communicate need not invent new legal standards but should rather call for enforcement of existing human rights standards.[40]

The second major controversy unfolding amongst civil society groups active in the WSIS process concerned the relation between human rights and development. In the process of finalizing the civil society declaration for the Geneva Summit, a number of organizations claimed that the issue of development (poverty reduction, and economic and social development) was to take priority over human rights, thus refusing to have the civil society declaration open with a section on the commitment to human rights standards. Advocates of the development perspective argued that development and human rights represent different spheres with diverging

---

[38] At the onset of WSIS, organizations that had been involved in the NWICO and newcomers gathered around the CRIS campaign, this time not calling for a state- or industry-led effort to create new global orders, but instead advocating for democratization of media and communication. For a discussion of the role of the CRIS campaign in the WSIS process see Mueller et al. (2007); Ó Siochrú and Alegre (2005).

[39] As part of a larger civil society coalition that came together around WSIS, a group of civil society organizations concerned with getting human rights on the WSIS agenda launched the Human Rights Caucus at the first preparatory conference in July 2002. See www.iris.sgdg.org/actions/smsi/hr-wsis/, retrieved 10 July 2012.

[40] This was iterated during the World Forum on Communication Rights, organized as a side event at the Geneva Summit in 2003 (Marzouki and Joergensen 2004).

objectives and policy agendas, whereas human rights groups argued that rights are the normative foundation for any society, independent of the level of development. In the last days leading up to the Geneva Summit, several heated discussions took place among the civil society organizations participating in the summit, and in the end a compromise was reached. It was decided to open the declaration with a section on *Social Justice and People-Centered Sustainable Development*, followed by a section on *The Centrality of Human Rights* (Marzouki and Joergensen 2004).

The debate is indicative of the perceived dichotomy between the development and human rights spheres that existed until the late 1980s, and where even UN agencies were reluctant to recognize the relationship between the two. The formal recognition of the convergence between development and human rights came at the 1993 World Conference on Human Rights held in Vienna, and in 1997 when the UN Secretary-General called for the integration of human rights into all principal UN activities and programmes (Filmer-Wilson 2005: 214–15).

While WSIS has been one of the major civil society spaces concerned with ICT and human rights, numerous other spaces exist. Below is a brief outline of two other civil society initiatives, namely the Public Voice Initiative and the Access to Knowledge (A2K) movement. Futher, the former Freedom of Expression project and the international network of national human rights institutions are mentioned.

The Public Voice Initiative is organized by the US-based Electronic Privacy Information Center (EPIC), in order to facilitate a civil society platform for engagement in information society policy.[41] The platform has been running since 1996, and has conducted a number of teleconferences debating issues of concern to the participants. In addition the Public Voice Initiative coordinated a coalition of civil society groups that came together around the Organization for Economic Cooperation and Development (OECD) ministerial conference on the Information Economy in Seoul in June 2008.[42] As a contribution to the ministerial conference, the civil society coalition drafted the Seoul Declaration, which details policy principles that are to guide the information economy. The declaration has human rights and the rule of law as one of its guiding principles, just as it reaffirms the commitment to international human rights treaties.[43] More recently,

[41] See http://thepublicvoice.org/, retrieved 10 July 2012.

[42] In 2009 the coalition formalized into the Civil Society Information Society Advisory Committee (SCISAC), which provides input to the development of OECD policies related to the internet. See http://csisac.org/, retrieved 10 July 2012.

[43] 'Compliance with international human rights standards and respect for the rule of law, as well as effective human rights protection, must be the baseline for assessing global information society policies' (Civil Society – TUAC 16 June 2008: 1).

the OECD has released a Communiqué on Principles for Internet Policy-Making (OECD 2011a). The Civil Society Information Society Advisory Committee (CSISAC) as well as other groups declined to endorse the communiqué due to the concern, among others, that the document would push internet intermediaries to police and enforce laws on their networks and services (CSISAC 28 June 2011: 1).

The Access to Knowledge (A2K) movement was initiated in 2004 by US-based Knowledge Ecology International (previously called CPTech) and is a consolidation of various local and global social movements.[44] The movement is concerned with fairness in structures-of-knowledge access, more specifically copyright law and other regulations that affect access to information and the digital commons. One element of the initiative has been the drafting of a proposal for a treaty to protect and promote access to knowledge.[45] The Access to Knowledge movement increasingly frame their issues as 'a struggle for the protection of human rights online', with the Anti-Counterfeiting Trade Agreement (ACTA) campaign as a recent example.[46] The techniques employed in recent access-to-knowledge activism are presented in *Winning the Web* (Hogge, May 2009), including how the movement has taken intellectual property issues to a wider audience.

The Freedom of Expression project (active in 2006–2008) was organized by UK-based Global Partners as a global collaboration to research and develop public policy principles for the networked communication environment.[47] The project suggested four values – accessibility, independence, diversity, and navigability – as guiding principles for the networked communication environment. Moreover, analysis has been made suggesting how each value is underpinned by human rights standards and how they may conflict with one another (Lipson 2008). The analysis provides an

---

[44] See http://keionline.org/, retrieved 12 October 2012.

[45] The draft treaty suggests provisions regarding limitations and exceptions to copyrights and related rights. The treaty stipulates a number of uses of creative works that should not be inhibited by exclusive intellectual property rights (for example, in the area of education, science, or preservation) as well as use by groups with special needs and interests such as persons with disabilities, distance education institutions, the media, or developing countries (Knowledge Ecology International, 9 May 2005).

[46] Interview with Vera Franz who heads the Information Policy and Intellectual Property Reform initiatives at the Open Society Information Program, available at: http://www.soros.org/voices/rise-access-knowledge-movement-interview-vera-franz, retrieved 14 August 2012.

[47] See http://www.freedomofexpression.org.uk/resources/about+the+project, retrieved 10 July 2012.

overview of the interface between human rights standards and each of the four principles, based on human rights case law.

A final group to be mentioned are the national human rights institutions (NHRIs). The NHRIs represent the national presence of the international human rights regime and ideally serve as a human rights resource for civil society groups at local level. Until now, the human rights implications of communication technology has only sporadically been covered by these organizations, and the vast majority have not participated in global policy processes such as the WSIS or the IGF. Currently there is little exchange between the policy spaces where ICT policy is debated and the NHRI community. Only a limited number of people cross-cut the various communities and, as in general, they have different professional references. Whereas the NHRIs are rooted in a legal regime, and tend to focus on long-established areas of human rights work, the organizations concerned with communication policy often have a stronger media and technology constituency and focus.

In summary, various civil society groups, especially from the media and cyber rights arena, have addressed ICT policy with reference to human rights and social justice arguments. Despite the overall human rights framing of issues such as media concentration, and online censorship and surveillance, the concrete use of human rights standards is often limited to either a general framework without specific human rights analysis, or referencing the right to freedom of expression and the right to privacy only. While few of the organizations develop detailed analysis based on human rights case law or frame their issues with reference to the broader array of rights, this is gradually changing, with APC as one example. Concerning the national human rights institutions, there has been limited focus on the human rights issues arising from global ICT policy and practice except for some attention to issues of privacy and data protection. Leaving for now the civil society arena, human rights and ICT is next considered from the perspective of international organizations.

An Institutional Perspective

Intergovernmental institutions concerned with ICT policy increasingly draw upon a human rights framing, starting with the WSIS process. However, despite many programmatic commitments to the human rights framework, a rights-based approach to ICT policies has not been substantiated. The strongest example of a rights-based approach is found within the Council of Europe, which is not surprising as it represents the European human rights system, including the European Court of Human Rights. As expressed by the Council of Europe on its website: 'The constant developments in the information society give Council [*sic*] of Europe the challenge of defending and maintaining its fundamental principles in new environments.'[48]

Starting with the WSIS as a space for intergovernmental policy deliberation, there were two human rights issues on the agenda that were especially controversial. The first was to establish the International Bill of Human Rights as the overarching framework for the WSIS Declaration of Principles and Plan of Action. The second issue was the treatment of specific information society topics related to human rights. The reaffirmation of the International Bill of Human Rights in the Declaration of Principles was realized, however, only in the final days of the negotiations, and as a result of strong pressure from the Western group of delegates (Drake and Jørgensen 2006: 31). The Declaration of Principles reaffirms the universality, indivisibility, interdependence, and interrelation of all human rights and fundamental freedoms, including the right to development. It further stresses that democracy, sustainable development, and respect for human rights and fundamental freedoms, as well as good governance, are interdependent and mutually reinforcing (World Summit on the Information Society 2003: Paragraph 3). This commitment to human rights was reaffirmed in the Tunis Commitment and the Tunis Agenda, at WSIS Phase Two. Moreover, the Tunis Agenda has an explicit linkage between human rights and internet governance (World Summit on the Information Society 2005: Paragraph 42). While the policy documents adopted at WSIS acknowledged the importance of international human rights agreements and principles, there was little intergovernmental debate on how human rights might apply to specific ICT policy issues. During the plenary sessions and working group negotiations, the Human Rights Caucus and other groups presented numerous interventions suggesting the incorporation of specific human rights standards within the Geneva Declaration of Principles in relation to issues including, among others, discrimination, data protection, labour rights, regulatory environment, press freedom, and information access. However, human rights considerations hardly figured in the states' negotiations on these issues (Drake and Jørgensen 2006: 31–3). Therefore, the WSIS process demonstrated that for many government officials the linkage between human rights and ICT policy issues is far from obvious. The human rights references that did make their way into the final version of the Geneva Declaration of Principles were references to the right to freedom of expression (UDHR Article 19) and to the due recognition and respect for the rights and freedoms of others (UDHR Article 29), plus more general references to the rights of children, the rights of

---

[48] See www.coe.int/t/dghl/standardsetting/media/, retrieved 1 May 2012.

authors and artists, the principle of non-discrimination, and the right to privacy.[49]

With regard to follow-up, the Tunis Summit decided on various mechanisms: the Internet Governance Forum, a UN coordination group on the information society within the UN's Chief Executives Board, and a mechanism for stock-taking and implementation under the UN Economic and Social Council's Commission on Science and Technology for Development (Jørgensen 2006: Afterword).

While preparing for the WSIS+10 (to be held in 2015), however, the state commitment to human rights is still short of benchmarks. Several human rights themes have been addresses by multi-stakeholder arrangements in the form of Dynamic Coalitions; however, few results have emerged from this process.[50] One result is the Draft Charter of Human Rights and Principles on the internet, produced by the Dynamic Coalition on Internet Rights and principles in a collective and global process. Against the backdrop of the Universal Declaration of Human Rights, the Charter applies human rights standards to an internet era.[51] In addition, an important milestone was reached in 2012, when the Human Rights Council adopted by consensus a resolution on promotion, protection, and enjoyment of human rights on the internet. Presented by Sweden, the resolution affirms that 'the same rights people have offline must also be protected online' (United Nations Human Rights Council 5 July 2012).

The UN agencies that were active during and after WSIS, especially the International Telecommunication Union (ITU), the United Nations Development Programme (UNDP) and UNESCO, play a central role as overall coordinators of the Geneva Plan of Action. Of particular relevance to communication policy is UNESCO, which is responsible for initiatives related to access to information, cultural diversity, e-learning, ethical dimensions, and media. UNESCO traditionally has a strong human rights focus on its communication policies, with particular emphasis on freedom of expression, and has at strategy level stressed that it applies a human rights approach to its projects.[52] In addition, the UNDP has,

---

49 See the Preamble and Paragraphs 3, 4, 5, 11, 18, 36, 52, and 58 of the Geneva Declaration of Principles (World Summit on the Information Society 2003).

50 For a list of Dynamic Coalitions see: http://www.intgovforum.org/cms/index.php/dynamiccoalitions, retrieved 10 July 2012.

51 See http://irpcharter.org/charter/, retrieved October 10, 2012.

52 'Overall, the Organization will pursue in all its fields of competence a human rights-based approach to programming.' UNESCO Medium-Term Strategy 2008–2013 (UNESCO 2008: 8).

since 2000, declared a rights-based approach to its development activities.[53] The UNDP is involved in capacity building, enabling environments for the telecom sector (including how ICT may be used as a tool for development), e-government, and international and regional cooperation. Despite UNESCO and UNDP's respective human rights framing, neither have substantiated analysis in their policy areas with respect to human rights. Regarding ITU, the agency is involved in infrastructure, security, e-learning, enabling environments for the telecom sector, and several other areas, but with no particular human rights framing of the agency's activities.[54]

A final UN mechanism to be mentioned is the UN Special Rapporteur on the promotion and protection of the right to freedom of opinion and expression, who on several occasions has stressed the importance of protecting freedom of expression in an online environment and has urged that information technology must also be made accessible for the developing world.[55] As previously mentioned, the Human Rights Council for the first time in 2011 addressed a report by the Special Rapporteur specifically focused on challenges related to the protection of freedom of expression on the internet.

Other intergovernmental organizations concerned with human rights and communication technology include the Organization for Security and Co-operation in Europe (OSCE) and the Council of Europe (CoE).

The OSCE works on security, conflict prevention, and post-conflict rehabilitation amongst 56 participating states, and has a special representative on

---

[53] 'Adopting a human rights-based approach may not necessarily change what we do, but it will raise questions about how we do it. As stated before, a human rights-based approach provides both a vision of what development should strive to achieve (to secure the freedom, well-being and dignity of all people everywhere), and a set of tools and essential references (human rights standards and principles). It is essentially based on the values, standards and principles captured in the UN Charter, the Universal Declaration of Human Rights and subsequent legally binding human rights conventions/treaties' (UNDP 2001: 2). See also Filmer-Wilson (2005: 214–16).

[54] An overview of all WSIS action lines is available at: http://www.itu.int/wsis/implementation/facilitators.html, retrieved 10 July 2012.

[55] 'The Special Rapporteur believes that guaranteeing freedom of opinion and expression on the internet and other new communication tools is the central challenge for the future. The achievement of a global information society, in which the poor can also have access to modern technologies, may represent a leap forward for mankind, opening new paths for human and economic development. Should the information society miss the opportunity of making technologies available globally, the social and economic cleavage between developed and developing countries will deepen' (Ligabo, 17 December 2004: paragraph 57).

Freedom of the Media.[56] The representative has developed several recommendations and best practices with regard to the protection and promotion of freedom of expression online. Most recently, a study on government efforts to regulate the internet in the OSCE area has been conducted (Akdeniz for the OSCE Representative on Freedom of the Media 8 July 2011).

The Council of Europe is one of the regional organizations that has conducted more comprehensive work in the area of human rights and ICT policy. Based in Strasbourg, the CoE covers the entire European continent and seeks to develop common principles based on the European Convention on Human Rights and related human rights documents. The CoE has been active in information society standard setting since the 1980s, not least in relation to data protection, cybercrime,[57] protection of children online, internet governance, and freedom of expression/media freedoms.[58]

Since 2005 the CoE has had specialized working groups on human rights and information society issues (that is, Group of Specialists on Public Service Media, Media Diversity, and Information Society), which have produced a number of standard-setting documents. In 2009 the groups were replaced by ad hoc advisory groups: Public Service Media Governance, Cross-border Internet, Protection of Neighbouring Rights of

---

[56] The OECD representative on Freedom of the Media regularly publishes joint declarations on freedom of expression on the internet. See, for example, the joint declaration from June 2011, available at: http://www.osce.org/fom/78309, retrieved 30 October 2012.

[57] Some of the CoE's standard setting has been criticized substantively by civil society groups for being overly invasive on individual freedoms, not least the Cybercrime Convention. See, for example, the critique by EPIC available at: http://epic.org/privacy/intl/ccc.html, retrieved 10 July 2012.

[58] See, for example, the CoE Convention on the Protection of Individuals with Regard to Automatic Processing of Personal Data (1981); Convention on Cybercrime (2001); Declaration of the Committee of Ministers on Human Rights and the Rule of Law in the Information Society (2005); Recommendation on Promoting Freedom of Expression in the New Information and Communication Environment (2007); Recommendation on Measures to Promote the Respect for Freedom of Expression and Information with Regard to Internet Filters (2008); Resolution on Internet Governance and Critical Internet Resources (2009); Declaration of the Committee of Ministers on Network Neutrality (2010); Recommendation of the Committee of Ministers on the Protection and Promotion of the Universality, Integrity and Openness of the Internet (2011); Recommendation of the Committee of Ministers to Member States on the Protection of Human Rights with Regard to Search Engines (2012). For a full list of CoE standard-setting documents pertaining to the information society please refer to: http://www.coe.int/t/dghl/standardsetting/media/, retrieved 15 August 2012. A summary: Recent Achievements of the Media and Information Society Division (October 2010) is also available at the CoE website.

Broadcasting Organizations, and Committee of Experts on New Media. In 2012 the CoE established a Committee of Experts on Rights of Internet Users.[59] The CoE also focuses on public participation in internet governance processes, and has drafted a code of good practice on information, participation, and transparency in internet governance, in cooperation with the United Nations Economic Commission for Europe (UNECE) and APC (APC et al. June 2010).

In the follow-up to WSIS, the CoE has increasingly elaborated the relationship between human rights and internet policy through a number of recommendations. The CoE *Recommendation on Measures to Promote The Public Service Value of the Internet* and its appended recommendations present various internet communication principles within a framework of human rights, democracy, and the rule of law, and is one of the more specific attempts to spell out a human rights approach to global ICT policy (Council of Europe 2007). Another example is the CoE contribution to the first IGF in Athens, where the CoE argued that states need to prepare themselves to deal with, for example, situations related to ECHR Article 2 (the right to life) or Article 3 (prohibition of inhuman or degrading treatment) with regard to incitement on websites to suicide or self-harm; to Article 8 (the right to private life and correspondence) with regard to disseminating other people's personal information or illegal eavesdropping or control of communication; or to Article 10 (the right to freedom of expression and information) when confronted with online hate speech inciting violence in blogs (Council of Europe 2006: 16). The document also emphasizes that the security and stability aspects of the internet may be interpreted in a human rights context, and can involve state responsibility under the ECHR, if it can be established that the state has failed to take appropriate measures within its powers to protect those under its jurisdiction from personality theft, online fraud, or e-attacks causing loss or damage (for example through spam or viruses) (Council of Europe 2006: 17).

An important part of the CoE system is the European Court of Human Rights (ECtHR), which has jurisdiction to rule, through binding judgments, on individual and interstate applications alleging violations of human rights.

In relation to communication technology the ECtHR has issued judgments, particularly in connection to ECHR Article 8, stressing that the human rights standards apply to communication via email or the internet.

---

[59] For more information on these advisory groups please refer to: http://www.coe.int/t/dghl/standardsetting/media/MC-S-PG/default_en.asp, retrieved 15 August 2012.

With regard to the privacy of communication, the ECtHR has for instance dealt with the unlawful monitoring of a civil servant's telephone, email, and internet usage.[60] In this case the Court held that emails sent from the workplace should engage the principles of 'private life' and 'correspondence', as should information obtained from the monitoring of personal internet use. As the applicant had been given no warning that their calls would be liable to monitoring, they had a reasonable expectation of privacy with regard to their emails and use of the internet. More generally, the Court stated that surveillance measures may constitute a violation of the right to privacy, especially if the offences that might justify such surveillance are not clearly defined.[61] The UN Human Rights Committee has also made a general comment on the right to privacy, which stresses that the protection of the Article covers all forms of communications, electronic or otherwise.[62]

With regard to freedom of expression, the ECtHR has frequently emphasized the importance of press freedom and debate on matters of public interest as inherent characteristics and necessary conditions for a democratic society. Case law that considers human rights provisions in the light of the internet is still limited.[63] However, it gives no indication that the Court considers the internet as a regime unto itself and/or beyond the realm of human rights. On the contrary, it is emphasized that 'the internet in its very essence is comparable to other means of content delivery' (Anne Sofie Greve quoted in Council of Europe 2006: 11).[64] In one of its first internet cases, the ECtHR underlined the right of member states to take action to stop illegal internet content. The Court held that it was proportionate for the authorities to resort to criminal prosecution for publishing obscene content on an internet site, as this pursued the legitimate aim of

---

60 See *Copland* v. *United Kingdom* (3 April 2007).

61 See, for example, *Kruslin* v. *France* (24 April 1990) and *Amann* v. *Switzerland* (16 February 2000).

62 'Compliance with (ICCPR) Article 17 requires that the integrity and confidentiality of correspondence should be guaranteed de jure and de facto. Correspondence should be delivered to the addressee without interception and without being opened or otherwise read. Surveillance whether electronic or otherwise, interceptions of telephonic, telegraphic and other forms of communication, wire-tapping and recording of conversations should be prohibited' (United Nations Human Rights Committee 1988).

63 See European Court of Human Rights (2011) for an overview of internet-related judgments.

64 Anne Sofie Greve is a former judge of the European Court of Human Rights.

protecting morals and the rights of others, and it considered this as necessary in a democratic society.[65]

Finally, a couple of initiatives from the European Parliament are worth mentioning. The first is a study on ICT and Human Rights requested by the European Parliament's Subcommittee on Human Rights. The study proposes a number of measures that the EU should take to support and expand human rights in the internet era. These include (1) Creative and coherent diplomacy and standard setting, (2) promoting awareness and understanding of the issues, (3) fostering multi-stakeholder collaboration and problem solving, and (4) providing expertise and direct support (Horner et al., June 2010: 11). The second is a briefing paper prepared for the European Parliament's Subcommittee on Human Rights. The paper addresses human rights and the internet in European foreign policy on the basis of internet-related cases in Tunisia, Egypt, Syria, Libya, and Bahrain (Wagner, July 2012). It also includes policy recommendations in response to issues raised during the Arab Spring, for example support to European telecom operators in order to mitigate state requests that violate human rights standards such as turning off the internet in third countries.

In summary, a number of intergovernmental organizations have addressed ICT policy with reference to human rights; and organizations such as UNESCO and UNDP explicitly subscribe to a rights-based approach to their activities. However, few of the organizations have engaged with substantive analysis of policy issues from a human rights perspective. The Council of Europe is one of the few organizations that have contributed more comprehensive human right analysis and recommendations on standards to guide global internet policy, based on case law from the European Court of Human Rights.

A Business Perspective

The human rights due diligence of private companies is a rapidly growing field, not least as it concerns companies in the ICT sector.

In 2011 the most important standard-setting document concerning the human rights responsibility of private companies was adopted, namely the Guiding Principles on Business and Human Rights endorsed by the

---

[65] In *Perrin* v. *United Kingdom* (18 October 2005), the applicant challenged a 30-month prison sentence in connection with pornographic material exhibited on a US-based website. The ECtHR held that the fact that the dissemination of the images in question may have been legal in the USA did not mean that, in proscribing such dissemination within its own territory and in prosecuting and convicting the applicant, the UK had exceeded the margin of appreciation afforded to it.

UN Human Rights Council in June 2011.[66] The guiding principles were developed in a year-long consultative process conducted by the former UN Special Representative for Business and Human Rights John Ruggie. The Human Rights Council resolution that endorsed the Guiding Principles also established a Working Group on business and human rights consisting of five independent experts, including Margaret Jungk from the Danish Institute for Human Rights. The working group will work on the dissemination and implementation of the guiding principles over a three-year period.[67] Prior to joining the working group, Jungk headed the Human Rights and Business Department of the Danish Institute for Human Rights, which provides tools for businesses to assess their human rights performance, currently used by 200-plus companies.[68] Other organizations in the field include the US/UK-based Human Rights and Business Resource Centre,[69] the UK-based Institute for Human Rights and Business,[70] and the US-based organization Access.[71]

The UN Guiding Principles on Business and Human Rights build on prior initiatives in the field, not least the UN-driven Global Compact Initiative that targets the business community at large. The Global Compact Initiative is structured as a public–private partnership and seeks to promote voluntary commitment amongst corporations to align their operations with universally accepted principles in the areas of human rights, labour, environment, and anti-corruption.[72]

Another important standard-setting document is the OECD Guidelines for Multinational Enterprises. In the most recent update of the guidelines from 2011, freedom of expression on the internet was included as a topic. The guidelines are part of the OECD Declaration on International Investment and Multinational Enterprises from 1976, and contain recommendations on a number of areas, including human rights and labour relations. The Guidelines represent the most comprehensive voluntary code of conduct developed by states.[73]

---

66 The Guiding Principles are available at: http://www.business-humanrights.org/SpecialRepPortal/Home/Protect-Respect-Remedy-Framework/GuidingPrinciples, retrieved 25 August 2011.

67 See http://www.ohchr.org/EN/Issues/Business/Pages/WGHRandtransnationalcorporationsandotherbusiness.aspx, retrieved 15 August 2012.

68 See www.humanrightsbusiness.org, retrieved 2 August 2012.

69 See http://www.business-humanrights.org/Aboutus/Staff, retrieved 15 August 2012.

70 See http://www.ihrb.org/, retrieved 15 August 2012.

71 See https://www.accessnow.org/, retrieved 15 August 2012.

72 See http://www.unglobalcompact.org/, retrieved 15 August 2012,

73 See http://www.oecd.org/daf/internationalinvestment/guidelinesformultinationalenterprises/, retrieved 30 October 2012.

Related to the ICT sector, one of the first human rights-related initiatives was the Global Network Initiative (GNI) initiated in 2008. GNI is a multi-stakeholder partnership between companies, civil society groups, and academics, set up to promote human rights standards among companies. Up to now, the initiative has been largely dominated by civil society groups and academia, while only four companies have joined, namely Yahoo, Microsoft, Google and Facebook (Facebook joined most recently in May 2013).[74] The project was initiated in response to state pressure on companies to comply with domestic laws and policies in ways that may conflict with human rights standards of freedom of expression and privacy. The GNI has developed principles and implementation guidelines related to those rights that inform a voluntary code of conduct for ICT companies. The group held its first public forum in 2008 in conjunction with the Business Leaders Initiative on Human Rights (BLIHR) chaired by former UN High Commissioner on Human Rights Mary Robinson.[75]

Since the formation of the GNI, other networks within the field of communication technology have emerged, including the Telecommunications Industry Dialogue on Freedom of Expression and Privacy, which was established in 2011.[76] The Industry Dialogue and GNI have, since 2013, cooperated to advance human rights compliance within the ICT sector.

At EU level, the European Commission's Directorate-General for Enterprise and Industry in 2012 decided that the ICT sector is one of three business sectors that will receive sector-specific guidance on corporate responsibility and human rights. The project is directly linked to the UN Guiding Principles and aims to provide guidance on how these principles should work in the ICT sector. The initiative is part of a renewed EU strategy 2011–14 for Corporate Social Responsibility.[77]

As illustrated, the human rights responsibility of private companies is increasingly high on the international agenda, not least concerning the ICT sector. Moreover, coalitions such as the Global Network Initiative and the Telecommunications' Industry Dialogue illustrate that technology companies increasingly address the role they play vis-à-vis human rights,

---

[74] For a full list of current members of the GNI please refer to http://www.globalnetworkinitiative.org/, retrieved 10 July 2012.

[75] BLIHR was active from 2003 to 2009. See www.blihr.org, retrieved 10 July 2012.

[76] See www.teliasonera.com/en/newsroom/news/2012/telecommunications-industry-dialogue-selects-five-host-organisations-as-potential-addresses/, retrieved 15 August 2012.

[77] See http://ec.europa.eu/enterprise/policies/sustainable-business/corporate-social-responsibility/index_en.htm, retrieved 15 August 2012.

in particular the right to freedom of expression and the right to privacy. These business-driven initiatives, however, are based on voluntary commitment, leaving the level of human rights protection up to the company itself. Moreover, the global nature of the communication environment makes the enforcement of human rights standards on private companies increasingly complex, not least in the area of privacy and data protection. International companies may experience pressure from states to comply with national laws that conflict with international human rights standards, as reported by the Global Network Initiative, whereas the experience of citizens is that the protection of their rights is in the hands of private companies located abroad and subject to varying legal regimes. Recent years have exposed a number of cases where companies such as Google, Yahoo, and Facebook have been criticized for violating their users' rights to privacy or their right to freely seek information, and where national enforcement of human rights standards is complicated by the transnational nature of these companies. As such, the global character of the internet forces a direct collision between diverse national legal cultures and ways of balancing competing human rights standards. Although states have an obligation to protect their citizens' enjoyment of human rights, including in the realm of private parties, the global character of the internet makes it legally and practically complex to enforce this principle.[78]

A Research Perspective

The research field concerned with the human rights implications of communication technology is steadily growing, but remains scattered across many disciplines. Below follows a brief – and by no means comprehensive – outline of some of the institutions with research agendas in this field.

The WSIS process provided a meeting point for many of the scholars interested in ICT policy, and various publications dealing with information society issues were produced as a result of this encounter.[79] By contrast,

---

[78] Another area of increasing attention is technology companies' export of dual-use products that may facilitate human rights violations, for instance products used to target surveillance of internet use. See the resolution adopted by the European Parliament in 2011 on dual-use technology, available at: http://www.europarl.europa.eu/news/en/pressroom/content/20110927IPR27586/html/Controlling-dual-use-exports, retrieved 15 August 2012.

[79] Several of the WSIS publications represent a mixture of academic and activist contributors, such as Heinrich Böll Foundation (2003, 2005); CRIS Campaign (September 2005); Ambrosi et al. (2005); Lovink and Zehle (2005); Jørgensen (2006). However, academic publications were also produced, for example, Kleinwachter

few legal scholars in the field of human rights participated in the WSIS. This is indicative of the challenge of combining research fields, which currently have few cross-cutting research themes and agendas.

In terms of academic institutions combining human rights and ICT issues, some of the most well known are the Berkman Center for Internet and Society (Harvard University), and the Stanford Center for Internet and Society (Stanford University), both affiliated with law schools. However, at both institutions emphasis is placed on national legal standards rather than on international human rights law. Likewise, research institutions such as the Oxford Internet Institute (Oxford University) and the School of Information Studies (Syracuse University) are prominent in specific fields of internet research, but rarely with a human rights framing.

One of the projects that have conducted extensive empirical research related to violations of online freedom of expression and privacy is the Open Net Initiative (ONI).[80] ONI is a partnership between the Citizen Lab at the Munk Centre for International Studies (University of Toronto), the Security Group at Cambridge Computer Laboratory (University of Cambridge), the Berkman Center for Internet and Society, as well as the Oxford Internet Institute. As for information and communication law, numerous legal departments deal with this topic, such as the Institute for Information Law (University of Amsterdam), which claims to be the largest research facility in the field in Europe.

With regard to human rights law, countless faculties specialize in the field,[81] but with limited focus on communication technology, though there are exceptions such as the Institute of International Law and International Relations (University of Graz). Privacy and data protection is one area where specific research combining human rights and technology is conducted. The institutions active in this field include (among many others) the Information Law Institute (New York University School of Law), the Cyberspace Law & Policy Centre (University of New South Wales), the Canadian Internet Policy and Public Interest Clinic (University of Ottawa), the Department of Management and the Department of Law (London

(2004); Best et al. (2004); Raboy and Schtern (2005); Flyverbom (2006); Mueller et al. (2007).

80 See www.opennet.net, retrieved 2 August 2012.

81 See, for example, the network of academic institutions affiliated with the European Master in Human Rights and Democratization Programme, carried out jointly by more than forty European Universities, available at: http://www.eiuc.org/, retrieved 2 May 2013.

School of Economics and Political Science), and the George Washington University Law School.

In summary, while the practice and regulation of communication technology is subject to research from a variety of technical, legal, and social science perspectives, the efforts to combine such research with human rights studies are relatively limited. The human rights research community has not, by and large, taken on the global communications environment as a research topic. For information science or communications scholars the topic of human rights is often dealt with as a normative framework at a very general level or in relation to a few specific rights only.

The Impact of Human Rights on ICT Policy

As outlined in the previous sections, the human rights perspective appears visible but not operationally applied in global ICT policy debates. References to the human rights regime, especially to the Universal Declaration of Human Rights, have been made on many policy occasions; however, this has been mostly in a very general form or with reference to selected rights only. The right to freedom of expression has been iterated time and again, and is by far the most debated human right in relation to communication technology debates. The emphasis on freedom of expression is not surprising, since the right protects freedoms related to both individuals and media, and as such is key to debates on the global communication environment. The enjoyment of freedom of expression, however, must be seen in conjunction with the whole human rights regime pertaining to multiple dimensions and contexts of social life, for example: the right to a minimum standard of living; the right to basic education; the right to health; the right to not be discriminated against based on, for instance, one's gender, ethnicity, or religion; the right to enjoy one's own culture; the right to political participation; and so forth. The protection and promotion of a broad range of rights may be affected in a negative manner by the ways in which the global communication environment is used and governed by both public- and private-sector actors.

Moreover, assessing ICT policy from the baseline of human rights standards may point toward policies and practices that are substantially different from the approaches currently being pursued. First, this implies ensuring that states refrain from establishing national or international laws, policies, and practices that erode the agreed-upon human rights standards. For instance, the UN Special Rapporteur on the promotion and protection of human rights and fundamental freedoms, while countering terrorism, has pointed to the erosion of the right to privacy in the fight against terrorism (Scheinin 2009: 2). Similarly, the UN Special Rapporteur on the promotion and protection of the right to freedom of opinion and expression has stressed that the arbitrary use of criminal law to sanction legitimate online expression constitutes one of the gravest forms of restriction on the right to freedom of expression, as it not only creates a 'chilling effect', but also leads to other human rights violations, such as arbitrary detention and torture and other forms of cruel, inhuman, or degrading treatment or punishment (La Rue 2011: Paragraph 28).

Second, states must proactively take steps to create conditions in which rights can be realized more fully and effectively. Currently national, regional, and global ICT policies are routinely being formulated with limited attention to the relevance of, or impact on, human rights standards. Increasingly important in the latter connection is the need to establish frameworks that encourage companies to protect and promote human rights standards. These challenges are further addressed in the chapters that follow.

PART II

Framing the net

Many scholars have stressed that the evolving story of internet politics essentially reflects a struggle between openness and control (Lessig 1999; Castells 2001; Rasmussen 2007). This struggle, however, takes many forms and shapes depending on how topics are framed and challenges articulated. In this second part of the book, four metaphors are used to organize the debate on human rights in the internet era. As previously indicated, this is not to suggest that just these four framings cover all facets of the internet; however, they represent recurring themes in internet-related literature and policy debate, and each point to current human rights controversies. The metaphors speak to the internet as infrastructure, public sphere, medium, and culture respectively.

The infrastructure metaphor differs from the others by being closely related to the technology that carries the internet – and thus to a more technical discourse – whereas the public sphere, medium, and culture metaphors each have a strong counterpart within political science, media/communication studies, and cultural studies. The public sphere and culture metaphor are elaborated in slightly more detail, compared to the infrastructure and medium metaphor, since these are deployed in the case studies presented in the third part of the book.

4. The internet as infrastructure

> We need to start by recognizing that the Net is infrastructure, in the sense that it is a real thing that we can build on, and depend on. It is also public in the sense that nobody owns it and everybody can use it ... this is a very different kind of infrastructure than anything civilization has ever seen before, or attempted to regulate.
>
> (Searls 2010: 1)

Many scholars have described the internet as an infrastructure (Finnemann 2005; Hindman 2009; Bowker et al. 2010). The concept of infrastructure is generally used to describe the underlying foundation or basic framework of a system or organization. Examples include transportation systems such as highways, railways, and airline systems; communication systems such as telephone networks and postal services; governance systems such as court systems; and basic public services and facilities such as schools and water systems (Frischmann 2012: 4). Infrastructure often exists as an invisible, taken-for-granted resource, whereas a breakdown in the infrastructure can make its design and effects visible (Bowker et al. 2010: 97–8). The government has in most contexts played a role in ensuring the provision of infrastructures, and these systems have, irrespective of the public or private ownership model, been required to serve the public on a non-discriminatory basis (Frischmann 2012: 5). When 'information' is added, infrastructure refers to digital facilities and services usually associated with the internet, just as global information infrastructure refers to communication of data across national boundaries (Bowker et al. 2010: 97–8). Whilst science and technology studies (STS) are concerned with infrastructure design,[1] information infrastructure is an emerging research arena that cross-cuts disciplines such as computer science, information science, cognitive science, and STS (Bowker et al. 2010: 112).

The internet is frequently pictured as a mass of lines that connect computers worldwide and explained by means of other infrastructures such as the highway system. 'One helpful way is to think of the National Information Infrastructure as a network of highways – much like the interstate begun in

1 See, for example, Hughes (1987); Ribes and Baker (2007).

the fifties' (Gore quoted in Stefik 1996: xv).[2] Speaking of the internet as an infrastructure highlights that it is a foundation for something else: a public resource to be provided to all on a non-discriminatory basis.

At policy level, The World Bank,[3] the UN International Telecommunication Union (ITU),[4] and the Organization for Economic Co-operation and Development (OECD)[5] are examples of international organizations that refer to the internet as a fundamental infrastructure crucial for development, for delivery of services such as health and education, and as a prerequisite for economic growth in a globalized world. The infrastructure metaphor also shows up in the discourse related to internet governance. Scholars such as DeNardis have suggested an infrastructure-based theory of internet governance, arguing that infrastructure design and administration internalize the political and economic values that ultimately influence the extent of online freedom and innovation (DeNardis 2012: 721). Dutton and Peltu (November 2005: 7) have developed a typology of internet governance issues that addresses, among others, the development of the internet infrastructure.

Like other infrastructures, the internet's technical layer was constructed at a certain point in time, and is now operated and developed on an ongoing basis. The history of how the internet evolved has been told numerous times, and will not be repeated here.[6] This chapter will, however, draw out a few highlights from this narrative to emphasize that the internet started as a private initiative, developed into a public utility, and increasingly is being debated as a global public good. Moreover, it will illustrate some of the human-rights challenges pertaining to the internet as an infrastructure.

---

[2] Stefik (1996: xix) elaborates how the highway metaphor carries misleading connotations when talking about the computer network since the highway is planned and designed, whereas the internet is self-organized with no central planner.

[3] See http://data.worldbank.org/about/world-development-indicators-data/infrastructure, retrieved 23 August 2012.

[4] See, for example, the ITU overview of the Global Information Infrastructure standards development at: http://www.itu.int/rec/T-REC-Y, retrieved 21 August 2012.

[5] See, for example, Chapter 5 on Internet Infrastructure in OECD (2011b).

[6] See, for example, Abbate (1999) or Rasmussen (2007). Rasmussen distinguishes between four internet phases. The first phase is from the Second World War to 1972, during which the ARPANET project was realized. The second phase is from 1972 until *c.*1990, in which the TCP/IP protocol was developed. A third phase starting in the early 1990s and with no ending date is characterized by the advent of the World Wide Web, and a current fourth phase is characterized by increasing regulatory and political intervention in a number of issues related to the internet (Rasmussen 2007: 18).

Governance of the internet's technical resources was *the* most contested issue during the second phase of the World Summit on the Information Society (WSIS), and post WSIS continues to be on the agenda at every Internet Governance Forum (IGF). The controversies address the interface between technical coordination and public policy issues,[7] including the USA's unilateral control of a global resource, as addressed in more detail below.

1. FROM MILITARY RESEARCH TO PUBLIC UTILITY

The internet arose out of research sponsored by the United States and other governments, and its early use was largely confined to the military and academic sector. It began as a research project of the US Defense Advanced Research Projects Agency in the early 1970s. The project (ARPANET) showed the utility of breaking up digitized information into packets of information that could be relayed from one computer to another, thus exploring methods for interconnecting an arbitrary collection of packet-switched networks so that computers connected to any of the networks could communicate with one another in an end-to-end fashion (Cerf 2004: 1). On 24 October 1995 the body responsible for internet policy in the USA, the Federal Networking Council, adopted the following definition of the internet:

> The Federal Networking Council (FNC) agrees that the following language reflects our definition of the term 'Internet'. 'Internet' refers to the global information system that –
>
> (i) is logically linked together by a globally unique address space based on the Internet Protocol (IP) or its subsequent extensions/follow-ons;
> (ii) is able to support communications using the Transmission Control Protocol/Internet Protocol (TCP/IP) suite or its subsequent extensions/follow-ons, and/or other IP-compatible protocols; and
> (iii) provides, uses or makes accessible, either publicly or privately, high level services layered on the communications and related infrastructure described herein.
>
> (Cerf 2004: 1–2)[8]

---

[7] Public policy refers to government activities, whether acting directly or through agents, that has an influence on the life of citizens (Peters 2006).

[8] At the time of the definition there was a distinction made between the term 'Internet' and the term 'internet'. The capitalized version referred to the publicly available system and the lower case version referred to private copies, hence what we today call intranet (Cerf 2004: 2). Today the lower case 'internet' is largely used for the public internet.

On the technical level, the internet works through packet-switching where a computer originates a 'post card', addressing it to a destination computer somewhere in the network. In addition to the routing and forwarding functions at the IP layer, the internet also includes a Domain Name System that associates domain names with IP addresses. Domain names are often presented as the real estate of the internet, though this analogy first and foremost may be for the convenience of intellectual property advocates, rather than technical accuracy (Rasmussen 2007: 177). IP addresses define exactly where a host computer is in the topology of the global internet. Since the networks all adhere to the same set of communication protocol standards, this allows the internet to function as an apparently uniform collaboration of hundreds of thousands of networks (Cerf 2004: 3).

The internet thus represents a grand network consisting of numerous operators, including companies, individuals, non-governmental organizations, and various branches of national governments, situated in various local jurisdictions. While its creation arose out of government-sponsored research, the provision of its services to the general public has been largely through private sector initiatives. The internet that began as a private network using dedicated circuits leased from telecom service providers is today 'an enormous, sprawling and rapidly evolving, public utility' (Cerf 2004: 2).

2. OPERATING THE INTERNET

There are several hierarchical mechanisms that are critical to the operation of the internet, namely the Domain Name System (DNS), the allocation and assignment of IP addresses, and the maintenance of other unique parameters associated with the internet protocols (Cerf 2004: 6). Operation of the DNS has policy implications, not least since it represents the access point for central control of the internet, as further addressed below.

Prior to the Internet Corporation for Assigned Names and Numbers (ICANN), the Internet Assigned Numbers Authority (IANA) was responsible for the overall coordination and management of the DNS, as described in Request for Comments (RFC) 1591.[9] IANA and Network Solutions (NSI), a private company, handled the DNS administration, and received US government funds to support their operation, however without any legal basis that provided these bodies or the US government with the right to set policy regarding domain names on the internet. The DNS functioned on the basis of agreed practice and not law, and this self-regulatory practice

[9] The Request for Comments (RFC) series archives and codifies internet protocols and standards.

extended to other policy questions such as payment for domain names. NSI thus demanded payment for registration of domain names without guidelines as to which other conditions could reasonably be imposed as a prerequisite for domain name registration.[10]

In June 1998 the US Department of Commerce and a task force headed by US Presidential Adviser Ira Magaziner issued a 'Statement of Policy on the Management of Internet Names and Addresses', known as the DNS White Paper (United States Department of Commerce 5 June 1998). The White Paper called for the creation of a private non-profit corporation to take over the DNS and institute various reforms. In the run-up to the establishment of this corporation, some of its institutional designers argued that the decentralized decision making that created the internet at a technical level should be used as a model for 'collective governance' of the global internet. The core of the argument was:

> (1) By decentralized decision making, the internet itself solves an immensely difficult collective action problem: how to get large numbers of individual computer networks, running diverse operating systems, to communicate with one another for the common good;[11]
> (2) decentralized decision making is the most cost effective and accurate means of reflecting the real preferences and experiences of the users; and
> (3) decentralized decision making is light work compared with the task of projecting local views into a centralized policy making process.
>
> (Johnson and Post 1997: 73–81)[12]

---

[10] 'Thus, no one can now say that any given condition must, may, or may not be imposed as a minimum requirement for this particular passport to "netizenship". Nor do any of the many different private and governmental organizations that are currently discussing a range of questions in this area … have an uncontested or clearly legitimate claim to the authority to decide these matters unilaterally' (Johnson and Post 1997: 64).

[11] '[T]he net is really nothing more than a set of voluntary standards regarding message transmission, routing, and reception. There is not now and never was a central governmental body that decreed or voted to adopt a law stating that TCP/IP is required to be used by those wishing to communicate electronically on a global scale, or that HTTP is required to be used if you wish to communicate over a particular portion of the global network (the World Wide Web). If you connect to a neighboring host and send out packets of data that conform to the protocol, your messages can be heard by others who have adopted the protocol. All are free to decline to follow the standard and to obey some other protocol, and they will communicate only to those who, literally, speak their language. Many people and groups have, in fact, seceded (or declined to join) the global net, forming local area, or proprietary wide area, networks' (Cerf 2004: 7).

[12] Johnson was advisor to Network Solutions during the formative stages of ICANN's development, and his ideas directly influenced Magaziner and others (Mueller 2002: 213).

In October 1998 ICANN was established as a private non-profit corporation under California law, representing the global 'internet community'. ICANN undertook its responsibilities under the auspices of the US Department of Commerce (DOC) by way of a Memorandum of Understanding between ICANN and the DOC. The organizational design was based on the idea that providers and users of internet services should have decision-making capacity, while governments should have an advisory role (Kleinwachter 2004: 38).[13] ICANN's claim to legitimacy is thus based on the assertion that it functions as the internet community's instrument for self-governance. ICANN's role was to 'carry out the oversight and information management functions needed to assure unique allocation of domain names, IP addresses and other protocol identifiers' (Cerf 2004: 6). This includes management of the top-level root zone file, whereas the process of allocating and assigning internet addresses to users is delegated to local internet registries. ICANN has since its inception been subject to extensive criticism, not least concerning its lack of adherence to the principles upon which it was founded.[14]

3. GOVERNING THE INTERNET

The term 'internet governance' has been debated since the formation of ICANN. Whereas some interpreted the term as the technical and operational arrangements for managing the DNS root, others pointed to ICANN's potential for exercising internet control, since control of the root implies control of access to the internet (Mueller 2002: 7). With the growing importance of the internet as a global resource, the role and mandate of ICANN has become an increasingly contested issue amongst states. This is not surprising since ICANN represents 'the only globally visible body charged with any kind of oversight for the Internet' (Cerf 2004: 9).[15]

---

[13] According to the initial agreement, the US supervision over ICANN was supposed to terminate after two years. However, ICANN still remains on contract with the US government. The current agreement that entered into force in October 2009 has strengthened the reporting obligations towards the international community and the review role of the Governmental Advisory Committee (United States Department of Commerce and ICANN, 30 September 2009).

[14] The role of ICANN and various critiques related to its constituency and modus operandi has been covered by, for example, MacLean (2004b); Drake (2005); Hofmann (2007); Mueller (2009).

[15] At the WSIS second phase, 'internet governance' was defined more broadly than the functions performed by ICANN, thus as: 'the development and application by Governments, the private sector and civil society, in their respective roles, of shared principles, norms, rules, decision-making procedures, and programmes

The WSIS brought to a head the profound disagreement between the USA and many other governments, including those of the EU, concerning the US control over the DNS root and, via contract, over ICANN.[16] In the course of this debate it was argued that ICANN's operation of internet resources entails matters of public policy, and that these should be separated from technical coordination. This would imply either an entirely different organization in charge of operating the internet, or a revision of ICANN to differentiate more clearly between technical coordination and matters of public policy. It was also stressed that ICANN needs to be more publicly accountable.[17] The debate echoed a number of the regulatory challenges and models for governing the internet that were discussed prior to the establishment of ICANN, including the following:

> (1) existing territorial sovereigns may extend their jurisdiction to govern actions on the internet that have impact on their own citizens;
> (2) sovereigns may enter multi-lateral agreements and establish new rules specifically applicable to the internet;
> (3) a new international organization may attempt to establish new rules; and
> (4) de facto rules emerge as a result of the interplay of decisions by domain name and IP address registries.
>
> (Johnson and Post 1997: 69–75)

Not surprisingly, the US government refuses to alter their unilateral control over the internet, and their position is by and large supported by the technical community around ICANN.[18] Most recently, the World Conference on International Telecommunications, which aimed to update a 1988 treaty on international telecommunications, was viewed by many actors as an attempt by the ITU to assert more control over the internet. As a result, 55 member states, including the USA, Canada, and several European countries, declined to endorse the final documents when the meeting ended on 14 December 2012.[19]

---

that shape the evolution and use of the Internet' (Working Group on Internet Governance 2005: 4).

[16] For a detailed account of the WSIS controversy over internet governance see Mueller (2010: Chapter 4).

[17] The accountability of ICANN is addressed in Mueller (2009), and in a review from the Berkman Center for Internet and Society at Harvard University (20 October 2010).

[18] A common argument in favour of the current model has been 'if it ain't broke why fix it?', implying that the operation of the internet has worked well, and that including more states in this process risks undermining the stability and freedoms of it. See Mueller (2010: 75–7) for an elaborated account of this controversy.

[19] The final document is available at: http://wftp3.itu.int/pub/epub_shared/GS/WCIT-12/E/web/flipviewerxpress.html, retrieved 18 December 2012. For an

On a final note, a few remarks on the internet as a global public good are required. Scholars and civil society groups have increasingly proposed that the internet should be regulated as a global public good.[20] The notion of a global public good refers to 'a benefit providing utility that, in principle, is available to the global population' (Morrissey quoted in Binger 2003: 4). The concept derives from economic theory, and became widely known with the UNDP publication *Global Public Goods: International Cooperation in the 21st Century* (Kaul et al. 1999).[21] Several authors have argued that the internet has dimensions of a global public good; however, the policy implication of this claim is largely unexplored.[22]

In summary, the infrastructure metaphor highlights that the internet offers a global standard for communication, connects resources worldwide, in principle enables universal access, and at the technical level does not discriminate between traffic or users. The internet has been widely spoken of as an infrastructure, among others, in the discourse on the operation and governance of the internet's technical resources. With reference to the public and private models, this discourse associates with the liberal model, stressing that control over the internet's technical resources should remain with a private corporation, with states taking an advisory role. This infrastructure-framing points to specific human rights issues, which is the topic to be considered next.

4. HUMAN RIGHTS ISSUES RELATED TO THE INTERNET AS INFRASTRUCTURE

Introduction

As stressed by several scholars, there are different layers involved in operating the internet (Mueller 2002; MacLean 2004a). First, there is the technical layer, which controls and coordinates the uniqueness of names and

---

overview of endorsing states see: http://www.itu.int/osg/wcit-12/highlights/signatories.html, retrieved 19 December 2012.

[20] At the 2007 IGF in Rio, APC Director Anriette Esterhuysen stated in the Opening Ceremony that the 'Internet is a public good and should be governed based on public interest principles including human rights, free expression, open standards, privacy, balanced intellectual property, interoperability, creativity, transparency, and accountability' (Esterhuysen 2007). The statement can be heard at www.ipjustice.org/Audio/Anriette-IGF2007.MP3, retrieved 12 November 2012.

[21] For an account of controversies related to the definition and scope of the concept see, for example, Binger (2003: 4–6).

[22] See, for example, Spar (1999); Accuosto and Johnson (2004); Raboy and Schtern (2005).

addresses. Second, there is the economic layer, which takes decisions about rationing scarcity. Third, there is the layer that defines policies regarding the rights to names (Mueller 2002: 19).[23] Since there is a principal difference between technical coordination (layer one) and rules and judgements related to rationing scarcity or defining and enforcing rights to names (layers two and three), much of the internet governance debate concerns how public policy issues may be identified and extracted from technical and operational coordination. Furthermore, it may be argued that all three layers are de facto subject to public policy, since their operation is based on a contract with the US government. As such, the internet is currently administered as an area of public policy, despite the fact that the 'day-to-day' operation is delegated to ICANN.

Some of the criticism that has been raised against ICANN stresses that it does not primarily operate through user self-governance, but rather through its professional staff who may control the policy agenda unilaterally, for example by drafting contracts with registries and registrars (Mueller 2002: 215).[24] The technical standard coordination (IETF), after which ICANN was modelled, had incentives for consensus-based processes, since it relied on coordination amongst many, whereas the situation with ICANN is different.[25] ICANN de facto controls the root zone file, a small but critical file that determines the entire address system of the internet, and thereby has a monopoly over an essential resource. This has led scholars to describe ICANN as a global regulatory regime with exclusive control of a critical input into an industry, which it uses to regulate that industry (Mueller 2002: 218). 'ICANN's control of the root is used to make and enforce policy in three broad areas: defining and enforcing rights to names; regulation of the domain name supply industry; and the linkage of online identity to law enforcement' (Mueller 2002). At least two of these areas are linked to human rights such as freedom of expression and the right to privacy.

As previously stressed, the whole system of human rights protection builds on state commitment to – and implementation of – human

---

[23] MacLean (2004: 88–90) has also developed a number of models illustrating the various policy layers and actors involved in internet governance.

[24] 'With a single point of control (the root), and competition for the political and economic benefits that can be derived from it, it was inevitable that political strength, not a communitarian commitment to rough consensus, would drive decisions' (Mueller 2002: 215).

[25] Mueller notes that ICANN's agreed practice whereby internet service providers point at the ICANN root has to be seen in light of powerful network externalities. Thus it is not necessarily a voluntary regime just because it is based on a contract (Mueller 2002: 216).

rights standards, which can then be invoked by the individual toward the state. Even when areas of operation are delegated to private parties, it remains the duty of the state to assert and secure the appropriate level of human rights protection. ICANN's Articles of Incorporation note the need to comply with relevant principles of international law (ICANN, 21 November 1998: Paragraph 4) and as stated by the Council of Europe: 'ICANN operates *de facto* by delegation on behalf of the international community and, ultimately, on behalf of each of the states and other stakeholders that make up the internet community' (Council of Europe 2006: 25). However, since ICANN is a US-based corporation, it is essentially the US government that is the contracting party with respect to human rights treaties. This raises human rights problems related to the rule of law, the right to privacy and the right to freedom of expression, as further explained below.

The Rule of Law

> To date, the rule of law has been lacking in ICANN's practices. Rules for decision making are frequently amended, often disregarded, and not reliably enforced. More powerful government(s) have more influence than less powerful governments, and more powerful private interests have more influence than their less powerful counterparts. If cyberspace is the 'electronic frontier', ICANN has created a 'wild west' culture of politicized decision making. The time has come to establish the rule of law.
>
> (Klein 2005: 1)

There is nothing unusual about a private organization having an impact on human rights. As argued in the previous chapter, there is a whole arena of actors occupied with the human rights responsibility of private actors. What is unusual in relation to the internet is the fact that a private US corporation has control over a global resource, including the power to impact the protection of human rights such as freedom of expression and the right to privacy for users worldwide. This raises a number of interrelated issues.

An overarching issue relates to the rule of law. Since ICANN's control over the root zone file implies that it has to make decisions with human rights implications, it is crucial to ensure that these decisions are based on international human rights law. Human rights standards related to the rule of law stipulate that interference with, for example, the right to privacy or the right to freedom of expression should have a legal basis, serve a legitimate purpose, and be proportionate to the goal pursued. Moreover, the law must be available to the public and be reasonably predictable to avoid arbitrary restrictions in fundamental rights (La Rue 2011: 8).

In contrast, there is no legislative instrument that spells out ICANN's mandate. The closest thing to 'an ICANN law' is the Memorandum of Understanding (MoU) with the US Department of Commerce, which defines various policy parameters for ICANN's operation. The MoU is subject to frequent and non-transparent modification (Klein 2005: 3). ICANN is subject to political oversight by the US Department of Commerce, while other governments may exercise political pressure via the Governmental Advisory Committee (GAC), which is the ICANN entity that represents governments. 'The majority of governments, however, have no voice in oversight, despite the fact that ICANN oversees a critical global infrastructure' (Klein 2005: 4). With regard to judicial review of decisions taken by ICANN, this can only be undertaken by state courts in California, where ICANN is incorporated.

These factors combined create a human rights vacuum where decisions concerning a global resource are taken by a private US corporation based on its internal by-laws and an MoU; where formal oversight is the responsibility of one powerful government, while other (powerful) governments may influence decisions via the GAC; where there are no means of judicial review outside the court of California; and with limited transparency regarding the internal processes that guide decision making. In contrast, proponents of the current model, in particular the US government and the technical community around ICANN, stress that US control ensures a free flow of information, whereas international control would include states with a track record of human rights violations.[26]

In response to this dilemma, scholars have suggested keeping the current organizational set-up, but ensuring that ICANN be revised and based on a legal framework that stipulates the public policy principles that are to guide its operation (Mueller et al. 2009). Such a legal framework could have a clear reference to international human rights standards, and include mechanisms for independent oversight and judicial review of ICANN's decisions. This would ensure that any ICANN decision with public policy implications was regulated by law rather than by internal by-laws and a Memorandum of Understanding.

One of the public policy principles suggested for governing the internet is the norm of net neutrality (Mueller et al. 2009). In this context, net neutrality is based on an end-to-end argument, which implies universal and reciprocal access to internet resources, thus the ability of any internet

---

[26] At the UN General Assembly in October 2011, India proposed to move the governance of the internet's technical resources to a UN body. India's statement is available at: http://cis-india.org/internet-governance/blog/india-statement-un-cirp, 22 retrieved August 2012.

user to connect to any lawful content or services on the internet.[27] The norm would thus preserve the non-discriminatory access to services associated with other types of infrastructures. As part of a legal framework for ICANN, the norm would indicate that the coordination of internet names and addresses should be a neutral enabling function, and that decisions that may impact on users' fundamental rights and freedoms (examples below) are subject to review. Debate about the applicability of the net neutrality norm to ICANN's activities already plays a role in the politics of ICANN (Mueller et al. 2009: 1).

Privacy and WHOIS

The right to privacy is one of the rights directly affected by the current operation of the internet's technical resources. One of the widely debated issues has been the level of privacy protection afforded to users registered in the Domain Name Registration Data Directory Service – the co-called WHOIS database.[28] The WHOIS database consists of – among other things – domain name registrants' contact information, and domain name and servers, and is publicly accessible for anyone with internet access. ICANN-accredited domain name registrars are obligated to provide accurate information about all registrants via WHOIS.[29]

The WHOIS database was originally intended to enable network administrators to easily locate and remedy network problems, but is increasingly used for a variety of purposes including to assist law enforcement authorities, to combat fraud, and to enforce property rights. WHOIS has been subject to debate concerning its privacy and data protection practices for the past 10-plus years. The concerns raised include, among others, that the purposes of the collection and publication of personal data are not sufficiently specified; that the amount

---

[27] The notion of network neutrality carries at least two different meanings in the public debate. One is focused on the regulation of bandwidth, and is concerned with the way network operators differentiate the speeds with which packets are delivered, while the other is concerned with users' ability to access any lawful content or services on the internet. The norm of net neutrality has been addressed in a comparative broadband study from around the world conducted by the Berkman Center for Internet and Society at Harvard University (2009), with Yochai Benkler as principal investigator.

[28] The WHOIS protocol is documented in RFC 3912, available at: http://tools.ietf.org/html/rfc3912, retrieved 22 August 2012.

[29] See http://www.icann.org/en/resources/registrars/raa/ra-agreement-21may09-en.htm, retrieved 22 August 2012.

of data collected and made publicly available should be restricted to what is essential to fulfil the purpose specified; and that any secondary use incompatible with the original purpose specified should be based on informed consent.[30] In other words, WHOIS should comply with international data protection principles such as the *OECD Guidelines on the Protection of Privacy and Transborder Flows of Personal Data* from 1980. In an opinion from 2003, the EU data protection authorities found that the original purpose of making data publicly available, that is technical remedy, was legitimate. However, concerns are raised about the much wider purposes for which data are being used today. It is also questioned whether the publication of registrants' contact information is relevant to the original purpose (Article 29 – Data Protection Working Party, 13 June 2003).

In order to enhance the privacy of WHOIS, some registrars and third-party providers have started to offer privacy services that publish alternative contact information. Other providers act as 'proxies' by registering domain names that users may access and use through a separate arrangement with the provider (Souter, March 2012: 4). The use of proxy and privacy services has become a battleground between privacy and data protection advocates and law enforcement and intellectual property interests over access to personal data on the domain name registrant (Souter, March 2012). As part of this, ICANN's Generic Names Supporting Organization (GNSO) Council has commissioned several studies on WHOIS deployment and use, including how proxy and privacy services affect the access to data on domain name registrants.

In summary, the WHOIS database was not designed with international use in mind. However, due to the global scope of the internet this is now the case. The data is located in the USA, and protected according to the domestic standard for privacy in the USA, which has raised concern from, for example, the EU data protection authorities. In addition, personal data contained in WHOIS may be transferred to the US government for law enforcement purposes without the legal safeguards entailed in the EU data protection regime. As such the USA enforces a privacy standard on a global resource that is lower than the level of protection guaranteed to users elsewhere. Moreover, there are no means for redress for non-US citizens.

[30] For an account of this debate see the WHOIS resource page provided by the Electronic Privacy Information Center (EPIC), available at: http://epic.org/privacy/whois/, retrieved 22 August 2012.

Freedom of Expression and Domain Names

Freedom of expression is another human right affected by the current operation of the internet. One of the controversial issues in this regard has concerned ICANN's role when approving new generic top-level domain names (gTLD). One example of this controversy was the process around the proposed generic top-level domain name '.xxx', signifying pornographic or 'adult' content. The triple-x domain faced strong opposition from some states and conservative groups, and was rejected several times by the ICANN board before finally being approved in March 2011 following a long process of complaints, review, and consultation with governments.[31]

In the course of the triple-x controversy, ICANN revised its policy so that applications for new generic top-level domain names would be evaluated on the basis of their semantic meaning. According to ICANN's recently finalized policy in this area, proposed gTLD strings must not be contrary to 'generally accepted legal norms of morality and public order that are recognized under principles of international law' (ICANN, Version of 4 June 2012: 3–20).

ICANN's evaluation of proposed gTLDs includes consultation with ICANN's Governmental Advisory Committee. 'The process for GAC Advice on new gTLDs is intended to address applications that are identified by governments to be problematic, for example that potentially violate national law or raise sensitivities' (ICANN, Version of 4 June 2012: 3–2). As part of the process GAC may issue an early warning notice indicating that the proposed string is seen as potentially sensitive or problematic by one or more governments, thus the application could be subject to a formal objection. The evaluation also includes a dispute resolution process, whereby an objecting party may have its objection considered before 'a panel of experts' (ICANN, Version of 4 June 2012: 3–4).

ICANN's role in evaluating proposed gTLD strings has been criticized by scholars and civil society groups as an example of privatized censorship and as indicative of the way ICANN transfers its role as technical coordinator into one of making public policy (Mueller 2010: 71–3).

There are several freedom of expression issues related to this issue. First, despite the fact that ICCPR standards on freedom of expression allow for law-based restrictions on the grounds of public order and morality, there is no such thing as one global standard for morality and public order, as

---

[31] For a detailed account of the .xxx incident see Mueller (2010: 71–3). See also the coverage in CircleID, 18 March 2011, available at: http://www.circleid.com/posts/20110318_icann_approves_xxx/, retrieved 10 August 2012.

human rights are interpreted differently in various national contexts. Any proposed top-level domain name might contradict public morals in country A, whereas it would be a legitimate expression in country B. Deciding whether a given domain name complies with 'global standards for morality and public order' is thus legally complex and risks undermining freedom of expression standards in some countries. Moreover, since ICANN's decision-making process is influenced by advice from national governments, it risks being highly politicized.

Second, if ICANN de facto works on the basis of delegation by the international community (as suggested by the Council of Europe, above), it is important that decisions with human rights implications are subject to independent judicial control, and that access to remedies are provided for. In the current example ICANN has mandated itself to judge on the content of domain names vis-à-vis international law, including human rights law, without any democratic control or means of judicial review. This example illustrates how the current operation of the internet's technical resources have carried with it decisions that may have an adverse human rights impact on internet users worldwide.[32]

5. CONCLUSION

In summary, this chapter illustrates some of the debates that speak to the internet as a global infrastructure, including policy controversies related to operating and governing this infrastructure. Table 4.1 summarizes some of the notions, policy themes, and human rights issues connected to this perspective on the internet. The first row indicates commonly used notions that refer to the internet as infrastructure, for example 'global information highway' and 'public utility'. The second row highlights that the potential for social change encompassed by this framing relates to the universal and non-discriminatory character of the internet. Third, with reference to the public and private models, the prevailing discourse addressing the internet as a global resource argues that the technical infrastructure should remain in the hands of a private corporation with minimal state interference. Next, coordination and governance of internet resources are suggested as some of the key themes associated with this framing. The fifth row indicates that

---

32 A related freedom of expression issue concerns ICANN's cooperation with authorities in the take-down of content presumed to infringe on copyright. See, for example, the coverage by EDRI-gram, 28 March 2012, available at: http://www.edri.org/edrigram/number10.6/icann-ipr-enforcement-takedown, retrieved 10 August 2012.

Table 4.1 Summary of the internet as infrastructure

	The internet as infrastructure
Infrastructure notions	'Global information highway', 'public utility', 'backbone'
Potential for social change	Universal and non-discriminatory access
Public–private framing	The liberal model: the internet as a privately run service
Key policy themes	Coordination of internet resources Governance of internet resources
Policy controversies	Technical coordination versus public policy US control over a global resource
Human rights issues	Rule of law Protection of user data in WHOIS Potential censorship of domain name strings

policy controversies relate to, for example, the distinction between public policy and technical coordination as well as US control over a global resource. The last row summarizes the human rights challenges addressed. These relate to the rule of law, protection of user data in the WHOIS database, and the potential censorship of controversial domain names.

5. The internet as public sphere

> It does seem to me as if the public internet, the space just beyond whatever default home screen you've neglected to change, is a public sphere. It seems like sphere-crossing to commodify it entirely – to make it into a private sphere.
>
> (Crawford, 10 October 2005: 2)

A large cluster of internet-related research has addressed the internet as a new or extended public sphere (Graham 1999; Papacharissi 2002; Barnett 2003; Goode 2005; Benkler 2006; Dahlberg 2007; Hindman 2009). The idea of a public sphere runs through modern democratic theory, as a space in which the public discourse takes place. The public discourse is typically presented as the articulation of the citizens' opinions, priorities, and criticism with respect to the democratic rule of a country. The notion of the public sphere is linked to a democratic norm that presupposes the presence and participation of the public in political debate and decision making. The public only appears in moments of representation that hold in reserve its full representation (Barnett 2003: 23).

Speaking of the internet as a public sphere highlights it as a space for public debate and political mobilization, including the new modalities for public participation that the internet represents. Research with a public sphere perspective on the internet often implies or challenges an underlying presumption of the internet's ability to democratize and strengthen participation of individuals in public and political life.

1. THE NOTION OF A PUBLIC SPHERE

Habermas's ideal model of the public sphere has been setting the agenda for debate on public discourse/public sphere since it was published in 1989. The theory emphasizes the public sphere as a state-independent realm used to shape public issue, and is inspired by the struggle against the feudal state in Europe in the eighteenth century (initiated in the UK in the seventeenth century). 'Only in the light of the public sphere did that which existed become revealed, did everything become visible to all. In the discussion among citizens, issues were made topical and took on shape' (Habermas 1989: 4). The public sphere has four main characteristics:

(1) it is a public of private individuals who debate issues of public concern;
(2) the debate follows a practice of rational-critical discourse;
(3) it is an inclusive sphere that disregards status/ranks ruled by the power of the better argument; and
(4) it is a sphere for criticism of public authority, which asserts itself as the only legitimate source of law.

(Calhoun 1992: 7–9)[1]

The emphasis on communicative action as central to democratic practice was in line with a wider linguistic turn in the social sciences. Further, the use of the spatial metaphor of the sphere, and the link to freedom of expression as a civil and political right that is key to democracy, addressed a number of perceived empirical problems related to media-saturated politics and to constructing the practices of democracy in newly democratized countries at both state and civil society level (Garnham 2000: 169). Habermas's notion of the public sphere is closely related to the concept of civil society, drawing on the following definition:

> Civil society embraces a multiplicity of ostensibly 'private' yet potentially autonomous public arenas distinct from the state. The activities of such actors are regulated by various associations existing within them, preventing the society from degenerating into a shapeless mass. In a civil society, these sectors are not embedded in closed, ascriptive or corporate settings; they are open-ended and overlapping. Each has autonomous access to the central political arena, and a certain degree of commitment to that setting.
>
> (Eisenstadt quoted in Habermas 1996: 367)

The public sphere is thus rooted in the associational network of civil society, which ideally functions as a warning system with sensors throughout society.[2] The communication channels of the public sphere (civil society)

---

[1] Habermas represents a normative, action-oriented approach associated with the Frankfurt School of thought. His theory stresses the inherent rationality in communicative acts, thus the inherent potential for understanding and reaching common agreement. Habermas's theory has met strong criticism but remains a very influential framework for research concerning civil society, communication, and the public sphere. The main criticism of the public sphere model is: (1) its procedural rules are too rationalistic, for example, persuasive use of rhetoric should not be excluded from political communication; (2) the distinction drawn between private and public excludes to a large extent women and private matters of public concern, for example, domestic violence; (3) it values general agreement around universal values, which understate differences or normative conflicts within modern multicultural societies (Garnham 2000: 170). Thompson (1995: 71–5) has also summarized the critique of Habermas's public sphere model.

[2] The notion of civil society has shifted from a focus on the private sphere (market and family) to a focus on the public sphere (civil society). 'What is meant

are linked to private spheres – to the network of interaction found in families and circles of friends as well as to the looser contacts with neighbours, work, colleagues, acquaintances, and so on (Habermas 1996: 365–6). Through these networks civil society ideally distils and transmits reactions to societal problems from the private sphere to the public sphere. In consequence, the public sphere is not just a place for opinion formation and consensus building, but equally important as a space for civil society deliberations on how these opinions can influence the actions of the state. It is a concept for understanding the conditions for effective leverage by citizens on the state and other powerful institutions (Calhoun 1993: 269, 279). This is in line with the definition applied by the former Centre for Civil Society at the London School of Economics, which defines civil society as the sphere of institutions, organizations, and individuals located between the family, the state, and the market, in which people associate voluntarily to advance common interests (Anheier and Carlson 2002: 1).

The notion of a public sphere has been subject to numerous debates. One cluster of debates concerns the relation between one/many, strong/weak, and national/international public spheres (Robbins 1993; Fraser 1997). A second debate concerns the need to replace the rather static public sphere notion with a more processual and agent-oriented notion such as 'public life' (Benoit-Barné 1999; Hauser 1999). A third debate suggests that the classical focus on the state as *the* political power should be supplemented by a broader understanding of decentred political authority (Hoff et al. 2006: 10). The debates are addressed below, but first let us consider the internet as a public sphere.

2. THE INTERNET AS A PUBLIC SPHERE

Habermas's ideal norm for public opinion formation may partly explain why many scholars and activists speak of the internet as a revised public sphere. W. Mills, Habermas characterizes the formation of public opinion by:

> (1) virtually as many people express opinions as receive them. (2) public communications are so organised that there is a chance immediately and effectively

---

by civil society today, in contrast to its usage in the Marxist tradition, no longer includes the economy as constituted by private law and steered through markets in labour, capital and commodities. Rather, its institutional core comprises those nongovernmental and non economic connections and voluntary associations that anchor the communication structures of the public sphere in the society component of the lifeworld' (Habermas 1996: 366–7).

> to answer back any opinion expressed in public. Opinion formed by such discussion (3) readily finds an outlet in effective action, even against – if necessary – the prevailing system of authority. And (4) authoritative institutions do not penetrate the public, which is thus more or less autonomous in its operation.
>
> (Habermas 1989: 249)

Further, opinions cease to be public opinions when they are entangled in the communicative structure of 'mass'. This is due to the characteristics of mass such as:

> (1) far fewer people express opinions than receive them; for the community of publics becomes an abstract collection of individuals who receive impressions from the mass media. (2) The communications that prevail are so organised that it is difficult or impossible for the individual to answer back immediately or with any effect. (3) The realisation of opinion in action is controlled by authorities who organise and control the channels of such action. (4) The mass has no autonomy from institutions; on the contrary, agents of authorised institutions penetrate this mass, reducing any autonomy it may have in the formation of opinion by discussion.
>
> (Habermas 1989: 249)

Some of these characteristics, particularly the equal possibility of receiving and expressing opinions, are features where the internet differs from conventional media. As the internet has no central editorial control, it in principle allows everyone to appear and express themselves publicly. Consequently the internet facilitates a stronger diversity of opinions and highlights issues of concern as they actually exist in society. A positive interpretation of the internet's role may thus stress that the decentralization of information control has increased the number of available discourses. Cardon has argued that the internet's democratic potential is related to its ability to embrace both freedom and selection. The claim for freedom is related to everyone's ability to express themselves without prior editorial control, whereas ongoing mechanisms of selection ensure that only some expressions are circulated. As an example, only blogs with some appeal are recirculated, whereas the others in principle remain invisible. This selection takes place 'post-publishing' by the individual, rather than 'prior-publishing' by an editor (Cardon 2010).

As previously mentioned, a large cluster of internet research addresses the internet's potential vis-à-vis democratic life and public participation. These debates are related to the internet's ability to enable social change, for example to allow new groups to enter political arenas, to democratize and strengthen participation in public discourse, to provide access to information from a variety of sources, and to mobilize civil society across themes and borders. A core question raised in this line of research is whether and how the internet contributes to a new kind of public sphere and thus to a new kind of democracy. This includes research concerned with new digitized methods of state–citizen interaction (Hoff and Storgaard 2005), and more generally the internet's effect on local or national democracy (Benkler 2006; Hansen and Hoff 2006; Rasmussen 2008; Coleman and Blumler 2009; Hindman 2009). Moreover, it has been suggested that the increasing mobile access to the internet may lead to a fusion of physical and online public spheres, making them more spontaneous and action-oriented, as illustrated by the Arab spring (Hansen 2011).

Benkler is one of the scholars who argues that the internet and the networked information economy provide us with distinct improvements in the structure of the public sphere over the mass media, precisely due to some of the characteristics discussed above (Benkler 2006: 212–14). This is not least due to the information produced by, and cultural activity of, non-market actors, which the internet enables, and which essentially allow a large number of actors to see themselves as potential contributors to public discourse and as potential actors in political arenas (Benkler 2006: 220). 'The network allows all citizens to change their relationship to the public sphere. They no longer need to be consumers and passive spectators. They can become creators and primary subjects. It is in this sense that the internet democratizes' (Benkler 2006: 272).[3] Coleman and Blumler agree on the internet's potential to improve public communication and enrich democracy. However, they stress that policy intervention is needed in order to realize this potential, mainly because the online sphere has not been integrated into the constitutional structures and processes of liberal democracies (Coleman and Blumler 2009: 11).

Other recent research based on US politics argues that while the internet has democratized politics, it has also fuelled the creation of new political elites and has done little to expand the voice of the ordinary citizen (Hindman 2009: 4–8). Hindman's empirical material suggests that the internet is shifting the bar of exclusivity from the production of information (fewer gatekeepers) to the filtering of information (the difficulty of being heard online), leading to increased marginalization and an elitist tendency. In consequence the internet may lead to greater segmentation of the public, with damaging consequences for political dialogue, and for the social and political community (Hindman 2009). While the internet

---

[3] These arguments are also elaborated in Benkler's presentation on 'SOPA/PIPA: A Case Study in Networked Discourse and Activism' from the Personal Democracy Forum, 11–12 June 2012 in New York, available at: http://www.youtube.com/watch?v=LNP9f8geCWA, retrieved 21 November 2012.

is allowing new forms of political organization, there is limited research that highlights the larger impact of these changes (Hindman 2009: 10). In addition, Habermas has argued that he considers the online publics to have relatively limited impact on national political processes, while mass media remain a key channel of influence. Whereas the internet's democratic significance for undermining censorship of authoritarian regimes is recognized, Habermas is concerned about the way the internet may fragment focused audiences 'into a huge number of isolated issue publics' (Habermas 2006: 423).

As part of the Media and Democracy in the Network Society (MODINET) research project, scholars have asserted how the internet complements, undermines or refigures existing public spheres in Denmark (Hansen and Hoff 2006: Chapters 8–10). A case study of a Danish municipality (Odder) suggests that the internet has opened new channels of communication between local politicians, administration, and citizens, thereby expanding the political public sphere, and has enabled a more direct and continuous dialogue between citizens and politicians (Hoff 2006: 296–7). In contrast, studies of two other municipalities (Hals and Søllerød) conclude that the internet has only had a modest impact on participation in local governance in both municipalities.[4]

In summary, the research to date suggests that the impact of the internet on political deliberations has had only a moderate effect (Olsen et al. 2006; Coleman and Blumler 2009; Hindman 2009; Morozov 2011). However, the research field is expanding rapidly, reflecting a variety of new empirical cases. The limited effect until now may suggest that expectations have been too high or premature, and that some of the early research in the field implies that democratic practices emerge from inherent technology features, rather than grow out of social practices (Bohman 2004: 131). It may also suggest that the early optimism related to the internet as a public sphere has been replaced by a citizen-centred perspective focusing on the new opportunities to connect the private sphere to a multitude of political spaces, as discussed by Papacharissi (2010) and Loader and Mercea (2011).

Parts of the debate related to the character of the public sphere are further explored below.

---

[4] In the case study the notion of political participation is applied to include not only the involvement of citizens in the formal political processes, but also the broad spectrum of participation and engagement with public policy issues (Olsen et al. 2006: 302).

Multiple Publics

The idea of the public as a single collective subject has been contested by several scholars, who in turn have argued for 'multiple public spheres', stressing the plural and diverse character of public communication.

> Within the concept of the public sphere, there is an unresolved and perhaps unresolvable tension, between a tight authoritative singleness (the public as object of a quest for a universal collective subject or a privileged area of struggle) and a more relaxed, decentered pluralism (publicness as something spread liberally through many irreducibly different collectives).
>
> (Robbins 1993: xxi)

Also, Habermas has modified his original public sphere model and increasingly speaks of the diversification of the public sphere in a variety of functional and thematic publics.[5] Fraser has elaborated this diversification and argues for a distinction between strong and weak public spheres (Fraser 1997: 89–92), whereas Keane speaks of 'a plurality of sometimes overlapping, sometimes conflicting definitions of public opinion and the public good within a variety of power-ridden contexts containing differently-sized public spheres – public spheres at the micro, meso, and macro levels' (Keane 1999: 18). The multitude of functional and thematic publics is a relevant point not least with regard to the internet, which provides for a variety of spaces for public debate at national, regional, and global level. Moreover, the online sphere differs from the physical sphere in relation to visibility. On the one hand, the internet provides for a common space in which a large number of individuals, organizations, business, governments, and so on have a presence, and thus are visible to one another. On the other hand, 'the other' is more invisible compared to a public meeting or a television show. The internet thus provides for a communicative sphere that is shared amongst all, locally as well as globally, while allowing for invisible presence in this publicly shared sphere.

---

[5] 'The public sphere cannot be conceived as an institution and certainly not as an organization. It is not even a framework of norms with differentiated competencies and roles, membership regulations, and so on. Just as little does it represent a system; although it permits one to draw internal boundaries, outwardly it is characterized by open, permeable, and shifting horizons. The public sphere can best be described as a network for communicating information and points of view (i.e. opinion expressing affirmative or negative attitudes); the streams of communication are, in the process, filtered and synthesized in such a way that they coalesce into bundles of topically specified public opinions' (Habermas 1996: 360).

Decentred Political Authority

Another line of argument examining the role and function of the public sphere argues that political authority is increasingly decentralized and that the online public sphere is part of a fundamental change with regard to the construction of political authorities (Hoff 2004: 40). This implies a transformation from the classical models of democracy to a network model, where the state is decentred and a number of political arenas develop across the various functional and thematic public spheres (Hoff and Storgaard 2005: 29). The networked model is presented as a necessary response to the growing level of societal complexity, leading to new types of political authorities with attached issues of legitimacy and solidarity, as it becomes increasingly unclear who is accountable, and to whom. In consequence, a revised debate on the public sphere needs to address issues of inclusion in exclusion from the networks of politics, as well as to study the character of the citizen and interest groups that match the new power nodes (Hoff and Storgaard 2005: 26).

Public Sphere as Public Life

Finally, some scholars have suggested that the ‘public sphere’ notion be replaced by the notion of ‘public life’. The notion of public life emphasizes the processual and agent-oriented perspective in recent public sphere scholarship, and speaks to a broader understanding of what constitutes public political life (Benoit-Barné 2007: 212). Whereas the public sphere notion is spatial and linked to the processes of political decision making, the notion of public life implies a broader concept of citizens’ participation, which places emphasis on the processes by which public life unfolds. Related to the internet, the public life notion directs attention to the way the internet provides new means for individuals in their daily exercise of public life, which may be only indirectly linked to political agenda setting. Online public life may entail practices such as collaborative contributions to the public domain, participation in various thematic debates, producing and sourcing information and news, and so on – practices that may not be perceived as political per se, but rather represent public life in a more general sense.

In summary, the public sphere framing stresses that the internet, in principle, allows anyone to contribute to public discourse; offers new courses for political agenda setting; makes available new means for observing and interacting with the state; and provides new ways of identifying, meeting with, and mobilizing various groups. The research field that addresses the internet as a public sphere covers, among other things, studies on the new modalities for public and political life that the internet facilitates. With reference to the public and private models this discourse speaks to the republican model, thus focusing on participation in the political realm of society. However, it also points to specific human rights challenges that occur when framing the internet as a public sphere, which is the topic to be considered next.

3. HUMAN RIGHTS ISSUES RELATED TO THE INTERNET AS PUBLIC SPHERE

Many of the civil society groups active in the WSIS process have more or less explicitly addressed the internet as a public sphere. The civil society plenary stressed time and again that the internet constitutes a communicative sphere, to which everyone should have access and the resources to participate in it, and in which basic freedoms should prevail. In consequence the civil society plenary advocated policy measures that would transform the internet's democratic potential into political realities via enabling regulation, as illustrated in the WSIS Civil Society Declaration:

> Everyone, everywhere, at any time should have the opportunity to participate in communication processes and no one should be excluded from their benefits. This implies that every person must have access to the means of communication and must be able to exercise their right to freedom of opinion and expression, which includes the right to hold opinions and to seek, receive and impart information and ideas through any media and regardless of frontiers. Similarly, the right to privacy, the right to access public information and the public domain of knowledge, and many other universal human rights of specific relevance to information and communication processes, must also be upheld. Together with access, all these communication rights and freedoms must be actively guaranteed for all in clearly written national laws and enforced with adequate technical requirements.
> (WSIS Civil Society Plenary 2003: Section 1)

Likewise, these themes have been prominent at the follow-up Internet Governance Forums (IGFs). At the 2009 IGF in Egypt, for example, access was a main theme in the plenary debate (as in previous IGFs) but increasingly addressed as something beyond infrastructure, that is the resources needed to participate.[6] In addition, the protection of rights and freedoms

---

[6] See the chairman's resume: 'The chairman stated that access included financial access, the relevance of literacy to access, political access which gave voice to linguistic access, and access by the disabled ... Issues concerned with infrastructure were now secondary, because advances had been made, specifically with mobile phones and Internet penetration in many parts of the world. True access would not be achieved without appropriate regulatory regimes being put in place.' (Internet Governance Forum 2009: 16)

in the internet era was a central theme in workshops and plenary debates alike.[7]

Internet Access – A Human Right?

The issue of access has been regularly invoked in ICT policy debates to address inequalities in access to communication technology generally and the internet specifically. Within this discourse, access implies access to internet infrastructure and is connected to issues of poverty, development, pricing schemes, and so on (Norris 2001; Coleman 2003). According to 2011 figures, one third of the world population has access to the internet. In developing countries 20 per cent of households have internet access, whereas 71 per cent of households in developed countries have internet access (International Telecommunication Union 2011). The current lack of access for a majority of the world's population, often referred to as the digital divide, is a reoccurring ICT policy theme and has been on the agenda of every IGF.[8] It is, however, increasingly addressed as an issue that goes beyond access to internet infrastructure.[9]

As previously discussed, access and rights to communicate were *the* main theme addressed by groups involved in the Communication Rights in the Information Society (CRIS) campaign. The groups advocating for rights to communicate were especially focused on media organization, regulation, and use,[10] but they also addressed civil society's participation in democratic life in a broader sense.[11]

---

[7] See the chairman's resumé: 'Another challenge concerned the issue that rights were currently protected by the constitutional nation state, yet people lived in a borderless global network. This meant there would need to be a human rights perspective beyond technological development and commercial developments. The interaction of all these elements was from a human rights policy and perspective, which would guarantee that the focus would be on human beings and their benefit' (Internet Governance Forum 2009: 12).

[8] The term digital divide has been strongly criticized for trying to find technological solutions to problems that are essentially socio-economic. See, for example, Parayil (2005); Pieterse (2006); Wildermuth (2010).

[9] La Rue (2011: Chapters IV–V) distinguishes between two aspects of internet access, namely access to content, and access to the technical infrastructure.

[10] As expressed by Garnham (1992: 365): 'In a situation of mediated communication, access to both channels and means depends on the mobilization of scarce material resources, the distribution of which is dependent upon the very structures of economic and political power that democratic processes of debate were intended to control.'

[11] See, for example, Hamelink (1995; 2002); Ó Siochrú and Alegre (2005); Mueller et al. (2007).

Drawing on Luhmann's terminology, access to the internet represents access or non-access to a society's system of communication. It follows that access or non-access to systems of communication is closely linked to power, since it gives access to processes and decisions whereby different actors seek to assert themselves as authorities (Hoff et al. 2006: 3). This relates to political authority in the classical sense but also includes public policy involvement and impact in a broader sense. As argued by Hoff et al. (2006: 21), power analysis in the network society differs not so much by the nature of power, but rather in relation to access to power. Presuming that the nature of political authorities is becoming more polycentric and complex, power is increasingly related to access to society's communicative processes rather than access to formal political authority per se. From this perspective, access to the internet is crucial in providing citizens with the means of accessing and influencing the communicative processes whereby values and priorities in society are negotiated. In line with this, scholars speak of new internet-based opportunity structures for citizens (Olsen et al. 2006: 302).

With reference to human rights, scholars and activists have argued that some version of 'communicative action'[12] lies at the heart of the theory and practice of democracy, and that this is not adapted to mediated societies (Hamelink 1995; Garnham 2000; Barnett 2003). In consequence, basic freedoms related to democratic life can no longer be assumed, and democratization of communication is needed for fundamental rights and freedoms to be fulfilled. An example of this is the right to freedom of expression, which assumes that everyone has access to means of communication, while in reality the majority do not have this access (Garnham 1992: 364).[13]

The study of internet practices in the Danish municipality Odder stressed that an increasing amount of communication between politicians, administrations, and citizens, and amongst the citizens themselves, were in the exclusive domain of citizens with internet access. While the internet practices of Odder municipality strengthened some groups of citizens, there were no mechanisms to ensure equal opportunities for all citizens (Hoff 2006: 296–7). The case study took place in one of the most internet-saturated countries in the world, and illustrates that despite a relatively

---

[12] The notion of communicative action refers to the work of Habermas, who defines it as a social, reflexive process oriented towards reaching understanding, as opposed to instrumental or strategic action (Habermas 1991–1992: 285 (I)).

[13] See also Balkin (2004, 2009), who examines the way the internet age has changed the conditions for exercising freedom of expression and argues that increasingly the exercise of freedom of expression will depend on the design of the technological infrastructure.

high internet penetration rate, lack of supporting policy structures may limit the general accessibility to the online public sphere.[14]

Recently, several countries have stipulated the right to access the internet in national legislation,[15] and having such a right has increasingly been proposed by a variety of actors. The EU Directive on Universal Service amended in 2009 (2009/136/EC) stresses that everyone within the EU must be able to access a minimum set of electronic communication services of good quality and at an affordable price. As regards rights of access to the internet, all reasonable requests for connection at a fixed location to a public communication network must be met by at least one operator.[16] In 2011 the UN Special Rapporteur on the promotion and protection of the right to freedom of opinion and expression recommended that universal internet access should be a priority for all states (La Rue 2011). Human rights scholars have also argued that access to the internet must be kept as cheap, easy, and non-discriminatory as possible as part of the right to participate in the cultural life of the community (UDHR Article 27) (Adalsteinsson and Thórhallson 1999: 593). In 2010 a BBC survey amongst 27 000 people in 26 different countries showed that four out of five believed internet access to be a basic human right (Rytter, 9 March 2010). Most recently, members of the Council of Europe's Parliamentary Assembly have suggested that the Assembly should investigate the issue of internet access as a human right and make a recommendation to the Committee of Ministers on how to ensure this right in member states (Pelkonen et al., 27 June 2012).

In a much-debated newspaper article from January 2012, Vincent Cerf – one of the fathers of the internet – argued that the right to access the

---

[14] In order to ensure widespread internet access, Danish libraries have been obliged to provide access to the internet free of charge since 2000. 'The public libraries are an important resource in the government's efforts to develop a network society for all. A new Act on library activities will give the population better possibilities of gaining access to information. In accordance with the Bill, public libraries will in addition to books and so on be under an obligation to provide access to the internet and digital information resources' (Ministry of Information Technology and Research 2000: Paragraph 11).

[15] Examples include the Estonian Telecommunication Act (2000), a ruling by the French Constitutional Court (2009), Amendment to the Finnish Communication Market Act (2010), a ruling by the Costa Rican Constitutional Court (2010), and an amendment to the Spanish Act on sustainable economy (2011). For further details please refer to Pollicino and Bassini (2011: 29).

[16] See section 1 of the *Code of EU Online Rights*, which draws on the Universal Service Directive. The Code is available at: https://ec.europa.eu/digital-agenda/sites/digital-agenda/files/Code%20EU%20online%20rights%20EN%20final%202.pdf, retrieved 19 December 2012.

internet is not a human right. The main argument of the article is that technology is an enabler, not a right in itself: 'There is a high bar for something to be considered a human right. Loosely put, it must be among the things we as humans need in order to lead healthy, meaningful lives, like freedom from torture or freedom of conscience. It is a mistake to place any technology in this exalted category' (Cerf, 4 January 2012). In response, others have agued that internet access is a precondition for enjoying a number of other human rights and should therefore be considered a right in itself (Edwards, 10 January 2012). This line of argument stresses the transformative nature of the internet not only to enable individuals to exercise their right to freedom of expression, but also to enjoy a range of other human rights, including the right to health, the right to education, the right to gender equality and so forth.[17]

So far the right to internet access has by and large been stipulated as part of the state's universal service obligations to meet the citizens' right to have access to a certain level of communicative infrastructure. Despite the increasing importance of the internet for the enjoyment of a broad range of human rights, there is no indication that internet access will be addressed by the UN system as a human right on its own merits. However, cutting off users from internet access, regardless of the justification provided, is considered to be disproportionate and a violation of the right to freedom of expression (La Rue 2011). In sum, users may have a reasonable expectation that internet access will be provided as part of the state's universal service obligation, however, it would be stretching the point to argue that internet access is recognized as a human right. Yet, once people are connected to the internet, the state has an obligation not to interrupt the user's ability to access it.

Gatekeepers in the Online Sphere

Another human rights issue related to the online sphere is that of the increasing power of private actors within this sphere. Free access to a diversity of information sources has long been under pressure as a result of the strong trend towards consolidation on the global online market, leading to a strong degree of concentration among key players (Hamelink 2000: 146). There are many private actors that influence participation in the online sphere (internet service providers, search engine providers, web portals,

[17] One example is the Draft Charter of Human Rights and Principles on the Internet, in which the right to access to the internet is presented as a human right, underpinning all other rights (Dynamic Coalition on Internet Rights and Principles 2010: Paragraph 1).

and so on) and the role of these companies is increasingly addressed as a human rights issue. The following section focuses on Google as one example of a significant player in the online domain.

Consolidation of the search engine market, and the dominance of Google in particular, has regularly been flagged as an issue of concern in public debate. The concern addresses the impact of search engines on the accessibility of information and on the values of diversity and pluralism in the public sphere, including whether they should be seen as strong gatekeepers or 'mere reflections of broader democratic social forces' (Hindman 2009: 59).[18] The founding corporate motto of Google – 'Don't be evil' – was originally used to disassociate the company from some of its competitors, and to stress its public-interest vision. This positive interpretation of the company has, however, increasingly been countered by more critical views on Google's alleged manipulation of search results and its extensive compilation of user data collected via its many services.

One of the challenges relates to the public/private character of the services presented by Google. This was illustrated by a court case decided by the Tribunal of Milan in 2010 (Case no. 1972/2010). In that case, three Italian Google executives were sentenced to six months in prison for failing to block a video showing an autistic boy being bullied by other students. The video was online for two months in 2006, and was removed after Google received a formal complaint. The case was raised under the Italian Data Protection Act, and the ruling concerned the privacy of the boy, and Google's 'collection and use of personal data' (Sartor and de Azevedo Cunha 2010). In this case Google argued that it merely provides a public platform (YouTube) for content uploaded by the users, whereas the court found it responsible for the data collection associated with the video in question. This case is indicative of the challenge of determining the various kinds of services offered online. According to Google, it should not be held responsible for a video shown in a public platform that it facilitates. According to the court, Google collects data as part of the service it provides, and is obliged to comply with data protection law.

The human rights responsibility of Google is complicated by its public utility role, since different norms pertain to a public utility as compared to a commercial service. Access to a public sphere and to search information within this sphere should arguably be structured by principles of equality and fairness, while companies to a greater extent are free to design their services according to commercial norms. The first challenge is thus

---

[18] For a critical account of the way search algorithms shape the users' search experience (the personalized internet) see Pariser (2011).

to decide upon the character of the service that an internet company such as Google provides. Is it merely a private company with a responsibility to protect human rights? Or does the character of its service entail special obligations due to its direct impact on the ability of individuals to participate in online public life? In other words, should internet companies that enable information searches in the public domain (or internet access for that matter) have an extra obligation to respect human rights standards?

Recent scholarship suggests that the human rights responsibilities of companies that have the capacity to impact democracy in a way traditionally reserved for public institutions should increase (Laidlaw 2012: 55). Laidlaw (2012: 62) distinguishes between micro-gatekeepers (certain content moderators), authority gatekeepers (Facebook, Wikipedia, portals), and macro-gatekeepers (internet service providers, search engines) with macro-gatekeepers having the greatest impact on democratic life. As previously mentioned, the UN Guiding Principles on Business and Human Rights focus on the potential and actual human rights impact of companies, and impose a requirement of due diligence on them (United Nations Human Rights Council, 21 March 2011). The unexplored question is whether some companies might invite additional corporate responsibilities beyond the duty to respect outlined in this framework. Laidlaw suggests that such an extra obligation could be placed on companies that are integral to the functioning of democracy, with search engines as an example: 'This scale of responsibility is reflected not only in the reach of the gatekeeper but in the infiltration of that information, process, site, or tool in democratic culture' (Laidlaw 2012: 55).

Another issue relates to the freedom-of-expression implications of search engine governance (and government interference with search engine providers), as addressed by Hoboken (2011). Hoboken points to third-party liability as one of the most pressing legal issues for search engine providers in Europe. Since search engines make illegal or unlawful information more easily accessible for internet users, this raises the question of the extent to which search engine providers can be held legally responsible for their role in facilitating such access (Hoboken 2011: 328) – a question that has yet to be answered clearly in a European context.[19] The legal uncertainty around liability may incentivize search engine providers to censor content when confronted with notices of alleged illegal or unlawful content in their index. It therefore makes self-regulatory frameworks problematic and has led to extra-legal pressure on search engines to self-regulate in the form

---

19 See Hoboken (2011: 328) for an elaboration of the legal problems with intermediary liability entailed in the EU Directive on E-Commerce and its safe harbour provisions.

of blocking or on the basis of blacklists. Moreover, the informalized role of public authorities in these self-regulatory frameworks may circumvent freedom of expression standards according to which any interference with freedom of expression should be prescribed by law (ICCPR Article 19).

With regard to the negative impact of dominant search engines on diversity and pluralism in the online sphere, Hoboken (2011: 330) concludes that there is not enough evidence to warrant regulatory action. On the contrary, the mere existence of general-purpose search engines such as Google can be considered positive (and necessary) for locating information and participating online. More concern, however, is raised in relation to the massive amounts of user data that search engines collect and process (Hoboken 2011: 323). These data collections are unprecedented in scale and, once collected, are valuable for a range of purposes unrelated to facilitating access to information. Moreover, data are typically accessible by law enforcement organizations under a range of national laws. This may warrant stricter data protection standards that specifically address the protection of data concerning an individual's information search behaviour.

The human rights implications of search engines were addressed in a recent Recommendation by the Council of Europe (Council of Europe, 4 April 2012). The Recommendation iterates that search engines can affect the exercise of freedom of expression and in particular impact on the individual's right to seek, receive, and impart information in the public domain.

The adverse impact on freedom of information is related to market concentration, to the way that search engines may select and index search results, and to lack of transparency about the selection process and ranking of results. Similarly, it is recognized that search engines have an impact on the right to privacy and the protection of personal data. The adverse impact on privacy may result from data collection and from search engines' ability to penetrate and index content that was not intended for mass communication.

To address these challenges, states are encouraged to, among other things, enhance transparency regarding the criteria according to which search results are selected, ranked, or removed, review search results for content not intended for mass communication, and to develop tools to minimize the collection and processing of personal data (Council of Europe, 4 April 2012).

Internet Freedoms

A third human rights theme related to the public sphere metaphor is that of internet freedoms. In this context, internet freedoms refers to the individual's ability to meet, interact, and debate freely in the online sphere without illegitimate state interference.

As previously discussed, a number of human rights support the individual's right to public and political life. Human rights enjoy the same level of protection online as offline, as stressed many times by the UN and European human rights system, and endorsed by the Human Rights Council in July 2012 (Human Rights Council, 5 July 2012). It follows from this that states have an obligation to protect, respect, and promote human rights standards on the internet. However, in practice there are numerous ways in which states around the world restrict individuals' fundamental rights and freedoms in the online domain. According to research by the OpenNet Initiative, the first generation of internet controls consist mainly of firewalls at key internet gateways, whereas the second generation aim to normalize (or even legalize) internet control. This includes, for example, targeted viruses, distributed denial-of-service (DDoS) attacks, surveillance at key points of the internet's infrastructure, and take-down notices (Deibert et al. 2010). La Rue (2011: Chapter IV) also provides an overview of some of the ways in which states restrict freedoms online, for example via arbitrary blocking or filtering of content; criminalization of legitimate expression; imposition of intermediary liability; disconnecting users from internet access; cyberattacks; and inadequate protection of the right to privacy and data protection. One example took place during the uprisings in Egypt in 2011, when the Egyptian government disrupted access to Facebook and Twitter, which were used to organize protests. In response, a group of UN Special Rapporteurs stressed that they were 'alarmed at increasing limitations on the right to freedom of expression and information imposed by Governments actively seeking to suppress the rising number of voices who wish to be heard' (United Nations, 3 February 2011).

The internet freedom debate has often targeted countries such as Cuba, China, Iran, Tunisia, Saudi Arabia, South Korea, Syria, and Uzbekistan, which are known for blocking and filtering of information, as well as imprisonment of human rights defenders and journalists. Groups such as the OpenNet Initiative, Amnesty International, Human Rights Watch, and Reporters sans Frontières regularly document online human rights violations. However, as previously discussed, there are numerous groups working in the area of internet freedoms.[20] Whereas it is relatively uncontroversial to condemn online censorship in non-democratic regimes, the topic becomes more tricky when applied to Western countries. In the following section the focus will be on internet freedom challenges in a democratic Western context rather than in one of 'the usual suspects'.

---

[20] See also the many examples of internet-related human rights violations provided by MacKinnon (2012).

Privatized Law Enforcement

The role and responsibility of internet service providers (ISPs)[21] is a key theme related to internet freedoms. Because ISPs control large chunks of the online domain, they have unprecedented influence over individuals' right to freedom of expression and access to information. Given the pressure exerted upon them by states, coupled with the fact that their primary motive is to generate profit, it is essential that they are aware of and respect human rights standards, and that they are prevented from assisting in human rights violations by states (La Rue 2011).

The role and regulation of ISPs has been subject to debate since the mid-1990s and raises some important points related to human rights. In the EU, ISPs are subject to limited liability for the third-party content they carry, whereas the individual speaker or publisher is responsible for her own communication.[22] In North African countries, by contrast, ISPs are held liable for content hosted on their servers, similar to the editorial liability applied to conventional media. This example illustrates how different metaphors (public sphere versus medium) show up in the regulation of these key actors on the internet.

Moreover, at EU level an increasing number of powers are delegated to the ISPs, as frequently raised by, for example, European Digital Rights (EDRI). 'Large chunks of the commission are actually inventing ways of pushing the enforcement of regulation, and therefore the understanding of law, into the private sphere' (McNamee quoted in Mahoney, 5 April 2011). Examples of this privatized law enforcement role include policing of peer-to-peer networks, and blocking of websites presumed to contain illegal content, without a court order (Mahoney, 5 April 2011). Hence despite a limited-liability approach to ISPs within the EU, these companies are increasingly encouraged to intervene in respect of alleged illegal action or content in the online domain.[23]

---

[21] Within the EU and CoE the term internet service provider is defined rather broadly, meaning (1) any public or private entity that provides to users of this service the ability to communicate by means of a computer system, and (2) any other entity that processes or stores computer data on behalf of such a communication service (European Commission 2011b: 1).

[22] The EU Directive on E-Commerce operates with limited liability, implying that ISPs are not to be held liable unless they become aware of illegal content and fail to take action. There is, however, a legal grey area surrounding the notification procedure (Van Eecke and Truyens, November 2009).

[23] For research on Europe-wide practices of self-regulation see, for example, Tambini et al. (2008).

The Europe-wide practice of delegating powers to ISPs has been criticized by civil society groups and scholars alike, as the decisions to sanction users and websites are taken administratively rather than judicially (Callahan et al. 2009; Brown 2010; Joe McNamee (EDRI) 2011). Current practices imply that companies that are in the business of providing access to, and services on, the internet de facto are being used to implement public policy with limited oversight:

> Internet Service Providers are commercial profit-making entities who are increasingly being asked to implement social policy without appropriate oversight or accountability. They operate in a very confusing situation with regards to competing and sometimes contradictory legal requirements. For example between providing high levels of quality of access to the Internet, on the one hand, and blocking access to services, on the other.
>
> (Callahan et al. 2009: 35)

Since internet blocking and filtering affects freedom of information, it is essential that any such practice follows the standards stipulated in human rights law. Any limitation to the right to freedom of expression must pass a three-part, cumulative test. It must be provided by law, which is clear and accessible to everyone (principles of predictability and transparency); it must pursue one of the purposes set out in Article 19, paragraph 3 of the ICCPR; and it must be proven as necessary and the least restrictive means required to achieve the purported aim (principles of necessity and proportionality). Moreover, any legislation restricting the right to freedom of expression must be applied by a body that is independent of any political, commercial, or other unwarranted influences in a manner that is neither arbitrary nor discriminatory, and with adequate safeguards against abuse, including the possibility of challenge and remedy against its abusive application (La Rue 2011: Paragraph 24).

The majority of filtering and blocking schemes applied across Europe have not been evaluated according to the above criteria. On 24 November 2011, however, the Court of Justice of the European Union ruled that generalized internet filtering violates Article 8 (Protection of Personal Data) and Article 11 (Freedom of Expression and Information) of the Charter of Fundamental Rights of the European Union.[24] The ruling concerned an action that the Belgian Society of Authors, Composers and Editors of Musical Works (SABAM) brought against Scarlet Extended, an ISP, over Scarlet's refusal to use filtering and blocking to prevent illegal downloading

---

[24] The ruling is available at: http://curia.europa.eu/juris/document/document.jsf?docid=115202&doclang=EN&mode=&part=1, retrieved 12 November 2012.

of music. The ruling concerned whether member states are allowed to order an ISP to install a system for filtering all electronic communications in order to identify electronic files in which the applicant claims to hold rights, and subsequently to block the files. The court held that such a generalized system of surveillance is not permitted. The ruling stated that the EU Directive on E-commerce 'prohibits national authorities from adopting measures which would require an ISP to carry out general monitoring of the information that it transmits on its network' (*SABAM* v. *Scarlet Extended*, 24 November 2011: Paragraph 35). Moreover, several Turkish cases concerning internet blocking and filtering are currently being tried before the European Court of Human Rights (ECtHR) in response to the government's blocking of, for example, YouTube, Last.fm, and Google sites (Akdeniz 4 March 2011). The first of these cases was decided in December 2012, where the ECtHR found a violation of Article 10 of the European Convention on Human Rights. The case concerned the state's alleged infringement of freedom of expression and freedom of information, since the blocking of a specific website with alleged illegal content had been carried out by blocking access to the service (Google Sites) that hosted the website. As a result, access to all other sites hosted by the service was blocked. The ruling found that the effects of the measure had been arbitrary and the judicial review of the blocking insufficient to prevent abuses.[25]

Online Privacy

Another theme related to internet freedoms concerns the right to privacy and data protection. Lack of privacy protection may have a negative impact on participation in the online sphere since it may chill individuals' online expressions and activities:

> Never has privacy been more important than today, in the age of the Internet, the World Wide Web and smart phones. In just the last decade, the Internet has enabled a renewal of direct political engagement by citizens around the globe and an explosion of commerce and innovation creating jobs of the future. Much of this innovation is enabled by novel uses of personal information. So, it is incumbent on us to do what we have done throughout history: apply our timeless privacy values to the new technologies and circumstances of our times.
>
> (The White House, 23 February 2012)

[25] The judgment in the case of *Ahmet Yıldırım* v. *Turkey* was released on 18 December 2012. The press release is available at: http://hudoc.echr.coe.int/sites/eng-press/pages/search.aspx?i=003-4202780-4985142, retrieved 18 December 2012.

The *OECD Guidelines on the Protection of Privacy and the Transborder Flows of Personal Data* (1980) represents the first international guidelines concerning data protection. The eight principles entailed in the Guidelines have provided the basis for international agreements and national laws around the world.[26] However, there is still no global standard for data protection. Scheinin, the former UN Special Rapporteur on the promotion and protection of human rights and fundamental freedoms while countering terrorism, has urged the UN Human Rights Council to recommend measures for the creation of a global declaration on data protection and data privacy (Scheinin 2009: Paragraph 73). Furthermore, he has recommended a new General Comment on the right to privacy (Scheinin 2009: Paragraph 74). The need for a global standard on privacy has also been iterated by the group of Data Protection and Privacy Commissioners at their annual meetings.[27]

Privacy International, Electronic Privacy Information Center, European Digital Rights, and many other groups have repeatedly stated that the right to privacy is threatened in the internet era.[28] In addition, Scheinin (mentioned above) has highlighted the erosion of the right to privacy in the fight against terrorism:

> This erosion takes place through the use of surveillance powers and new technologies, which are used without adequate legal safeguards. States have endangered the protection of the right to privacy by not extending pre-existing safeguards in their cooperation with third countries and private actors. These measures have not only led to violations of the right to privacy, but also have an impact on due process rights and the freedom of movement – especially at borders – and can have a chilling effect on the freedom of association and the freedom of expression.
>
> (Scheinin 2009: 2)

---

26 See the OECD Report *The Evolving Privacy Landscape: 30 Years After the OECD Privacy Guidelines* (2011c).

27 See, for example, the *Resolution on Development of International Standards*, adopted at the International Data Protection and Privacy Commissioners' Conference in Montreal, 2007 (International Data Protection and Privacy Commissioners' 29th Conference, 26–28 September 2007) and *The Madrid Privacy Declaration – Global Privacy Standards for a Global World*, which were signed by more than a hundred civil society organizations and privacy experts at the International Data Protection and Privacy Commissioners' Conference in Madrid, 2009 (Public Voice, 3 November 2009).

28 The debate around privacy is extremely broad, touching on new schemes for identity management, retention and use of personal data, surveillance and wiretapping, online behavioural mapping, RFID (radio frequency identification devices), body scanners and so forth. For an overview of topics see the 2010 report by Privacy International et al.

As illustrated by the above quote, the concerns point toward increased state surveillance, often carried out in cooperation between state and private parties. One example of this is the EU Directive on Data Retention 2006. According to the Directive, telecom and internet service providers are obliged to retain traffic data (data about phone, email, and web traffic) between individuals for a period from one to three years, and to deliver the data to the police for the purpose of criminal investigations. The criticism raised regarding the Directive concerns, among other things, the fact that data about citizens' communication and web practices is retained without a concrete suspicion of crime, thereby establishing a potential surveillance infrastructure:

> [T]he provisions of the Directive will have far reaching consequences for all European citizens and their privacy. The decision to retain communication data for the purpose of combating serious crime is an unprecedented one with a historical dimension. It encroaches into the daily life of every citizen and may endanger the fundamental values and freedoms all European citizens enjoy and cherish.
>
> (Article 29, Data Protection Working Party, 25 March 2006)[29]

Whereas the data retention regime is a EU-wide example of cooperation between states and private actors, there are many other examples from across the globe where state authorities request access to personal data that companies hold. For example, in 2008 Yahoo provided the Chinese state security authorities with data that helped to identify and convict a journalist who was critical of the state (MacKinnon, 3 January 2008). In 2010 Google announced that they would no longer comply with the requirement of the Chinese authorities to conduct censorship towards Chinese users, and threatened to pull out of China following attacks on the Gmail accounts of Chinese human rights activists (BBC News, 13 January 2010). As previously mentioned, the Global Network Initiative was set up in response to a growing number of cases where companies have been requested to assist national law enforcement in ways that potentially violate human rights standards on freedom of expression and the right to privacy.

Moreover, concern has been raised in relation to the collection by internet companies of personal data in the online sphere. One controversial case concerned the merger between Google and Doubleclick, which was approved by the US Federal Trade Commission in December 2007. The

---

[29] For other sources of critique towards the Directive see, for example, the Opinion by the European Data Protection Supervisor (31 May 2011) and the Europe-wide civil society campaign led by European Digital Rights, available at: http://www.edri.org/campaigns/dataretention, retrieved 22 August 2012.

merger raised concern, since Google's dominant position as a search engine and Doubleclick's dominant position in marketing profiling combines intensive knowledge of individuals' search habits with marketing data that may potentially lead to extensive user profiling. 'If the merger is approved, then Google's dominant service will transform radically from one with a search advertising function into one that collects both searches and browsing habits' (Privacy International, 5 November 2007). When approving the merger, the US Federal Trade Commission announced new privacy principles for online advertising in response to 'the need for greater transparency and consumer control regarding privacy issues raised by behavioral advertising' (Federal Trade Commission, 20 December 2007).

Most recently (March 2012) Google changed its privacy policy to be able to share data across the various services it provides, including embedded services in millions of third-party websites. The new privacy policy has been widely criticized and subsequently the EU data protection authorities wrote to Google with a number of concerns. The authorities iterate that Google have not demonstrated that it endorses key data protection principles such as purpose limitation, data quality, data minimization, proportionality, and right to object. On the contrary, 'the privacy policy suggests the absence of any limit concerning the scope of the collection and the potential uses of the personal data'.[30] This is just one of many examples where the right to privacy is threatened by potential negative impact on expressions and activities in the online sphere.

In summary, the theme of internet freedoms addresses some of the most debated and controversial issues related to human rights protection on the internet, and there is no indication that this is decreasing. On the contrary, new cases and issues continue to emerge.

Participation

A third human rights theme related to the public sphere metaphor concerns participation. The notion of participation has many connotations and competing definitions. According to Smith (1983), participation refers to various procedures designed to consult, involve, and inform the public to allow those affected by a decision to have an input into that decision. Public participation may refer to political participation in a narrow

---

30 The letter that is based on an investigation led by the French data protection authority (CNIL) is available at: http://www.cnil.fr/english/news-and-events/news/article/googles-new-privacy-policy-incomplete-information-and-uncontrolled-combination-of-data-across-ser/, retrieved 12 November 2012.

sense (voting, political parties, lobbying, and so on) or to participation in a broader sense (the various ways by which citizens may engage in public services). Recent years have seen a shift towards a more rights-based understanding of participation, emphasizing participation as part of citizenship and closely related to 'good governance'. The shift implies a move from beneficiary to citizen, from project to policy level, and from consultation to decision making (Cornwall et al. 2001: 52). In line with this move, the notion is increasingly linked to empowerment: participation as something that may redistribute power by enabling people to gain more control over their lives (Cornwall et al. 2001). Similarly Mäkinen (2006: 381) refers to digital empowerment as processes by which 'people gain new abilities and ways to express themselves in the networked society'.

From a human rights perspective, the right to take part in the conduct of public affairs is a right on its own merits as well as a right that is closely related to several other rights. The right to take part in the conduct of public affairs is enshrined in Article 25 of ICCPR. The Human Rights Committee has noted that the conduct of public affairs is a broad concept that 'covers all aspects of public administration, and the formulation and implementation of policy at international, national, regional and local levels' (UN Human Rights Committee, 12 July 1996: Paragraph 5). It is further stressed that participation is supported by ensuring freedom of expression, assembly, and association, as citizens take part in the conduct of public affairs 'by exerting influence through public debate and dialogue with their representatives or through their capacity to organize themselves' (UN Human Rights Committee, 12 July 1996: Paragraph 8). As such, the right to take part in the conduct of public affairs presupposes that the public is free to speak their mind, and to organize their voices via voluntary associations. The right to participate in the conduct of public affairs becomes meaningless without the possibility of forming independent opinions and expressing these views to others without interference.

The UN Special Rapporteur on the promotion and protection of the right to freedom of opinion and expression has stressed that he believes the internet to be one of the most powerful instruments of the twenty-first century for 'increasing transparency in the conduct of the powerful, access to information, and for facilitating active citizen participation in building democratic societies' (La Rue 2011: 4). As examples, the Special Rapporteur points to demonstrations in countries across the Middle East and North African region, which have illustrated the role of the internet in mobilizing the population in their call for better respect for human rights.[31]

---

[31] See also the APC Issue Paper *Internet Rights Are Human Rights – Freedom of Expression, Freedom of Association and Democracy: New Issues and Threats,*

The emphasis on participation in the online sphere was stressed by the Council of Europe in its contribution to the first IGF in Athens, where it emphasized that the right to participate in the information society includes 'not only the right to be connected to infrastructure, not only the right to gain access to the informational richness on the Net, but also the possibility for everybody to take part in the large discussion forum which the Internet does constitute' (Council of Europe 2006: 5). The quote refers to access to infrastructure, access to the online sphere of information, and the ability to participate in various discussions online.

At WSIS and subsequent IGFs, the ability of various individuals and groups to participate online and to engage in public debate and agenda-setting has largely been addressed as 'capacity building' (stipulated in the WSIS Plan of Action, section C4). The notion of capacity building is commonly used to describe a development approach, whereby the capacity of people to determine their own values and priorities, and to act on these, are strengthened (Eade 1997: 3). UNESCO in particular has initiated a number of projects focusing on ICT literacy and capacity building as part of its WSIS follow-up process: 'Everybody should have the opportunity to acquire the skills in order to understand, participate actively in, and benefit fully from the emerging knowledge societies.'[32] Civil society networks such as APC have also worked on ICT capacity building since the late 1990s, focusing especially on women in the developing world, but also in relation to civil society participation in ICT policy processes more generally.[33]

4. CONCLUSION

In summary, this chapter illustrates some of the debates that speak to the internet as a public sphere, including controversies related to rights and freedoms in this sphere. Table 5.1 summarizes some of the notions, policy themes, and human rights issues connected with this perspective on the internet. The first row indicates commonly used notions that refer to the internet as a public sphere, for example a communicative 'space' where people 'participate' and have 'conversations' about various topical issues. The second row points to the new modalities for public and political life as one

---

which discusses potential and real threats to internet-enabled public participation on the basis of cases from around the world (Liddicoat, March 2012).

32 UNESCO's Communication and Information portal at http://portal.unesco.org/ci/en/ev.php-URL_ID=19487&URL_DO=DO_TOPIC&URL_SECTION=201.html, retrieved 3 September 2012.

33 See for example *The APC ICT Policy Handbook* (Souter 2009).

Table 5.1 Summary of the internet as public sphere

	The internet as public sphere
Public sphere notions	'Space', 'conversation', 'participation'
Potential for social change	New modalities for public and political life
Public–private framing	The republican model: the internet as a space for public deliberation
Key policy themes	Access Internet freedoms Participation
Policy controversies	The role and powers of private parties in the online sphere
Human rights issues	Access as a fundamental rights Gatekeepers in the online sphere Protection of internet freedoms The right to participate

of the characteristics that is often emphasized in relation to the internet's potential for social change. Third, with reference to the public and private models, the public sphere metaphor refers to the republican model, stressing the online sphere as a space for public participation and deliberation. The fourth row indicates key themes associated with this framing such as access, freedoms, and participation, while the fifth row highlights policy controversies related to the role and powers of private parties in the online sphere. The last row summarizes the human rights issues discussed, that is access as a fundamental right, gatekeepers in the online sphere, internet freedoms, and the right to participate.

6. The internet as a medium

> New Media is a 21st Century catchall term used to define all that is related to the internet and the interplay between technology, images and sound. In fact, the definition of new media changes daily, and will continue to do so.
>
> (Socha and Eber-Schmid 2012)

The internet has been spoken of as 'new media', 'web-based media', 'electronic media', or 'digital media' in numerous publications from media and communication scholars (Rasmussen 2000; Hutchby 2001; Aarseth 2003; Gauntlett 2004, 2009; Liestol et al. 2004; Finnemann 2005; Jenkins 2006; Merrin 2009). Moreover, it has been argued that the internet added a much-needed kick to media studies, because of the ease by which media students may become media producers, thereby providing a more active engagement in questions of creation, distribution and audience (Gauntlett 2011/2007). The medium metaphor is in many ways linked to that of the public sphere. As discussed earlier, the public sphere is largely a mediated public sphere, since media connect the public with the state through a variety of mediating technologies from print, to broadcasting, to the internet. The role of media is thus closely related to the socio-political interaction between the state and the citizens.[1]

The notion of media has many competing definitions, for example, 'the range of tools that humans have used throughout history to communicate with each other about a shared reality. The most common reference is to the set of modern technologies – from the printing press to the Internet – which facilitates communication across space, time, and social collectives' (Bruhn Jensen 2008).[2] Addressing the internet as a medium highlights its ability to mediate symbols and meaning and thereby facilitate communication, in line with other types of media. The field of media theory stems

---

[1] In the Danish research programme, Media and Democracy in the Network Society (MODINET), new media theory was a central component in the attempt to formulate a theoretical position between social constructivism and technology determinism (Hoff et al. 2006: 13).

[2] Finnemann argues that all media are in fact bound to time and space, since all messages are realized in a physical space. They are, however, bound in different ways; thus it may be misleading or imprecise to emphasize their detachment from space and time as a general characteristic of media (Finnemann 2005: 84).

from a tradition of Canadian media theorists such as Innis (1977) and McLuhan (2002/1964), who articulated an evolving theory of communication and media that addresses the way a particular medium structures the communication and power equilibrium in a given society. Media theory stresses that communication is never a neutral process, hence each medium affects the message it is conveying in a different way, or as formulated by McLuhan, 'the medium is the message'.[3] This speaks to the entailments or specific affordances of different media (Deibert 1997). First-generation medium scholars such as Innis and McLuhan have been criticized for overemphasizing the medium's power over the individual (Deibert 1997: 7). From the mid-1980s the term new media theory was increasingly used to describe a second generation of media research, placing emphasis on the transmission and communicative space created by each medium (Tække 2006: 28).[4]

Below are some examples of research that address the internet from a medium perspective, including some of the work on how new media may transform publicness.

1. THE INTERNET AS A NEW MEDIUM

The focus on the media evolution and the inherent features of any particular medium is central to the work of Finnemann (2005), who conceptualizes and presents the internet as the most recent member of the media family.[5] Finnemann distinguishes between five historical media matrices: (1) oral, (2) oral and print, (3) oral, print, and publishing, (4) oral, print,

---

[3] McLuhan coined the 'global village' metaphor, thereby stressing the similarities between cyberspace and village communities, where everyone is communicatively within reach. The notion has been criticized for underestimating the complexity of global, synchronous communication. As the internet increases the discrepancy between possible and actually occurring communications, cyberspace will never become a global community (Qvortrup 2003: 174).

[4] The notion of media diffusion has been used to capture the role and interaction of conventional and new media platforms (Bechmann Petersen 2006). As argued by Jenkins (2001), people increasingly use all kinds of media in relation to one another, hence this complex media landscape should be the focal point of media-related analysis rather than presuming media convergence towards one common platform.

[5] In 1999 the United Nations Development Programme (UNDP) compared the internet to previous media and noted that the speed of internet penetration is significantly faster, making the internet the fastest-growing tool of communication ever. Whereas radio took 38 years to gain widespread acceptance and television

publishing, and energy-based, (5) oral, print, publishing, energy-based, and digital media (Finnemann 2005: 38). 'With internet the citizens have acquired a new media for public communication, and the public have acquired a new media matrix' (Finnemann 2005: 214, my translation). The internet is presented as the first medium in the history of mankind to combine a global communicative infrastructure with a global archive. It *entails* prior media such as print media, telephone, film, radio, and television, and *expands* these by allowing for, for example, individual publishing and broadcasting, interactive features, and social communities. Finnemann's analysis of the internet as a new medium is based on three dimensions: the internet as a societal infrastructure, the internet as a communicative space with a specific pattern of interaction, and the internet as a mediating form represented in specific contexts of meaning, for example news, games, blogs, and so on (Finnemann 2005: 120).

The 'infrastructure dimension' emphasizes the internet as a digital medium based on a large number of servers, communication protocols, interface applications, and globally distributed points of access, from where there is (in principle) unlimited public access to content on the connected servers, and to communication with other connected persons (Finnemann 2005: 125). This is summarized as a 'node-network-structure', thereby stressing the combined function of archive (node) and access to content or other people (network). Finnemann notes that civil society has played a major role in the development and use of this communicative infrastructure.[6]

The 'communicative space' dimension emphasizes the so-called 'cultural grammars', which are the characteristics formed by the actual uses of the internet. Finnemann points to six grammatical characteristics of the internet, which all build on electronic communication as a common premise: the interactive potential, the integration of communication and archive, the multi-semiotic potential, the potential for both public and private communication, the potential as a local, regional, national and transnational media, and the potential for differentiated communication (Finnemann 2005: 142). He further situates the internet beside and beyond previous media by comparing their core functions and narrative characteristics, and argues that the internet entails and expands

took 13 years, the World Wide Web has taken 4 years. UNDP define widespread acceptance as the years from inception to 50 million users (UNDP 1999: 58).

6 One example is Tim Berners-Lee, who in 1989 invented the World Wide Web, including the http protocol and the html format, at the same time as performing his official job at the European Organization for Nuclear Research (CERN).

well-known media characteristics. Lastly, when exploring the 'mediating form' of the internet, Finnemann argues that any use of the internet has three dimensions. The first concerns the digitized 'content', the second concerns 'communicative relations', and the third involves 'actor/institutions'. These dimensions are suggested as analytic categories for analysing concrete internet uses (Finnemann 2005: 198–9).

Another media-inspired account of the internet is presented by Slevin (2000), who uses Thompson's notion of a mediated publicness to examine how the internet may affect the public dimension of modern societies (Slevin 2000: 183–4). Slevin stresses the global reach, the dialogical interaction, the open-ended space and the plurality of content producers as central aspects in understanding how the internet differs from previous media and how it may provide for an extended publicness.[7] The 'global reach' dimension emphasizes that, as with mass media, the internet provides for a public space in which information can in principle be shared across various local contexts. However, whereas most mass media are local or regional, the internet has global reach. By 'dialogical space' it is stressed that unlike media such as print, radio, and television, the internet provides for dialogical interaction. The 'open-ended space' signifies that whereas the mediated publicness represents a somewhat uncontrollable space in which content is not entirely fixed in advance, the internet accentuates this open-ended space. As for the 'plurality of producers and recipients', this emphasizes that contrary to print and broadcasting media, in which most participants are only recipients of information, the internet provides for a plurality of content producers.

Additionally, the internet's effect on the media ecosystem and what this implies for media studies has been discussed (Gauntlett 2004; 2009; 2011/2007). One of the points raised in this line of research concerns the way the internet alters the individual's means of interacting with and contributing to media content, leading to a collapse of the conventional 'producer' and 'audience' categories. This signifies a shift from professional media production towards more participatory media structures, where an increasing number of people consider themselves broadcasters (Gauntlett 2009: 147).[8] Other accounts of these participatory media structures are

---

[7] These dimensions are somewhat similar to Gurak's characteristic of the internet as a medium. Gurak operates with speed, reach, interactivity, and anonymity as organizing categories (Gurak 2004: 24).

[8] A 2007 US survey targeting 2000 people between 13 and 75 years found that 32 per cent strongly or somewhat strongly agreed with the statement 'With all the technology available to me today, I actually consider myself to be a "broadcaster" of my own media' (Gauntlett 2009: 149).

presented by, for example, Shirky 2008 and Sunstein 2006, both with numerous practical examples such as the citizen journalism website *ohmynews.com*, a South Korean online newspaper that is based on daily contributions from thousands of citizen reporters. Another example is Global Voices, an international community of 500-plus bloggers who report on blogs and citizen media from around the world.[9]

2. MEDIA AND PUBLICNESS

Historically the model of publicness has been tied to dialogical interaction and a particular setting in time and space, derived from the assemblies of the Greek city-states (Thompson 1995: 244). When publicness is expressed through the use of media, the opposite is the case. Mediated publicness is constituted by *not* being tied to a particular spatial–temporal setting, and has been characterized by a non-dialogical interaction. In consequence, mediated publicness is defined as a non-localized, non-dialogical, open-ended space of the visible in which mediated symbolic forms can be expressed and received by a plurality of non-present others (Thompson 1995: 245). It is a publicness created through processes of symbolic exchange made available and visible in a public domain. A key point in Thompson's account of mediated publicness concerns the need to replace the Habermasian narrative of the spatial and dialogical publicness with one built on mediation (Thompson 1995: 132).[10] Another key theme concerns the media's role in transforming the so-called struggles for visibility, thus the struggle to be seen or heard on the public stage (Thompson 1995: 119–25). In the traditional model of publicness most people were invisible to one another. However, with mass media a new type of publicness occurs: a space of the visible. This fundamentally changes the conditions for exercising power, by altering the conditions for being or going public:

> There is nothing new about the concern of political rulers or leaders to construct their self-images and to control their self-presentation: the management of visibility is an ancient political art. But the development of communication media, and therewith the transformation in the nature of visibility, have changed the rules by which this art is practised.
>
> (Thompson 1995: 135)

---

9 See www.globalvoicesonline.org, retrieved 10 November 2012.

10 Related to this, Hjarvard (2009) has introduced the notion of mediatization, pointing to the way media increasingly penetrate institutions and practices of modern society.

The mediated form of presenting and accessing power is related to the changing modalities of political life addressed in the previous chapter, specifically how the internet provides new means for political agenda setting (Hoff and Bjerke 2004: 40).

The mutual relation between media and publicness is also addressed in Meyrowitz (1985), in particular how media transform the common understanding of public and private. Meyrowitz claims that the features of the 'information age' resemble the hunting and gathering society, where people had limited loyalty towards territory as a fixed physical setting, and generally no sense of place. As electronic media present and combine previously distinct social settings, for example home and work, the dividing line between public and private behaviour is in flux and previously private actions increasingly become public (Meyrowitz 1985: 308). This increasing lack of separation between domestic and public spheres signifies a more egalitarian society, where men and women alike take part in public decisions (Meyrowitz (1985: 315). A similar point is made by Barnett, who stresses the new communicative spaces created by new media. These spaces occur in the sense of a new material infrastructure of communication and in new spaces of communicative sociality, thereby potentially changing the ways in which people engage in a wider world of publicity (Barnett 2003: 53). Therefore, the advent and domestication of media has transformed the relationship between what is considered public and private. Broadcasting in particular has been key in reshaping relationships between public and private, developing distinctive new forms of intimate publicity (Barnett 2003: 43). The role of media in transforming the distinction between public and private is also central in the later work of Habermas, in which he elaborates how private communication (lifeworld) increasingly becomes public (Habermas. 1996).

In summary, framing the internet as a medium stresses that it is a communicative platform that, like other media, mediates symbols and meanings; enables individual publishing and broadcasting; entails one-to-many, one-to-one and many-to-many communication; and supports social communities (social media). The research field that addresses the internet as a medium covers, among other things, the socio-political perspectives on the role of media in society as well as the specific mediating form of the internet. Linking back to the public/private models, this discourse speaks to the public-as-open model, stressing the internet's open, participatory, and decentralized structures of producing and distributing content as one of the characteristics where it differs essentially from conventional media. Likewise, the openness of the internet is often emphasized when debating its potential for social change, for example its ability to provide a structural alternative to current media powers (Stalder 2005: 65). Framing the internet as a medium associates with specific human rights issues, which is the topic to be considered next.

3. HUMAN RIGHTS ISSUES RELATED TO THE INTERNET AS A MEDIUM

The medium metaphor has appeared in European internet policy discourse since the late 1990s, in particular in relation to the protection of children and youth. Whereas the public sphere metaphor associates with public discourse and participation, the medium metaphor is reflected in commonly used notions such as harmful content, positive online content, the public service value of the internet, online literacy, protection of youth audiences, and internet archives. Some examples of these policy discourses are examined below.

Content Regulation and Freedom of Expression

At EU level, regulation of potentially harmful and illegal content on the internet has been a highly prioritized policy area since the *Safer Internet Action Plan* in 1999.[11] The current *EU Safer Internet Programme 2009–2013* (European Commission 2009) has a budget of €35m and implements a number of actions that are concerned with how to protect the public, not least children, from illegal and harmful content and conduct. This includes measures such as public awareness-raising, transnational cooperation, providing the public with a network of contact points for reporting illegal and harmful content and conduct, promotion of self-regulatory initiatives, and so on. The programme is an example of European internet policy that frames the internet as a medium, as some of its main notions associate with 'publishing', 'harmful content', and decency standards for 'the digital media': '(1) … Measures should be adopted at EU level in order to protect the physical, mental and moral integrity of children, which might be impaired by their accessing inappropriate content' (European Commission 2008b: 1). Content rating, filters, blocking, and notice and take-down procedures are some of the means by which this content regulation is carried out.

Rating, together with classification and labelling, are three distinct but integrated steps in the process of categorizing content according to its

---

[11] Seehttp://ec.europa.eu/information_society/activities/sip/policy/programme/early_prog/index_En.htm, retrieved 10 July 2012.

suitability for minors and making the relevant criteria and age recommendations available to the user (European Commission 2008a: 4):

> One of the risks children face online is seeing inappropriate content (such as pornography or violent content). The ambition is to have a generally applicable, transparent, and consistent approach to age rating and content classification EU-wide, for a variety of content/services (including online games, apps and educational and other cultural content) and to explore innovative solutions (e.g. rating by users or automated rating).
>
> (European Commission 2012: Paragraph 2.3.3)

The notion of rating is imported from the conventional media domain and transferred to the broader complexity of social practices on the internet, as illustrated by the quote. It would thus seem awkward to rate 'discourse' within a public sphere, whereas film rating is common practice in Europe.

Filters and blocking systems are both ways of preventing the user from accessing certain content. Filters may be controlled by the users, for example parents, whereas blocking of access to websites is typically implemented at central (ISP) level. Whereas blocking systems initially was introduced to protect children, it is now practised and supported across Europe for a number of purposes (Callahan et al. 2009).

Notice and take-down procedures refer to a process whereby alleged illegal content is removed by the host (ISP) following notice to the owner of the content. So far the industry has not been able to agree on a common standard for these procedures.[12]

Content regulation entails several problems related to freedom of expression and the rule of law. First, the initiatives largely build on 'self-regulation' amongst the internet industry, which implies that companies are encouraged to assist with law enforcement. 'When it comes to fighting illegal and harmful content and conduct online, the Commission has always been a supporter of industry self-regulation which enables industry to create a system by which they can deal rapidly with any kind of new issues that might come up' (European Commission 2011c). The encouragement to self-regulate has frequently been criticized by civil society organizations as well as scholars. As concluded in a study on European practices: 'A comprehensive summary of internet blocking and the law especially relating to human rights, fundamental freedoms and civil liberties creates substantial concern about the currently implemented blocking systems ... The complexity of balancing rights which are in conflict needs to be assessed by

[12] In January 2012 the European Commission announced an initiative on 'notice-and-action' procedures in the Communication on e-commerce and other online services (COM(2011) 942 final).

judges, who are trained in managing such complexities' (Callahan et al. 2009: 34–5).[13] In Denmark, for example, blocking of specific websites has been deployed since 2005, starting with child sexual abuse content (child pornography), and later expanding to include file-sharing sites, for example AllofMP3, mp3sparks, and the pirate bay. The blocking of alleged child sexual abuse content is carried out in cooperation between Save the Children Denmark, the Danish National Police, and the ISPs. Save the Children runs a hotline where the public may report websites with alleged illegal content. Following an initial assessment the websites are reported to the National High Tech Crime Centre of the Danish National Police, which considers whether the content is prima facie illegal under national law and, if so, advises the ISPs to block access to the site. The practice is based on a voluntary Cooperation Agreement between the Danish National Police and the ISP (Rigspolitiet 2006). More recently, blocking of unauthorized online pharmacies as well as online games have been stipulated.[14]

In a recommendation on internet filters from 2008, the Council of Europe has stressed that blocking should only take place 'if the conditions of Article 10, paragraph 2, of the European Convention on Human Rights are fulfilled' and it concerns 'specific and clearly identifiable content, a competent national authority has taken a decision on its illegality and the decision can be reviewed by an independent and impartial tribunal or regulatory body, in accordance with the requirements of Article 6 of the European Convention on Human Rights' (Council of Europe 2008: section III).[15]

---

[13] See also the 2011 report *The Slide 'Self-regulation' to Corporate Censorship* by European Digital Rights (McNamee (EDRI) 2011).

[14] On 6 April 2011 the Danish Parliament hosted a public hearing addressing the various means of content blocking, in response to a critical letter from a number of organizations concerned with the principal and practical implications of content blocking for online freedom of expression. The hearing did not result in any changes in the current practice. The webcast of the hearing is available at: http://www.ft.dk/Folketinget/udvalg_delegationer_kommissioner/Udvalg/Udvalget_for_videnskab_og_teknologi/Hoeringer/Hoering_om_internetcensur.aspx (in Danish), retrieved 10 November 2012.

[15] In June 2011 the European Parliament, Council, and Commission negotiated EU-wide blocking in relation to child sexual abuse content; however, they decided not to make it mandatory. The negotiations have resulted in a new EU Directive on Combating Sexual Abuse (2011/93/EU), which stresses that measures to remove illegal content must provide adequate safeguards, and ensure that the restrictions are limited to what is necessary and proportionate, and that users are informed of the reason for the restriction (European Commission 2011a).

Second, it is crucial to distinguish between content that is illegal and content that is deemed harmful. Unlike illegal content, harmful content often implies content that is legal under national law, and thus protected under freedom of expression standards. The distinction between harmful and illegal content was emphasized in the first major internet court case concerning the US Communication Decency Act.[16] The ruling compared the internet to mass media such as radio and television and stressed the essentially different nature of internet communication. In relation to conventional media, the right to freedom of expression does not include a general right to broadcast, since mass media have scarcity in broadcasting channels and broadcasting time, making it legitimate to restrict content via the editing process. By contrast, the internet in principle provides for unlimited 'airtime' for every individual. According to the court these characteristics eliminate the justification for restricting content as long as it is legal, despite the fact that it may be perceived as harmful. The ruling stressed that the internet is a wholly new means for human communication, which combines, adds to, and differs essentially from previous media. In consequence, internet policies that seek to restrict legal but unwanted content may constitute violations of freedom of expression standards, whether the restriction is deployed through content policies or via technical measures such as blocking and filters (*Reno et al.* v. *American Civil Liberties Union et al.*, 26 June 1997).[17]

As pointed to by Garnham (2000), two communication models have been central to debates on internet regulation, inspired by mass media and telecommunication respectively. The first model, applied to internet service providers (ISPs), follows standards of private communication. This implies that regulation of the networks (for example to ensure universal access) are legitimate but that interference with the content has been

---

16 The US Communication Decency Act (CDA) was passed as part of the Telecommunications Act in 1996, and later ruled unconstitutional by the US Supreme Court. The CDA sought to impose criminal penalties on anyone who used the internet to communicate material that, under contemporary community standards, would be deemed patently offensive to minors under 18 years of age (*Reno et al.* v. *American Civil Liberties Union et al.*, 26 June 1997).

17 Ironically, primary schools and public libraries in the USA were in 2000 mandated to protect youth via internet filters as a precondition for receiving federal funding, as stipulated in the Children's Internet Protection Act (CIPA). CIPA was subsequently challenged by the American Library Association, but according to a Supreme Court ruling, public libraries' use of filters does not violate their patrons' First Amendment rights, as a library can easily disable the filter or unblock a site in response to an adult patron's request to do so, as stated in the ruling from the US Supreme Court (*United States* v. *American Library Association*, 23 June 2003).

regarded as an illegitimate infringement of individual freedoms such as privacy and freedom of expression. The second model, applied to mass media, sees media as caretakers of public communication/public interest and thus subject to a varying degree of public policy intervention, while respecting the freedom of the press (Garnham 2000: 173–4). Whereas ISPs in Europe from the outset are regulated according to the standards of private communication, the above examples illustrate how ISPs in a number of cases are encouraged to interfere with the content they carry on their networks.[18] As stressed by the Communication Decency Act ruling, as well as by CoE standards, measures to remove or block content on the internet requires that the content is identified as illegal by a national authority. The justification for content regulation that conventional media entail do not transfer to the internet.

The policy of the Council of Europe (CoE) represents another European example of internet policy with a medium framing. CoE internet-related policy is situated in the Information Society Division and entails various initiatives related to the internet as a new medium. This includes the previously mentioned Committee of Experts on New Media and various working groups concerned with media diversity, public service media, public service media governance, and so on. In addition, the issue of internet literacy and the promotion of standards and strategies to protect children against harmful content has been a recurring policy topic within the CoE in recent years, as addressed in standard-setting documents such as the *Recommendation on Measures to Protect Children against Harmful Content and Behaviour and to Promote their Active Participation in the New Information and Communications Environment* (Council of Europe 2009) and the *Recommendation on Measures to Promote the Respect for Freedom of Expression and Information with Regard to Internet Filters* (Council of Europe 2008). In line with the EU Safer Internet Programme, the commonly used notions of content, literacy, and public service speak to the internet as a medium, and likewise suggest areas where policy intervention is needed in order to educate or protect the public when using this new medium. As a most recent example of the medium framing, the CoE has adopted a *Recommendation on a New Notion of Media* (Council of Europe 2011), addressing the various elements and actors in 'the media ecosystem':

> Despite the changes in its ecosystem, the role of the media in a democratic society, albeit with additional tools (i.e. interaction and engagement), has not

---

[18] As mentioned in the previous chapter, ISPs may be held liable if they become aware of illegal content and fail to take action.

> changed. Media-related policy must therefore take full account of these and future developments, embracing a notion of media which is appropriate for such a fluid and multi-dimensional reality … The response should be graduated and differentiated according to the part that media services play in content production and dissemination processes.
>
> (Council of Europe 2011: Paragraph 7).[19]

The recommendation suggests that member states adopt a new, broad notion of media that encompasses all actors involved in the production and dissemination of content as well as applications that facilitate 'interactive mass communication (for example social networks) or other content-based large-scale interactive experiences (for example online games), while retaining (in all these cases) editorial control or oversight of the contents' (Council of Europe 2011: Paragraph 7).

As illustrated by the quote, the various features of the internet (social network sites, games, blogs, and so on) are described along the lines of other media, as means of content production and content dissemination with additional tools such as 'interaction and engagement', and subject to editorial control or oversight along the lines seen in conventional media.

Publicly Available vis-à-vis the Right to Privacy

Framing the internet as a new medium also has implications with regard to the right to privacy. From a conventional media perspective, documents, statements, and so on that are publicly available may be utilized without any claim of privacy by the individual concerned. However, on the internet the distinction between what is public and what is private is more complex. As suggested by Svenningsson (2009: 75), the various areas on the internet represent public, semi-public, semi-private, and private environments. This differentiation is relevant for the protection of users' privacy, for example in relation to the archiving of various 'internet editions' as practised in several countries.[20] In Denmark, net archiving was initiated in July 2005 and is carried

---

[19] The Recommendation was adopted by the Committee of Ministers on 21 September 2011 and is available at https://wcd.coe.int/ViewDoc.jsp?id=1835645&Site=CM, retrieved 12 September 2012.

[20] In the USA the national internet archive offers 'permanent access for researchers and scholars to historical collections that exist in digital format'. The archive was founded in 1996 and is run by a non-profit organization. It includes texts, audio, moving images, and software as well as archived web pages in its collections. The archive is available at: www.archive.org, retrieved 19 September 2012.

out by the State Library and the Royal Danish Library, which retain copies of the Danish part of the internet using so-called web crawlers.[21] Copies of the Danish part of the internet are produced four times a year and kept at the State Library. The archive contains information that is public, semi-public, and semi-private according to the definition above.[22] The archive is not open to the general public, and as a general rule may only be accessed for research purposes and following an application to the Data Protection Agency (DPA). This restricted access is mandated by the DPA, which in its response to the project stressed that the archive may contain information that is protected under national data protection law. The practice of restricted access is contrary to the initial project design, whereby it was foreseen that the archive should be perceived as already published text and thus include general access for the public to study 'previous internet editions'.[23]

The case is an example of competing claims and perceptions as to the level of publicness of the various types of content on the internet. Seen from a conventional media perspective, any content that is generally available on the internet is public, and should therefore be accessible for future audiences, as with any other published text. Seen from a privacy perspective, a more differentiated definition of public is needed in order to accommodate the new forms of sociability that the internet represents; for example, covering information that is provided in so-called semi-public or semi-private communities, where membership is required, and where users may have a different expectation of privacy and not perceive their communication as publishing (Svenningsson 2009: 83). As argued by some scholars, the fact that something is publicly available on the internet does not per se make it published information.[24] In fact such a one-to-one interpretation based on previous media standards may interfere with users' right to privacy when communicating on semi-public and semi-private platforms.

---

[21] See www.netarkivet.dk (in Danish), retrieved 19 September 2012.

[22] The archive covers 'published material', which is understood as any material that is made generally available to the public, including material with restricted access, as long as the access requirements, for example payment, might in principle be met by everyone. See Netarkivet.dk (June 2005: 3).

[23] The case was presented by Niels Ole Finnemann at the NordForsk Seminar in Helsinki, 15 August 2007.

[24] Clay Shirky in *Facebook Killed the Private Life*, on SwitchedShow, 11 June 2007, available at: http://www.youtube.com/watch?v=azIW1xjSTCo, retrieved 19 September 2012.

4. CONCLUSION

Table 6.1 Summary of the internet as a medium

	The internet as a medium
Media notions	'Content', 'audience', 'literacy', 'archive'
Potential for social change	Democratization of publishing and broadcasting
Public–private framing	The public-as-open model: internet as an open medium
Key policy themes	Harmful and illegal content Protection of youth audiences Internet literacy Internet archives
Policy controversies	Various means of content regulation
Human rights issues	Content regulation and freedom of expression Publicly available information and the right to privacy

In summary, the medium metaphor points to human rights controversies concerning at least two points. The first point touches on the open and unedited nature of the internet compared to previous media, which has led to various means of content regulation with freedom of information and rule of law implications. The second point concerns the difficulty of categorizing information as public merely because it is available online, iterating that a standard for published information based on conventional media may conflict with users' right to privacy in a number of cases.

A vast amount of European internet policy implies a medium metaphor and focuses on ensuring a safe media environment through increased online literacy, public awareness-raising, and rating, filtering, and take-down of content via industry self-regulation. Another example is internet archiving, in line with other publications; something one would not consider in a public space, for example the recording of all oral conversations taking place in a public piazza. Whereas the public sphere metaphor is mainly spatial (the internet as a public space), the medium metaphor speaks to internet content to some extent as published text.

Table 6.1 summarizes some of the notions, policy themes, and human rights issues considered in this chapter. The first row indicates examples of commonly used notions that refer to the internet as a medium: 'content', 'audience', 'literacy', and 'archive'. The second row points to the democratization of publishing and broadcasting as one of the commonly claimed potentials for social change relating to this framing. Third, with reference to the public and private models, the medium metaphor refers to the public-as-open model, stressing the open character of the internet medium as one of its key features. In the fourth row harmful and illegal content, protection of youth audiences, online literacy, and internet archives are indicated as some of the key policy themes. With regard to policy controversies, the various means of restricting online content are highlighted, for example blocking of access to specific content. Finally, illustrations of human rights issues related to the medium metaphor are provided: the conflict between content regulation and freedom of expression, and between 'publicly available information' and the right to privacy.

7. The internet as culture

> The Internet has unleashed an extraordinary possibility for many to participate in the process of building and cultivating a culture that reaches far beyond local boundaries. That power has changed the marketplace for making and cultivating culture generally, and that change in turn threatens established content industries.
>
> (Lessig 2004: Introduction)

The culture metaphor shows up in notions such as 'cyberculture', 'internet communities', 'digital natives', and 'free internet culture', which associate the internet with specific cultural and social practices. As with the previous metaphors, the culture metaphor is reflected in a large body of research that explores the internet from the perspective of its cultural practices, focusing on various examples of internet communities, including their norms and values, identity formation, sharing and collaboration, means of social control, and so forth (Rheingold 1993; Turkle 1995; Paccagnella 1997; Smith and Kollock 1999; Miller 2000; Silver 2000; Bell 2001; Lessig 2004; Benkler 2006; Shirky 2008).

1. CYBERCULTURE

Amongst many competing definitions, culture may be defined as 'the integrated system of socially acquired values, beliefs, and rules of conduct which delimit the range of accepted behaviors in any given society' (Columbia Encyclopedia 2008). Cyberculture as a research topic took off in the mid- to late 1990s with a large number of contributions especially from US scholars, starting with Rheingold's *The Virtual Community* in 1993.[1] The major works on cyberculture may be divided roughly into three stages (Silver 2000). The first stage is popular cyberculture, which has journalistic origins and uses 'the internet as a symbol for a new frontier'. This narrative typically took the form of either a dystopian or utopian story,

[1] *The Virtual Community* focuses on a particular online community, the Whole Earth Lectronic Link (the WELL), and the interactions that take place within the WELL.

linked to deteriorating literacy and social fragmentation, or to a new and more democratic frontier of civilization. Some argued that the internet provides individuals with a richer choice of communities to which they may belong, and that online spaces potentially revitalize the notion of community. In the words of Rheingold (1999: 418), virtual communities are 'a natural response to the hunger for community that has followed the disintegration of traditional communities around the world'. Others were more sceptical and argued that internet communities are pale substitutes for real communities, among other reasons for the lack of face-to-face interaction (Bell 2001: 97).

The second stage cyberculture studies, focused largely on 'virtual communities and online identities', and thus how people interact within a given social space. Cyberspace is here defined as 'incontrovertibly social spaces in which people still meet face-to-face, but under new definitions of both "meet" and "face"' (Stone 1991).[2] The focus is on the new opportunities that cyberspace offers for collective communities and individual identities. Cyberculture studies were at this point mostly articulated positively, as a space of empowerment and creativity. However, as the internet mainstreamed into various academic fields as a research topic, scholars from a vast array of disciplines contributed with new methods and perspectives, for example Smith and Kollock (1999), who in *Communities in Cyberspace* investigated how the idea of community is being challenged and rewritten by online interaction.

By the late 1990s the third stage, critical cyberculture studies, had arrived. Critical cyberculture studies expanded the notion of cyberculture to include 'the social, cultural, and economic context of the online communities' and the policy discourses related to these contexts such as exclusion and inclusion, commercialization, surveillance, as well as the critical analysis of interface design. In 1999/2000 the Association of Internet Researchers (AoIR) was formed and the notion of *internet studies* became the common umbrella for what was previously known as cyberculture studies (Gurak 2004: 24).[3]

---

[2] The term cyberspace originates from the American author William Gibson: 'Cyberspace. A consensual hallucination experienced daily by billions of legitimate operators, in every nation, by children being taught mathematical concepts. A graphic representation of data abstracted from the banks of every computer in the human system. Unthinkable complexity. Lines of light ranged in the non-space of the mind, clusters and constellations of data. Like city lights, receding' (Gibson 1984: 51).

[3] The scope and boundaries of 'internet studies', including whether they constitute a research field of their own, is still being debated.

The research presented at, for example, the annual AoIR conference is still dominated by studies of internet communities, thus focusing on the values, identities, and practices of various communities *on* the internet.[4] Online communities are defined in many ways but definitions typically address communication among a group of people 'who come together for a particular purpose, and who are guided by policies (including norms and rules) and supported by software' (Preece and Maloney-Krichmar 2006). Online communities have frequently been characterized as open and exchange-oriented rather then control/permission-oriented (Lessig 2001; Raymond 2001; Stalder 2005).

In recent years the investigation of internet communities has started to focus on the economics and virtues of 'commons-based peer-production' (Benkler 2006; Benkler and Nissenbaum 2006), as well as social network sites and youth practices more broadly (boyd 2008; Palfrey and Gasser 2008). Social network sites essentially allow individuals to construct a public or semi-public profile within a bounded system, and to articulate and make visible their connection with other people within this system (boyd and Ellison 2007: 2). The social network sites support a wide range of interests and activities, either by supporting pre-existing social networks, or by connecting strangers based on shared interests. We might thus be at a fourth stage of cyberculture/internet studies, which entails elements from the previous three stages but includes a broader range of participants and social domains, due to the fact that internet use is inherent in a much broader area of social practices. Whereas the study of specific internet communities was dominant in the previous stages, research increasingly speaks of the role of networked publics, how people socialize in the various online domains, tensions between public and private, and so on (Benkler 2006; boyd 2008). Moreover, despite the obvious global and local divides in internet use, the notion of 'digital natives' is now applied to describe generations who have grown up with the internet as an inherent element of their social life (Palfrey and Gasser 2008).

Online versus Physical Public Spaces

Whereas numerous studies have examined the social and cultural practices of various online communities, fewer have focused on the way these spaces add to or diverge from physical public spaces. As stressed by boyd (2007), online public spaces diverge from physical public spaces in many regards. They are mediated, and potentially global. They are searchable, and the

---

4 See http://aoir.org/conferences/, retrieved 20 September 2012.

interaction may be recorded or copied. Further, they may have invisible audiences or audiences who were not present at the time of the conversation (boyd 2007: 2–3). Also, most of the environments are multifaceted and consist of different communication modes, which permit different degrees of publicness vis-à-vis privacy (Sveningsson 2009: 75). Studies of, for example, self-help communities suggest that online spaces may represent new ways of bringing the private sphere into the public both in terms of topics and in terms of the participants being in a public or semi-public space while at home.[5] As discussed earlier, the distinction between whether an online space is public or private is often blurred, and communities may comprise public, private, and semi-public spaces alike. A case study of *Cyworld* (one of the largest online communities in South Korea) concludes that the users regard the community as a distinct third place (Oldenburg 2001), separate from both home and work, and labels it 'informal public life' comparable to a party between friends happening in a public park (Lee 2007: 5).

The Internet and the Formation of Identity

Another cultural take on the internet relates to how online practices affect the formation of identity. One example is Miller and Slater's research on internet use in Trinidad, which summarizes the dynamics between identity and the internet in four dimensions. One is expansive realization, stressing the internet as a means through which the individual can enact a version of him/her self. Through the global interconnections 'a Trinidadian may feel able to act as the Hindu he or she "really is" (but could not be within the confines of Trinidad) by participating in worldwide Hindu networks that can be integrated into their everyday local reality' (Miller and Slater 2000: 10–11). In this regard, the internet is helping people to deliver on pledges they have made to themselves. These findings correspond to some of the early research on online identity. In *Life on the Screen: Identity in the Age of the Internet*, Turkle (1995) finds that while some use cyberspace to repress an otherwise less than functional 'real' or offline life, most use the internet to exercise a more

[5] In self-help communities members share sensitive information and sentiments related to topics such as, for example, mental or physical diseases, civil war and conflicts, and so on. The communities often provide a space for people who have never met in real life to gather, exchange, and support each other, while remaining in their private domestic sphere. See for example Orgad (2006) and Kimby (2006).

true identity, or a multiplicity of identities.[6] Social network sites may be seen as an example of this multi-identity tendency, which is related to a networked individualism, stressing that individual self-identity can no longer be separated from one's position within one or many relational networks (Castells 2001).

The 'expansive potential' is a second dimension addressed in the Trinidad study, referring to the dynamics whereby the numerous encounters that the internet offers allow the individual to create a new vision of what he or she could be. The focus is thus the internet as a means of imagining a future (Miller 2000: 13). A third dimension is the dynamics of 'mediation', thus how people come to understand, frame, and make use of the internet as a medium. A key issue in the mediation dynamic is the need to 'disaggregate' the internet by looking at a variety of practices by which people assemble the technical possibilities that make up 'their internet'. Finally the study finds 'normative freedom' as a fourth dynamic, referring to the way the internet stands as a symbol of potential freedoms. At least two contrasting sets of freedoms are part of this vision: the free-market ideologies of neo-liberalism and the 'cyber libertarianism' mentioned below.

The Internet as Cultural Transmission

The internet has also been examined as part of a broader cultural transmission. One example is Slevin (2000), who draws on especially Thompson (1995), Baumann (1995) and Giddens (1984) in his attempt to sketch out a social theory of the internet and its impact on modern culture and communities. Thompson's four characteristics of mass communication are used to argue for the inadequacy in capturing the functions of the internet from the perspective of mass media, whereas it is proposed to conceptualize the internet as a modality of cultural transmission.[7] This implies an analytical

---

6 There are several accounts of how the internet allows people to realize different identities, thus construct and reconstruct different selves. Gray (2009) examines how rural youth explore and carve out online spaces to fashion their emerging queer identities. Gauntlett (2004: 19) suggests that the internet's potential for identity play fits with contemporary queer theory, which suggests that people do not have a fixed essence and that identity is a performance. In relation to games, Taylor (2006) has studied how the online game culture in 'Everquest' relates to online and offline roles and identity.

7 Thompson's four characteristics are (1) the institutionalized production and diffusion of symbolic forms, (2) the instituted break between production and reception, (3) the extension of availability in time-space, and (4) the public circulation of symbolic forms (Slevin 2000: 73).

framework that focuses on the way in which the internet provides for new forms of actions and interactions. The argument is based on three types of interaction: 'face-to-face interaction', 'mediated interaction', and 'mediated quasi-interaction', combined with 'arenas of circulation' (Thompson 1995) and 'repertoires of possibilities' (Bourdieu and Johnson 1993). It is argued that that the internet potentially changes all three types of interaction, as well as expanding the arenas of circulation and repertoires of possibilities.

Inspired by Giddens (1990), Slevin suggests that the internet enables specific characteristics of late modernity, such as reflexive and open-ended social interaction. The internet may enrich and transform processes of self-formation by:

> (1) increasing the opportunities for negotiating mediated experience, that is making available, acquire [*sic*] and reembed [*sic*] symbolic content;
> (2) facilitate [*sic*] the reappropriation of knowledge and skills by use of the technology;
> (3) forge [*sic*] commitment and mutuality by gaining more involvement with the outer social world; and
> (4) be used [*sic*] to track risk and uncertainty and transcend conflict, by increasing individuals' contact with contexts far from their own.
>
> (Slevin 2000: 177)

The analysis is presented as contrary to the trend of postmodernism that is found in many of the cyber community studies, such as Reid (1999) and Turkle (1995) (Slevin 2000: 115–16).

In the following section key notions associated with online cultural practices are examined, in particular community, free culture, collaboration, and self-regulation.

2. COMMUNITY

There are many definitions of community, typically referring to community as either a specific space (territorial definition) and/or a specific sharing of interest (relational definition). An often-referenced piece of work is by Tönnies (1887/1955), who has suggested 'gemeinschaft' and 'gesellschaft' as two different types of community. The former is the fully integrated, face-to-face community, where everyone knows and helps everyone (for example, the small town), whereas the latter is described as the disintegrated, partly anonymous, and transitory community (for example, the city). Another distinction is proposed by Schmidt, who refers to 'communality' as a non-articulated sociality based on shared taste or interest, whereas community refers to articulated membership (Schmidt quoted in

Bjerke 2006: 176). According to McMillan and Chavis (1986: 9): 'A sense of community is a feeling that members have of belonging, a feeling that members matter to one another and to the group, and a shared faith that members' needs will be met through commitment to be together'. This notion of community emphasizes belonging and sharing (sharing of space, sharing of values, sharing of rules, and so on) within a distinct social system and is thus a subcategory of the broader concept of public life.

3. FREE CULTURE

The early utopian narrative of the internet framed it as a new frontier: 'a kind of society that real space could never allow – freedom without anarchy, control without government, consensus without power' (Lessig 1999: 4) In 1996 John Perry Barlow (co-founder of the Electronic Frontier Foundation)[8] formulated this vision in *A Declaration of the Independence of Cyberspace*:

> Governments of the Industrial World, you weary giants of flesh and steel, I come from Cyberspace, the new home of Mind. On behalf of the future, I ask you of the past to leave us alone. You are not welcome among us. You have no sovereignty where we gather … We will create a civilization of the Mind in Cyberspace. May it be more humane and fair than the world your governments have made before.[9]

As the internet has become more widespread, the claim for a new government-free frontier was replaced by claims for upholding values of openness and sharing. Within the research community, Lessig became one of the leading scholars to consolidate the link between the architecture of the internet and values of openness and sharing, promoted as a free culture movement (Lessig 2004).[10] According to this line of thinking, the internet and the social practices associated with it represent a creative revolution fostering new means for participation in cultural production, thereby challenging a more passive consumer era (Lessig 2004).[11]

---

[8] EFF was one of the first organizations to frame civil liberties in cyberspace. See www.eff.org, retrieved 20 September 2012.

[9] The Declaration is available at: http://homes.eff.org/~barlow/Declaration-Final.html, retrieved 4 September 2012.

[10] See, for example, the Free Culture Research Workshop organized by the Berkman Center for Internet and Society at Harvard University in October 2009, available at: http://cyber.law.harvard.edu/fcrw/Main_Page, retrieved 10 July 2012.

[11] Historically, there have been at least two different approaches to cultural practices: an object-oriented and an exchange-oriented approach (Stalder 2005).

One proponent of this sharing culture is the Free and Open Source Software movement (FOSS), to whom freedom and sharing are key components of software development. According to FOSS, software is a cultural product, which anyone should have access to use, study, and improve.[12] This implies that anyone should have the freedom to run the program, for any purpose (freedom 0); the freedom to study how the program works, and change it (freedom 1); the freedom to redistribute copies in order to help your neighbour (freedom 2); and the freedom to distribute copies of your modified versions to others (freedom 3).[13] One of the examinations of the open source community was carried out by Raymond (2001). Raymond compares the process of traditional software development with building cathedrals based on principles of central and detailed planning. As a contrasting metaphor, he proposes the metaphor of a bazaar to capture the open source software development processes: 'No quiet, reverent cathedral-building here – rather the Linux community seemed to resemble a great babbling bazaar of differing agendas and approaches ... out of which a coherent and stable system could seemingly emerge only by a succession of miracles' (Raymond 2001: 21–2). Other examples include collaborative platforms such as Wikipedia, as addressed in more detail below.

The notion of a gift culture is frequently associated with the free culture movement. By gift culture is meant a 'culture' in which 'social status is determined not by what you own but what you give away, thus prestige is acquired by giving time, creativity and ideas to the common good' (Hyde

---

The digital form fundamentally changes the distinction between fixed products and fluid forms, as still more people are able to access, remix, and distribute cultural products. 'Once fluid culture was realized as a fixed material object, for instance a book or a painting, it was almost impossible to convert it back into a fluid exchange because they are made to be passed around as objects' (Stalder 2005: 13).

[12] 'Proprietary software is like Kentucky Fried Chicken. Open source and free software is like Kentucky Fried Chicken sold with the "original secret recipe" printed in bold on the box' (Lessig quoted in Sunstein 2006: 165).

[13] See www.gnu.org/philosophy/free-sw.en.html, retrieved 20 September 2012. The Free Software Foundation was founded by Richard Stallman in 1985 with the aim of developing a free alternative to proprietary software. There is a long-lasting controversy between the proponents of free software and open source software. Whereas the free software movement, and not least Stallman, insist on the emphasis on 'free' (as in liberty), the open source community emphasize the open access to source code. At present, the open source terminology seems to have gained more currency, and many find 'open' a less confusing way to refer to products that may be bought and sold (Sunstein 2006: 171). The notion of free and open source software (F/OSS, FOSS, or FLOSS) is increasingly used as an accepted notion from both 'sides'. For literature see, for example, Stallman (2002); Grassmuck (2004); Sunstein 2006.

2007: Chapter 5). This is somewhat similar to Rheingold's (1993) study of the WELL that describes the community's online interaction as a gift economy in which help and information are offered without the expectation of a pay-back. The notion of gift culture (or gift economics) can also be found in many anthropological studies, where it is used to describe social practices based on three related obligations: 'the obligation to give, the obligation to accept, and the obligation to reciprocate' (Mauss qoted in Hyde 2007: xxi). Essentially, factors such as status, prestige, or esteem take the place of cash remuneration in communities characterized by gift exchange (Hyde 2007: 101).[14]

Another dimension is that of collectivism as opposed to individualism. In a comparative study of IBM workplace cultures, Hofstede (1991) develops four (later expanded to six) cultural dimensions, of which one addresses the extent to which members of a culture rely on and have allegiance to either themselves or to the group.[15] Scholars have found that the exchange-based practices on the internet imply a new balance between individuality and sociability; a new pattern of 'weak collaboration' (Cardon and Aguiton 2007).[16] The notion of weak collaboration stresses the self-directed and volunteer character of the work, thus the fact that many people cooperate with limited prior planning or direction. This allows for cooperation to begin at a lower level, compared to many previous types of cooperation.

4. ONLINE COLLABORATION

Collaboration refers to a process through which parties who see different aspects of a problem can constructively explore their differences and search for solutions that go beyond their own limited vision of what is possible (Gray quoted in London 1995: 5). The focus is thus directed towards

---

14 The scientific community is mentioned as an example of a community in which the sharing of ideas is linked to recognition and status.

15 As explained by Hofstede: 'Individualism on the one side versus its opposite, collectivism, that is the degree to which individuals are integrated into groups. On the individualist side we find societies in which the ties between individuals are loose: everyone is expected to look after him/herself and his/her immediate family. On the collectivist side, we find societies in which people from birth onwards are integrated into strong, cohesive in-groups, often extended families (with uncles, aunts and grandparents) which continue protecting them in exchange for unquestioning loyalty' (Hofstede quoted from his webpage at: http://www.geerthofstede.nl/dimensions-of-national-cultures, retrieved 10 September 2012).

16 Weak collaboration is used as a middle ground between acts of pure self-interest and selfless contributors to a collective effort.

the processes whereby community members cooperate towards a common goal. Commons-based collaboration indicates that the collaboration is based on resources that belong to the community or the public at large.[17]

Since 2004, the notion of *Web 2.0* has gained currency as a label to describe many of the collaborative practices currently unfolding online (O'Reilly 2005: 1).[18] The key point that distinguishes Web 2.0 from the previous era is the 'leverage of user-provided data'. There has been much debate about the actual substance and motivation behind this term, but in essence it refers to: 'a common web platform, users provide data, services as opposed to software, an architecture of participation, and harnessing collective intelligence' (O'Reilly 2005: 2).[19] Common to Web 2.0 services is the fact that the value of the software is proportional to the scale of the data it helps to manage or, put differently, a social network site becomes more valuable the more people who use it.

One of the scholars who have written extensively on online collaboration is Benkler, with a particular focus on commons-based peer production:

> Commons-based peer production is a socio-economic system of production that is emerging in the digitally networked environment. Facilitated by the technical infrastructure of the Internet, the hallmark of this socio-technical system is collaboration among large groups of individuals, sometimes in the order of tens or even hundreds of thousands, who cooperate effectively to provide information, knowledge or cultural goods without relying on either market pricing or managerial hierarchies to coordinate their common enterprise.
>
> (Benkler and Nissenbaum 2006: 394)

This type of collaboration relies on certain characteristics in order to be manageable. The object of peer-production must be modular for different people to work on different parts of it; the modules must be relatively small in size; and the integration of the modules into the whole must be at low cost (Benkler and Nissenbaum 2006: 400–401). Benkler addresses not only how these new forms of production transform conventional markets, but also the potential they hold for individual freedom (autonomy), for

---

17 Commons refers to a shared resource that is not owned privately but available to all members of a community (Stalder 2007: 43).

18 For a critical analysis of Web 2.0 business manifestos see Dijck and Nieborg (2009).

19 Current archetypal Web 2.0 services include Flickr, YouTube, Wikipedia, Facebook, LinkedIn, BitTorrent, and MySpace. The level of collaboration varies between sites such as MySpace, Flickr, or YouTube, which represent resource sharing on a public platform, and platforms such as Wikipedia where people cooperatively create a product, guided by a common vision. Mailing lists represent the oldest and most widely used form of collaborative platforms (Stalder 2005: 51).

creativity, and for virtues such as openness, trust, and fairness. Arguably, the new means of production represent richer models of human motivation besides personal wealth maximization, or, as formulated by one scholar, 'a preference for fairness that is more emotional than rational' (Shirky 2008: 134).[20] In summary, this line of research establishes a structural connection between the defining features of commons-based peer production and the possibility of engagement in autonomous, creative, generous, and collective undertakings.[21]

Sunstein is another scholar who addresses the new forms by which 'many minds produce knowledge', for example how these collaborative platforms can be so relatively successful; and why so many knowledgeable people are willing to contribute (Sunstein 2006: 151). One of the answers suggested is that the contributors have a distinctive attitude towards authorship, whereby no one considers themselves the owner of an entry, or claims any kind of authorship (Sunstein 2006: 153). Another point is that those committed to making collaboration work far outnumber those who try to disrupt or vandalize the platform. The modalities of Wikipedia's collaborative platform has been compared to Hayek's price theory,[22] in the sense that any particular article at any given time may be seen as a kind of 'price', a product of many minds, just as a price on

---

20 Benkler and Nissenbaum operate with four clusters of virtues. The first addresses autonomy (liberation) and is reflected when participants in peer-production exercise independence of will, initiative, self-reliance, discretion, and free-spiritedness. The second addresses creativity and is reflected in the practices of contributing thoughts, knowledge and know-how into creating meaningful, in contrast to passive, consuming. The third addresses generosity (altruism) reflected when participants in peer-production benefit others by contributing time and effort without receiving the conventional payments for their time and effort. Finally the fourth addresses sociability (cooperation), which involves giving to the commons, hence the participants' effort is part of a collective effort (Benkler and Nissenbaum 2006: Section III).

21 For a more critical take on peer production such as how these forms relate to inclusivity and accountability, see Kreiss et al. (2011). Lanier (2010) is also critical of the appraisal of peer-production and public sharing, and argues that these social models may in fact limit the creative accomplishment of the individual author/creator.

22 Hayek is an economist and political philosopher known for his defence of classical liberalism and free-market capitalism. He claims that the efficient exchange and use of resources can be maintained only through the price mechanism in free markets. In *The Use of Knowledge in Society*, Hayek (1945) argues that the price mechanism serves to share and synchronize local and personal knowledge, allowing society's members to achieve diverse, complicated ends through a principle of spontaneous self-organization.

a good is the result of the judgement of a large number of consumers (Sunstein 2006: 156–7). The entries thus aggregate information, which is widely dispersed and held by many people, without any central planner to orchestrate the process. However, unlike the market Wikipedia has no prices, trades, or mutually advantageous deals. Whereas markets are guided by economic incentives, Wikipedia is guided by different incentives. It is precisely these non-economic incentives that make the success of Wikipedia difficult to replicate. 'For many users participation is attributable not to self-interest, but to other motivations, including people's desire to see their words in print, the value of self-expression, and the apparently widespread desire to be helpful and constructive' (Sunstein 2006: 157).

The same is true of the FOSS movement that is driven by a commitment to values of openness and sharing rather than economic incentives. 'Making the software freely available, and opening up its code for inspection and change, transforms the character of software from a commodity into something like an environmental resource of the internet, similar to air in the physical environment' (Stalder 2005: 21). In return, those who use the code are required to make their improvements available under the same conditions.[23] Much like Wikipedia, the FOSS community aggregates knowledge beyond that which any smaller group of people could have accomplished. However, contrary to Wikipedia the community does not have the ability to modify the common product; rather it subscribes to a number of formal processes for approving software changes. As such it is an example of collaborative processes within a relatively tight system of control concerning the common product: the GNU/Linux operating system.

A final note on collaboration concerns the potential link to the field of computer-supported collaborated work (CSCW). Scholars such as Pfeil, Zahiris, and Ang (2006) link collaborative platforms such as Wikipedia to the theories of CSCW and argue that Wikipedia may be seen as an example of CSCW, since participants contribute whenever it is needed and wherever it is located (Lipnack and Stamps 1997). However, there are essential differences as the CSCW research field originates within conventional workplace settings, whereas Wikipedia is a voluntary, self-regulated, and open-ended project.

---

23 This is done via 'share-alike' licences that require adaptations of the work to be released under the same or similar licence as the original. For an elaboration of these licence principles see Sunstein (2006: 166–8).

5. SELF-REGULATION

The final theme, self-regulation, refers to a process whereby private actors agree to rules regulating their activities, defined and enacted via codes of conduct (Schulz and Held 2001: A-2). It is thus arrangements made between private parties based on voluntary commitment, without any interference by the state. Self-regulation within a community usually refers to a number of mechanisms that the community has developed and employed to regulate behaviour amongst its members. These mechanisms may include a formal structure that comprises various positions, arbitration mechanisms, voting procedures, and so on. They may also include more informal ways of regulating community behaviour such as principles and norms that the parties subscribe to. As the self-regulatory mechanisms represent the members' way of governing themselves, they are part of the power structure within the community. One of the points that have been emphasized in relation to Wikipedia's means of self-regulation is the community's faith in self-correction rather than sanctions and restrictions. Even in the extreme case of vandalism, the community usually responds in a rather low-key way, whereas sanctions are used only as a last resort (Benkler and Nissenbaum 2006: 397).

In summary, a cultural take on the internet stresses that the internet enables new forms of sociability; facilitates public life in a variety of forms; allows for new ways of creating cultural products; and underpins exchange-oriented practices. The research field that addresses the internet from this perspective covers, among others, the study of specific online communities, the cultural and social practices related to those spaces, and the way the internet may be part of a cultural transmission. With reference to the public and private models, the discourse speaks to the sociability model, with a focus on the cultural practices that constitute public life. Framing the internet as culture also points to specific human rights challenges. In the following section the focus is on two main themes, namely human rights versus intellectual property law, and protection of privacy in online public spaces.

6. HUMAN RIGHTS ISSUES RELATED TO THE INTERNET AS CULTURE

In the policy arena some of the most controversial issues related to internet regulation have concerned online practices of sharing vis-à-vis intellectual property (IP) law. Numerous campaigns by civil society groups and scholars have argued that regulation, such as the Agreement on Trade-Related Aspects of Intellectual Property Rights (TRIPS 1994),[24] the World Intellectual Property Organization (WIPO) Copyright Treaty (WIPO 1996),[25] the US Digital Millennium Copyright Act (DMCA 1998),[26] the EU Copyright Directive (2001/29/EC)[27] and the Anti-Counterfeiting Trade Agreement (ACTA 2011),[28] in an imbalanced way favours IP right-holders; that it expands a culture of permission; and that it discourages the dissemination of new ideas and creations into the public domain.[29] Recent examples of IP enforcement include the two US bills PROTECT-IP (PIPA) and Stop Online Piracy Act (SOPA), which in 2011 caused a public outcry, and eventually were withdrawn in their then current form.[30]

The IP debates vary depending on whether the topic is music, films, books, academic journals, or software, but essentially play out between advocates of expanding and enforcing existing IP regulation, for example media corporations, and advocates of an online culture based on sharing and exchange, for example the previously mentioned free culture movement.

The battle between proponents of free culture and IP rights is fought both at a legal level (expanding or narrowing IP law); at a technical level (promoting digital rights management systems or distribution and access technologies); and at the economic level (sale of products or provision of services) (Stalder 2005: 17–18). Moreover, since sharing of, for example, music and films takes place both within the private and public spheres, the enforcement of IP law increasingly needs to control actions within both spheres.

---

[24] Available at: http://www.wto.org/english/docs_e/legal_e/27-trips_01_e.htm, retrieved 12 July 2012.

[25] Available at: http://www.wipo.int/treaties/en/ip/wct/trtdocs_wo033.html, retrieved 12 July 2012.

[26] Available at: http://www.copyright.gov/legislation/dmca.pdf, retrieved 12 July 2012.

[27] Available at: http://eur-lex.europa.eu/LexUriServ/LexUriServ.do?uri=CELEX:32001L0029:EN:HTML, retrieved 12 July 2012.

[28] ACTA is a widely contested trade agreement, which was rejected by the European Parliament in July 2012. More information can be found at: http://www.europarl.europa.eu/news/en/pressroom/content/20120703IPR48247/html/European-Parliament-rejects-ACTA, retrieved 24 September 2012.

[29] Civil society organizations active in the IP field include, among many others, EFF (US-based), IP-Justice (US-based), the Free Software Foundation (US-based with sister organizations around the world), and European Digital Rights (European network).

[30] For an explanation of PIPA and SOPA see for example Newman (17–19 January 2012).

Human Rights versus Intellectual Property Rights

Traditionally, there has not been much interaction between human rights law and IP law. However, this is changing gradually and more scholars have started to examine the intersection between the two bodies of law.[31] One meeting point is UDHR Article 27 and the corresponding Article 15 of the International Covenant on Economic, Social, and Cultural Rights (ICESCR). Article 27 UDHR represents cultural rights and includes freedom of creative activity, freedom of scientific research, the right to enjoy culture, the right to enjoy the results of scientific advancements, and protection for authors (creators) of any scientific, literary, or artistic production. Article 27 offers protection for authors but also recognizes the public's right to benefit from the scientific and cultural progress that intellectual property products can engender (Helfer 2007: 976). Cultural rights are closely related to other rights such as freedom of expression, freedom of information, and the right to education. However, there has also been work to develop the distinct meaning of Article 27, not least from UNESCO, which has developed a number of standard-setting documents dealing with cultural rights.[32]

In a General Comment to ICESCR Article 15 it was stressed that whereas the right of authors to protection of the moral and material interests derived from their creative production is a human right, IP rights are *not* human rights but primarily regimes set up to protect corporate interest (United Nations and Committee on Economic Social and Cultural Rights 2005).[33] Regarding the right to enjoy one's own culture, this has mostly been addressed as the state's duty to create appropriate socio-economic conditions so that individuals or groups may freely obtain information,

---

[31] See, for example, Helfer (2007) and Yu (2008).

[32] See Adalsteinsson and Thórhallson (1999: Section 3) for an account of UNESCO work in this area.

[33] 'In contrast to human rights, intellectual property rights are generally of a temporary nature, and can be revoked, licensed or assigned to someone else … Whereas the human right to benefit from the protection of the moral and material interests resulting from one's scientific, literary and artistic productions safeguards the personal link between authors and their creations and between peoples, communities, or other groups and their collective cultural heritage, as well as their basic material interests which are necessary to enable authors to enjoy an adequate standard of living, intellectual property regimes primarily protect business and corporate interests and investments' (United Nations and Committee on Economic, Social and Cultural Rights 2005: Paragraph 2).

training, knowledge, and understanding. Further, individuals and groups should have opportunities to express themselves freely, to communicate, to act, and to engage in creative activities (UNESCO 1976). States thus have a duty to promote the democratization of access to, and participation in, all forms of culture, while also protecting the interests of authors.

Another intersection between the two bodies of law is to view IP law in light of its impact on the broad array of human rights, such as the right to health (medicine), the right to education (access to knowledge), the right to information, and so on. As argued by Yu (2008), there is a growing need to develop a human rights framework for IP, hence a more systematic approach to evaluating IP law in light of human rights law. One example of assessing IP rights from a broader societal perspective is WIPO's Development Agenda, which was initiated in response to the WSIS discourse on these issues. The WIPO Development Agenda was established in 2007, when WIPO's General Assembly adopted a set of recommendations to enhance the development dimension of the organization's activities.[34] The Development Agenda indicates a closer examination of the relation between IP law and development, including possible revision of existing regulation.

The regulation of IP is extremely complex, not least because the United States and European traditions are different. Below is a brief introduction to some of the arguments that are often raised in relation to the transposition of IP law to the digital domain.

A core argument raised in favour of the IP regime has been that the removal of economic incentives for product innovation and new artistic expressions will result in fewer people being creative, thus society will be poorer and more ignorant as a result (Sunstein 2006: 165). The challenge is thus to maximize access to and use of knowledge as widely as possible while at the same time ensuring the economic protection of authors. IP is protected through various means such as patent and copyright laws. Patent law protects the right to hold ideas in private hands in order to encourage innovation, whereas copyright law protects the principle of 'the original form' of expression, for example as a book or a painting. While it is impossible to infringe copyright without being familiar with the original work, it is easy to infringe patent rights without any knowledge of the protected idea.[35] The following mainly addresses copyright issues.

---

34 See http://www.wipo.int/ip-development/en/agenda/recommendations.html, retrieved 3 August 2012.

35 Protection of IP via patenting has been controversial especially in relation to software. The practice of patenting software has been subject to a heated

In Europe, copyright law is generally based on the protection of two sets of rights: the 'exclusive right', which is the protection of the original with respect to the production of copies, and the 'moral right' that requires that the author be credited whenever his/her work is used (Koktvedgaard 1996: Chapter II). The relationship between the original and the copy in particular is one of the characteristics distinguishing digital products from physical products. First, digital products do not differentiate between the original and a copy, just as their use by one person does not exclude use by other people. Second, everyone may share the same information irrespective of physical location. Third, copies are produced every time information is accessed. And fourth, there is minimal additional cost for further distribution of information. This potential for sharing information challenges the principle of 'exclusive right' and may essentially be accommodated in two ways. One approach is to enforce the principles of copyright law within the digital environment, that is to protect access and the use of material according to the principles of pay-per-copy. Another method would be to find new models for protecting the interest of the author. To date the policy response has been to enact legislation that transfers principles of copyright law to the internet era, and in some cases expands traditional limits to copyright by prolonging the time that content stays out of the public domain.[36] The policy measures that have been introduced to protect copyright include legal measures criminalizing file sharing as well as technical measures such as digital rights management systems that are used to enforce pay-per-use models.[37]

As part of the free culture movement, an increasing number of alternative models promote sharing in the public domain. One example is the Creative Commons (CC) initiative. Creative Commons is a global scheme that enables copyright holders to grant some or all of their rights to the

---

battle amongst the European Parliament, civil society groups, and the European Commission. The campaign against software patenting claims that patenting of software elements will have damaging effects on creativity and on software development practices, not least for smaller development teams and individual software developers. The campaign argues that the patenting of software is similar to patenting the ideas contained in a book and would pose a radical change to the ability to use and build on other people's ideas so long as credit is given to the author. The various software modules are seen as specific expressions protected by copyright law, but not as an 'invention' that may be excluded from general use. See http://www.nosoftwarepatents.com/en/m/intro/index.html, retrieved 10 November 2012.

[36] For an elaboration of these arguments see Lessig (2008: Chapter 5).

[37] One of the alternatives to pay-per-use is a cultural flat rate, which has been suggested as a way of compensating the authors whose work is distributed via the internet. See for example Grassmuck (2009).

public while retaining others through a number of licensing schemes. The permission to freely copy and distribute work along with the obligation to credit the author are mandatory in all CC licences, but authors can decide whether to allow the processing of their work and whether commercial use should be permitted or not. The CC licence thus provides for a public domain where work is freely available to the public whilst recognizing that it is subject to copyright. 'We use private rights to create public goods: creative works set free for certain uses. Like the free software and open-source movements, our ends are cooperative and community-minded, but our means are voluntary and libertarian.'[38] The Creative Commons network consists of 100-plus affiliates working in over 70 jurisdictions around the world. As of 2012, Creative Commons licences are translated to more than fifty national codes.[39] Another example of a sharing scheme is the Open Access (OA) project, which promotes unrestricted use and free availability to academic articles by removing price barriers (subscriptions, licensing fees, pay-per-view fees) and permission barriers (most copyright and licensing restrictions) by consent of the author. Authors declare their consent to the Open Access scheme by using one of the Creative Commons licences, or through other open-content licences. OA could in principle include any kind of digital content, but has so far focused on peer-reviewed journal articles and their preprints.[40] Additionally, there is the Public Domain Manifesto, launched in January 2010, which outlines a series of principles and recommendations to ensure that the public domain may continue to function in a meaningful way, not least with regard to education, cultural heritage, and scientific research.[41]

In summary, the free culture movement advocates a participatory and exchange-based culture rather than enforcing and expanding the permission culture implied in IP law. Despite a growing number of alternatives to IP rights, such as Creative Commons and Open Access, the deployment of IP law is still expanding worldwide. Likewise for the development of a human rights framework towards IP law: this is still in the early stages.

---

[38] See http://wiki.creativecommons.org/History, retrieved 10 July 2012.

[39] See http://wiki.creativecommons.org/CC_Affiliate_Network#The_Licensing_Suite, retrieved 4 July 2012.

[40] Most scholarly journals do not buy their articles or pay royalties to authors; hence researchers can consent to OA for their journal articles without losing revenue, which is contrary to the position of most musicians and movie-makers. See Suber's OA overview at: http://www.earlham.edu/~peters/fos/overview.htm, retrieved 10 August 2012.

[41] The Public Domain Manifesto is available at http://www.publicdomainmanifesto.org/, retrieved 24 September 2012.

Next is examined another human rights challenge related to the cultural and social practices that unfold on the internet, namely protection of privacy in online public spaces.

Protection of Privacy in Online Public Spaces

In the Web 2.0 environment, where users by and large contribute and share information within commercial platforms, social life becomes intimately connected with business. As an example, a study of MySpace found audiences to be employed as commodities, which are sold to advertisers, as well as being producers of site content (Morris 2007). Other scholars have iterated that online social spaces are subject to decisions based on economic incentives, rather than social norms (boyd 13 March 2010). In relation to privacy, this raises issues such as collection and control over data, how long data are retained, and under what circumstances data may be exchanged with other parties.

It is commonly claimed that if people valued their privacy, they would not share personal information as widely online as is currently the case. This has led many to assume that young people in particular disregard privacy, and that 'the age of privacy is over' (Facebook founder Mark Zuckerberg quoted in Read Write Web (Kirkpatrick, 9 January 2010)). Scholars have also argued that privacy is a lost cause, and that people increasingly seek exposure rather than privacy (Brin 1998). However, several privacy campaigns led by users of social network sites seem to contradict the assumption that public exposure implies a disregard for privacy protection.[42] On the contrary, these campaigns seem to emphasize that control over data is *the* central aspect, and thus the individual's ability to decide what information to convey to the world, rather than certain types of information being private per se. As expressed by one scholar:

> There's an assumption that teens don't care about privacy but this is completely inaccurate. Teens care deeply about privacy, but their conceptualization of what this means may not make sense in a setting where privacy settings are a binary. What teens care about is the ability to control information as it flows and to have the information necessary to adjust to a situation when information flows too far or in unexpected ways.
>
> (boyd 25 January 2010: 1)[43]

---

[42] Examples include Facebook groups such as 'Facebook: Do not sell my private pictures! Change your terms of use, NOW!' and the Facebook petition 'Facebook, stop invading my privacy!'.

[43] A similar conclusion was reached in a recent study based on interviews with teens across the USA (boyd and Marwick 2011).

A similar line of argument is found in a study on the reconceptualization of public and private in the blogosphere (Livejournal), which concludes that the individuals perceive privacy as a matter of information control, thus the ability to decide on who shall view any particular piece of information (Ford and Gammon 2007: 4). In addition, research on the Swedish community Lunarstorm suggests that what may seem private/sensitive to an observer is not necessarily understood as such by the individual who exposed the content (Sveningsson 2005).

In 2007 Privacy International (PI) started to investigate the storage, use, and exchange of user data by internet companies across the spectrum of search, email, e-commerce, and social networking sites (Privacy International 9 June 2007).[44] Based on the survey, PI concluded that 'Overall, the privacy standard of the key internet players is appalling, with some companies demonstrating either willful or a mindless disregard for the privacy rights of their customers' (Privacy International 9 June 2007: 9). This point was reiterated by other observers: 'These companies are continuing full steam ahead with a new generation of intrusive marketing practices that are based on unprecedented levels of data collection and personal profiling' (Montgomery quoted in Digital Journal (Engelen, 6 December 2007)). Since then, online privacy protection has been increasingly high on the internet policy agenda in the USA and in Europe. On occasion online companies have accommodated their users' privacy concerns, for example when Facebook agreed to a privacy resolution with the Office of the Privacy Commissioner of Canada (25 August 2009), and when they decided to close down their advertising system, Beacon.[45] However, since 2010 Facebook has insisted on public rather than private as the default setting. Recent research on Facebook concludes that the company's privacy policy and privacy design are guided by a belief system that encourages 'radical transparency' and is at odds with conventional understandings of privacy (Raynes-Goldie 2012).

---

[44] The survey included Amazon, AOL, Apple, BBC, Bebo, Ebay, Facebook, Friendster, Google, Hi5, last.fm, LinkedIn, LiveJournal, Microsoft, Myspace, Orkut, Reunion.com, Skype, Wikipedia, Windows Live Space, Xanga, Yahoo!, and YouTube. The selection of companies was based on criteria such as market share, services offered, number of users, and site traffic. Only English language services were included in the survey.

[45] The close-down of Beacon was in response to a large outcry by consumer groups and privacy advocates when they learned that Facebook recorded their users' activity on other sites and relayed those actions back to the users' friends on Facebook (Hood, 19 September 2009).

As previously mentioned, one of the European responses to these challenges has been a substantial data protection reform, including a 'right to be forgotten'. EU Commissioner Reding has stated that she 'cannot accept that individuals have no say over their data once it has been launched into cyberspace' (Reding quoted in Net York Times (Daley, 9 August 2011)). The privacy obligations of internet companies has also been addressed by the EU data protection authorities in an opinion on how social networking sites are affected by European data protection law (Article 29 Data Protection Working Party, 22 June 2009). Related initiatives in the USA include the Obama administration's recent launch of a new set of online privacy policies (White House, 23 February 2012).

In summary, several campaigns led by users, consumer groups, and privacy advocates have flagged a concern for the diminishing level of privacy protection in online spaces and have called for stricter control over the privacy practices of internet companies. In response, a substantial revision of the legal framework in Europe has been proposed, but in general the protection of privacy online is defied by the lack of a global standard for data protection. Moreover, the protection of online privacy is challenged by the fact that personal data represents commercial value to an extent not previously seen.

7. CONCLUSION

By framing the internet as culture, attention is directed towards the norms and practices unfolding in online spaces. The culture metaphor speaks to the ways the internet transforms sociability and adds to the spaces and modalities for public life. Moreover, these new modalities for public life influence the private sphere by offering new ways of playing with identity; of expressing oneself; of remixing and creating cultural products; of collaborating with peers, and socializing, in a variety of online spaces.

Table 7.1 summarizes some of the notions, policy themes, and human rights issues considered in this chapter. The first row points to commonly used notions that refer to the internet as culture such as 'free culture', 'cyber culture', and 'community'. Next, the potential for a more participatory culture is suggested as the main theme related to social change. Third, in relation to the public and private models, the culture metaphor refers to the sociability model with a focus on the social and cultural practices unfolding on the internet. The next row suggests free culture, collaboration, and self-regulation as key themes associated with this perspective,

Table 7.1 Summary of the internet as culture

	The internet as culture
Culture notions	'Free culture', 'cyber culture', 'community'
Potential for social change	The potential for a more participatory culture
Public–private framing	The sociability model: the internet as social/cultural practices
Key themes	Free culture Collaboration Self-regulation
Policy controversies	Online practices of sharing versus IP rights
Human rights issues	The impact of IP rights on human rights Protection of privacy in online public spaces

and indicates the online practices of sharing in contrast to IP rights as the main policy controversy. Finally, two human rights issues are iterated: the impact of IP rights on human rights, and the protection of privacy in online public spaces.

This concludes the discussion of the four internet metaphors and leads to the third empirically oriented part of the book. A comparative summary of the metaphors are outlined in Appendix A.

PART III

ICT and social change

In this final part of the book, the focus is on ways in which civil society groups deploy communication technology to foster their causes. This is done via two case studies addressing women's organizations in Uganda and the German Wikipedia community. The studies apply the public sphere and culture metaphor to concrete spaces of social interaction, and examine in more detail the interrelation between ICT use and social change. Based on the findings, the concluding chapter will discuss the usefulness of the metaphorical framework, outline some cross-cutting challenges to human rights protection in the internet era, and suggest areas for future research.

8. ICT as a tool for empowerment in Uganda

The entry point of the first case study is the Women of Uganda Network (WOUGNET), a network of more than ninety women's groups, which have used and promoted ICT as a tool for women's empowerment since 2000. WOUGNET is occupied with the democratic potential of ICT and their strategies and initiatives address themes such as access to information, participation in public and political life, collective action, and communicative capacity building.

Inspired by the public sphere metaphor, the study focuses on three main themes when examining the use of ICT in Uganda. First, 'access', which addresses the women's access to basic infrastructure, to information, and to decision-making processes. Second, 'freedoms', referring to the women's ability to act and debate freely in the public sphere, thus to participate in public life. Third, resources to participate, which concern, for example, the women's familiarity with use of ICT and with expressing themselves publicly. The notion of ICT in this context refers to computers, the Web (internet), mobile phones, and radio alike.

Applying a public sphere perspective to a developing country such as Uganda has, for example, been done in a range of research concerning the relationship between digital media and democracy in Africa (Banda et al. 2009). This research points to the role of new media in supplementing conventional media, rather than replacing it: 'The value of new media thus lies in the extent to which they enmesh with old media to provide multimedia platforms that allow for greater democratic participation, inclusion and expression' (Banda et al. 2009: 2). The potential for greater democratic participation, inclusion, and expression was also emphasized in the current study, for example how women as voices in the private sphere increasingly appeared and expressed themselves in the public sphere.

1. CONTEXTUAL OVERVIEW

The Republic of Uganda is a landlocked country in East Africa, with a total population of approximately 34.5 million people.[1] Like many African countries, Uganda is described as a hybrid regime, situated at a crossroad between democratization and authoritarianism (Tripp 2010). The 1995 constitution established Uganda as a republic with executive, legislative, and judicial branches. The constitution provides for an executive president, to be elected every five years. President Yoweri Museveni, in power since 1986, was elected in 1996 and re-elected in 2001, 2006, and 2011 (US Department of State 2011). Following decades of economic and political instability, Uganda was one of the first sub-Saharan African countries to embark on liberalization and pro-market policies in the late 1980s. GDP growth has accelerated from an average of 6.5 per cent per year in the 1990s to over 7 per cent since 2000. The agriculture and fishing sectors provide approximately 80 per cent of employment in Uganda, and the country is Africa's second-leading producer of coffee, which accounted for about 17.9 per cent of the country's exports in 2009 (US Department of State 2011).

Regarding ICT, the government has developed a national policy framework to support ICT sector development and established a Rural Communication Development Fund to support infrastructure and ICT development in the rural areas (Government of Uganda, 13 February 2003). As of 30 June 2012, Uganda had approximately 4 376 672 internet users, representing 13 per cent of the population (Internet World Stats 2012). Tensions between the Ugandan government and the media have risen in recent years as the authorities have conducted raids on independent media outlets and arrested journalists on politically motivated charges. However, until recently governmental attempts to control information had not reached the internet (OpenNet Initiative, 30 September 2009). In April 2011, however, the government wrote to three of the country's major ISPs asking them to block Facebook and Twitter 'to eliminate the connection and sharing of information that incites the public' (Heacock, 18 April 2011). The request came after a week of protests over rising fuel and food prices that were widely advertised on Twitter.

Inequalities between men and women remain a major problem in Uganda. The number of females receiving education has remained considerably lower than that of males, causing high illiteracy levels among women, with rural–urban differentials (Kaddu 2007: 3). Despite the

---

[1] See http://www.worldbank.org/en/country/uganda, retrieved 6 January 2013.

government's efforts to promote gender-sensitive policies and laws (for example, the National Constitution and the National Gender Policy), the inequalities between men and women are still significant (Kaddu 2007: 4). Broadly speaking, men dominate decision making in both the public and private spheres, and many of the efforts made to empower women in Uganda essentially aim at improving women's means of generating income and their ability to participate in public and political life.[2] WOUGNET is an example of a local civil society network seeking to remedy this inequality by focusing explicitly on ICT as a tool to empower women.

2. THE WOMEN OF UGANDA NETWORK

The Women of Uganda Network (WOUGNET) was launched in 2000 by several women's organizations, with Dorothy Okello as the main initiator.[3] Prior to WOUGNET, Okello had maintained an email list whereby news was distributed to a number of women's organizations in addition to queries related to ICT use. Due to the increasing interest in the list, it was agreed that there was a need for a common platform to facilitate exchange between the women's organizations. WOUGNET was launched to develop the use of ICT among women as tools to share information and to address issues collectively, for the better being of Ugandan women.[4]

WOUGNET's organizational structure consists of a coordinator, an administrative board, and a small staff of employers and volunteers. The funding base is provided by organizations such as the Association for Progressive Communications (APC); The Humanist Institute for Development Cooperation (HIVOS); The Technical Centre for Agricultural and Rural Co-operation; Dimitra/Food and Agriculture Organization of the United Nations; Global Fund for Women; and the United Nations Development Program.[5] The activities are organized in three main programmes (outlined below) with health, agriculture, and entrepreneurship as cross-cutting themes. Regarding ICT, the emphasis is on email and the Web, and how these technologies may be integrated with conventional

---

[2] For an overview of the human rights situation in Uganda please refer to the annual report by the Uganda Human Rights Commission (2010).

[3] Dorothy Okello has a PhD in Electrical Engineering and is affiliated with Makerere University in Kampala.

[4] See http://wougnet.org/about/, retrieved 10 July 2012.

[5] Please refer to http://wougnet.org/about/ for further information on funding partners, retrieved 10 July 2012.

Table 8.1 Overview of WOUGNET's programmes and activities

Programme	Information Sharing and Networking	Technical Support[6]	Gender and ICT Policy Advocacy
Aim	Facilitate access to relevant information in urban and rural areas.	Provide technical support to the women in the region.	Advocate for the integration of gender issues in ICT policies and programmes.
Activities	• Maintain website and mailing list. • Provide newsletters. • Host online and face-to-face forums. • Participate in national and international events. • Build capacity of rural women to access and use ICT.	• Technical support to members. • Facilitate refurbished computer shipments. • Use of worldspace satellite radio.	• Build gender capacity of policy makers, ICT experts, and journalists. • Sensitize decision-makers on the need to integrate gender into policy processes. • Assess the Rural Communications Development Fund from a gender perspective.

media. 'While our emphasis is directed towards Internet technologies, we are also interested in how these technologies can be integrated with traditional means of information exchange and dissemination including radio, video, television and print media.'[7] WOUGNET's programmes and activities are summarized in Table 8.1.

ICT Strategy

WOUGNET was one of the first local groups to address ICT as a tool for women's empowerment. ICT usage in Uganda in the early 2000s was very limited, and WOUGNET provided a platform where women's groups

[6] WOUGNET's link to the Department of Technology at Makerere University (via Okello) was stressed as important for access to cutting-edge ICT knowledge (#3, WN). In the following, quotations from interviews are referenced by a number referring to the list of interviewed people in Appendix B, followed by affiliation. WOUGNET staff affiliation is referred to as WN.

[7] Quoted from http://www.WOUGNET.org/cms/content/view/20/33/, retrieved 3 August 2011.

could access and share information as well as receive basic technical support and training. The first members were mainly urban-based organizations with internet access:

> When we first started the idea was to get people to use email and the internet ... and so that is why there is focus on those particular areas and the more people that we got online the better ... it was a very simple process, and still it is a very simple process to get onboard, which is that you basically fill out this form and then we subscribe you to either the regular mailing list or the newsletter something like that, so that you are actually actively online.
>
> (#1, WN)

WOUGNET's first major evaluation in 2003 stressed that they were mainly targeting women in urban areas and excluding rural women. The evaluation showed that despite a general increase in awareness and participation of women in ICT-related activities, the benefits were limited to groups with access to the internet. In response, WOUGNET decided to reach out to women in rural areas (Okello 2007: 1). The focus on rural women implied that the scope of ICTs had to be broadened to include conventional media, and in 2005 a pilot project was established in the northern part of Uganda. WOUGNET also started to engage with ICT policy, in particular to promote gender mainstreaming via commenting on draft legislation.[8] The policy advocacy was coordinated via a broader civil society coalition (the Uganda Women's Caucus on ICT), which also fed into the WSIS process. The advocacy created some awareness, but few results in terms of concrete policy changes (#2, WN). One of the challenges was the lack of data to support the relevance of linking gender and ICT politics (#6, WN).

The WSIS process, however, was stressed as significant for WOUGNET's involvement with ICT policy nationally, since it provided nationally information that was barely available at national level. In particular, the importance of the WSIS process was attributed to being part of an international civil society network (APC).

> WSIS was a vehicle for us. We would not have been here ... if it wasn't for WSIS, because you know we were very APC so we could put [a spotlight] on these issues, we had access to tons of materials and we knew what was the hot issues.
>
> (#1, WN).[9]

---

[8] Gender mainstreaming refers to the (re)organization, improvement, development, and evaluation of policy processes, so that a gender-equality perspective is incorporated into all policies, at all levels, and at all stages by actors normally involved in policy making (Council of Europe 1998).

[9] WOUGNET and some of its partner organizations are still participating in WSIS follow-up via the Internet Governance Forum (IGF). Regarding IGF,

By 2007 ICT usage had matured in many of the women's organizations, and WOUGNET decided to concentrate their efforts on exploring best practices for using ICT.

> There was a growing support of the idea of us being the moderator for, you know, not necessarily new technology but maybe new ways of using existing technologies ... to really show people different ways of doing things. I think that is where our niche should be.
>
> (#1, WN)

In response, the Enhancing Access to Agricultural Information project in northern Uganda was initiated.

3. REACHING RURAL WOMEN IN NORTHERN UGANDA

Introduction

The Enhancing Access to Agricultural Information (EAAI) project was launched in 2005 in 12 parishes in the Apac District in Northern Uganda. The goal of the initiative was to develop communication systems that would enable easy access to agricultural information for rural women farmers. According to the local agricultural office, more than 90 per cent of the population in the district depended on agriculture for their livelihood, with the majority of the work being conducted by women (#27, local administrative officer). With regard to ICT, general access was very scarce in the region. Some households had radio, or were familiar with radio, but mostly the radio followed the man and was not available to the women on a regular basis. Additionally, the level of literacy was low, and for many farmers oral communication in the local language was *the* means of communication.

Prior to the project a baseline study amongst the farmers had identified some of the major constraints on farming activity. The study found that

---

the study iterated that Uganda is seen to have little impact on the overall political agenda, whereas a regional forum with a focus on the specific context and challenges in Africa would make more sense. 'I find it unfair to sit and talk along with someone from the UK, Canada, and Denmark where they have superb connectivity and then I am sitting in a panel with these people, and their issues are completely different from mine. I am not going to get anywhere, because they will start a discussion on a different target and how many Africans are at IGF to pull our issues? There are quite few' (#9, BROSDI).

the women's capacities to increase their income were limited by time, by customary prohibitions against women's rights to access and control their own economic resources, and by lack of information. The lack of information limited production, which again led to limited incomes and poverty (Beijuka 2007: 17–18).[10] An initial workshop showed that access to radio was seen as the main priority by the women, followed by mobile phones as a second priority, not least to communicate with agricultural extension workers.[11]

> What came out [of the workshop] was a priority because what they wanted was radio. We said that we could also call them to talk on radio and then they also said, if they could have access to phones, and the computer never came out at that time because many of them had never seen one and did not know how it works ... They also want to use a radio because it was audio you could listen and then the extension possibility to reach the villages and also the place is quite big so if you have two or three extension workers in the district they are not able to reach everybody.
>
> (#16, former KIC staff)[12]

On the basis of these priorities the project targeted 12 groups of 30 women farmers and equipped the groups with a radio and a mobile phone. The goal was to facilitate communication between the farmers and agricultural experts via mobile phones and community radio, thereby strengthening the women's access to information as well as their decision making power. Kubera Information Centre was also established in Apac town to ensure a local point of access for the farmers.[13]

Access

The role of ICT is discussed below, along three main lines pertaining to access: first, as a way to counter infrastructure challenges; second, as a means to enhance access to information; and third, as a facilitator for

---

[10] John K. Beijuka conducted an external evaluation of WOUGNET's work in late 2006/early 2007. The evaluation was based on meetings and interviews with more than 50 people, including the local farmers in the Apac district.

[11] Extension workers are local agricultural officers who provide support and advice to the farmers in the district.

[12] While emphasizing the radio as the preferred medium for receiving information, the analysis also showed that current radio usage was limited to personal announcements, question and answer sessions, and greeting programmes.

[13] See http://kic.WOUGNET.org. The staff at KIC all speak the local language, Luo, and were provided with computers, a printer, a television, a video deck, newspapers, and Worldspace Satellite Radio.

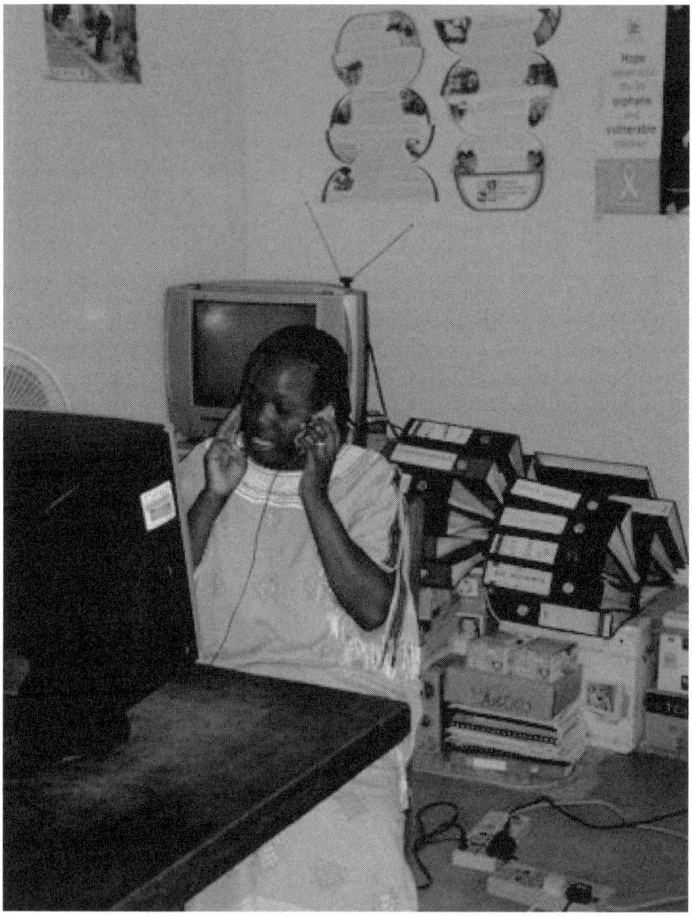

Figure 8.1 *Kubera Information Centre*

access to decision-making processes. The three levels of access are intertwined, with the third level most directly linked to power.

Access to infrastructure

In the context of Apac, the notion of infrastructure was used to speak of public resources such as public roads and power supply, as well as internet infrastructure and network coverage. The lack of these basic resources was a recurring theme in the study. The findings highlighted the bad condition of public roads, the few points of public internet access, the poor network coverage, and that community radio was unstable and of limited reach. Despite the shortcomings of community radio, it was emphasized as a useful alternative to travelling long distances on poor roads.

> ICT has improved service delivery because in those days you needed to move from one point to the other to inform farmer X that this is what is happening. Considering the resource constraint that we have, you must ride a motorcycle up to 30, 50 kilometres to go and talk to the community about the changes in production trends … Instead of going to do something we just go to the radio and say this is what is on the ground.
>
> (#19, VEDCO)

Also, the unstable power supply was frequently mentioned, implying regular power interruptions as well as complete lack of electricity in certain areas. In response, radio shows were recorded on audio cassettes to make them available irrespective of power supply and radio signals. Moreover, radio scripts were translated into the local language Luo. To ensure a local point of contact, Kubera Information Centre (KIC) was established in Apac town. It was decided to locate the information centre in a central marketplace to ensure that the farmers would frequently pass by its location.

> Basically what we did, we put up the information centre to be like a link … Twice a month, there is a market so everybody comes around there. They do ride their bicycles when there is a big market like that because people come from the neighbouring districts of Lira and the other far counties … so it is accessible it is easy for them also to come even if it is just to come and say hi, hello, how are you doing?
>
> (#16, former KIC staff)

In summary, the study pointed to limited access to public infrastructure as a key barrier that needed to be overcome in order to improve the farmers' livelihoods and means of participation in public life.

Access to information

The lack of access to information was one of the predominant themes in the study, covering a variety of issues. Initially the lack of agricultural information available to the farmers was a key concern. However, the scope soon expanded to include access to health and educational information as well.

> Initially it used to be only agricultural information. However, we realized that they do not only need the agricultural information to survive. Sometimes they need the information on health and probably even on education.
>
> (#17, KIC)

As indicated by the above quote, KIC perceived its role somewhat as an 'information broker', thus as someone that selected information for the farmers. In terms of locating contextual relevant information, KIC partnered with local organizations trained in providing agricultural information.[14]

> We go around and take market surveys, how much is it within the local market and then compare with the cross-district, the cross-border markets, so like yesterday I moved around and was making surveys on how much maize is, how much is beans, and how much is soya beans and then compare on radio ... because sometimes most of our farmers thought there are better markets across borders ... so this information we convey to them through radio.
>
> (#19, VEDCO)

The identification of contextual relevant information was based on the needs expressed in the initial survey supplemented with ad hoc visits to the farmers to assess their requirements. Due to the low level of literacy most information was translated into the local language and largely communicated through audio tapes and face-to-face meetings (#17, KIC). The survey had indicated that, to a large extent, relevant information was already available in the community; however, it was not communicated to the farmers. In response, priority was given to the provision of 'information channels', rather than producing new types of information.

> When we started with the farmers project the district had plenty of information, they were just waiting for an extension worker to go to the field ... this is why I think it worked so well. Because for us we did not have the information that we wanted to give, for people who had this information, we had all these channels to disseminate the information, the radio programmes, you know, whatever. And so you know it is like basically getting married, you know everyone was fitting together, but you know what brought us together was ICT.
>
> (#1, WN)

As illustrated by the preceding quote, ICT was spoken of as information channels used to disseminate information to the farmers. This indicates an understanding of communication as 'information transmission', whereas the actual practices were somewhat more nuanced. Examples of

---

[14] Partner organizations included the Agency for Sustainable Development Initiatives (ASDI) and Volunteer Efforts for Development Concerns (VEDCO), both NGOs based in Apac, FOODNET (an agricultural research and development network), The Radio and Internet Program (RANET), Uganda Metrological Department, and the Apac District Agricultural Office.

Figure 8.2 Radio Apac host

more participatory spaces included, for instance, community radio shows, a 'question and answer' service (QAS), and farmer group meetings, as further explained below.

The community radio shows included programmes such as *Farmer News* and *Morning Glory*.[15] The radio programmes debated current issues raised by the farmers, sometimes with the participation of extension workers and local farmers. Questions were raised during the programmes via text messages or phone calls from the farmers, or via direct participation in the programmes.

> For example we call a farmer to come and discuss something with the banana, like improved variety as opposed to the local variety, so these people come, and the experts come and talk about this.
>
> (#17, KIC)

[15] The involved radio station was Radio Apac, which serves the district together with Radio Wa.

> I always used to listen to the radio, about sunflower planting, and have radio at home. Now we listen and discuss together in the group.
>
> (#22, local farmer)

One farmer explained how the farmer group gathered in her home on Mondays between 4 pm and 5 pm and used the mobile phone to submit questions to the radio (#23, local farmer).

The Question and Answer Service (QAS) allowed the farmers to pose questions to agricultural experts in written form. Questions could address, for example:

> When we farm beans, soya, maize, the main problem is market. How do we get better access to the market?
>
> (#22, local farmer)

> As a woman what method can I use to improve soil fertility?
>
> (#23, local farmer)

> I've seen for long when planting soil and wanting to plant beans, they don't heal well. How to deal with this problem?
>
> (#24, local farmer)

In response to the first question, the women had received the following answer:

> Join group, groups have power, if you are one person the buyer will defeat you.
>
> (#22, local farmer)

The QAS service was coordinated by the information centre, which collected questions, submitted them to local experts, and provided the farmers with the answers in various forms. In some cases community-wide relay of the answers was provided via Radio Apac.

> For the QAS we have given different groups question forms in which the farmers fill out the forms on any question that may arise or any problem, and they send it back to the information centre here, whereby we process these forms, send them to the experts who answer the questions and we send the answers back to the women. Depending on their urgency we may send the answer by SMS, we may deliver the forms by hand or we may make a phone call.
>
> (#17, KIC)

The evaluation conducted in 2007 found that the new communicative practices had improved the farmers' access to information and that this had had a positive impact on their livelihood (Beijuka 2007: 22). These positive findings were generally confirmed in the current study. As an example, one of the local organizations mentioned a banana bacteria epidemic to

Figure 8.3 St Luke Farmer Women's Group meeting

which farmers were able to respond rapidly due to information received via community radio:

> like banana bacteria there was no way we could communicate on one like this going to the radio and informing the masses that please take care there is an epidemic … in fact that was the emphasis and many of them took it serious and they took on to destroy the affected plants and then managed and now the disease is reducing
>
> (#19, VEDCO)

Also, one the local farmer groups (St Luke Farmer Women's Group) stressed that increased access to information had led to new farming practices. One example was beekeeping, which was conducted as a new farming enterprise and organized as a profit-sharing venture within the group. The profit from the first two years of beekeeping had been used to pay for the entry of a local youth to university (#23, local farmer).[16]

---

[16] In their October 2009 newsletter, WOUGNET reported that the project is 'now progressing at a rate they [the rural women farmers] believe would drive them out of poverty'. An example mentioned is a group that had expanded its flock

Concerning the significance of increased access to information, the farmers indicated that by now the 'information resource' was more accessible than other resources such as, for example, seeds and implements (#24, local farmer). This had led to some frustration since information access was less valuable if other resources were unavailable or if working practices seemed difficult or impossible to improve beyond a marginal level.

In summary, improving access to information has been a key inspiration for WOUGNET's work in Apac. In response, various information and communication systems have been established, for example the QAS that enabled access to expert information, the weekly radio shows and, more generally, the new spaces for dialogue and problem solving that have been established between the farmers and local experts. The project has utilized structures that were already present in the community, for example farmer groups, Radio Apac, and local organizations, to facilitate ownership and access to contextualized information.

The study revealed some contradiction between the way ICT was spoken of and actual ICT practices. According to WOUGNET, ICTs were means to disseminate timely, accurate, and relevant information to the farmers, as illustrated by the quote: 'despite being the largest contributor to the country's economy, the agricultural sector still lacks knowledge dissemination innovations (ICTs) to facilitate timely, accurate and relevant information to farmers' (Okello 2007: 1). In contrast to this emphasis on effective information transmission, the study highlighted participatory spaces such as radio programmes where information was shared, debated, and challenged, rather than transmitted.

Access to decision-making processes

One of the main findings related to decision-making processes concerned the way the new communicative spaces had influenced gender divides in the district. While the project initially targeted women farmers, men soon participated and sat side by side with the women at the group meetings. Moreover, the men were frequent users when it came to visiting the information centre, for example to source information.

> You know that the women are in some places and men in some places but now when they go to, for example, the dissemination meeting, you have both men and women, they are both in the same place, maybe the only difference is that

---

of goats from 6 to 40 and bought 30 beehives from income generated by farming activities. The group had also bought an accumulator that charges the group's phone and powers the radio (WOUGNET, October 2009).

> the men sit on the chairs and the women sit down you see, but then you have a discussion and everyone can contribute to that.
>
> (#1, WN)

More generally, the farmers indicated that ICT had strengthened their ability to make decisions on what to grow, how to tackle crop diseases, and how to counter bad weather or varying market prices (#22, #24, local farmers). Further, as part of the group structure, the women increasingly negotiated market prices as a collective, which had enhanced their bargaining power towards the middlemen buying their products.

> We produce together, market together, and share the profit. There is easier access to the market and to negotiate when you are a group.
>
> (#23, local farmer)

As an example, the women were now connected with the district farmer association linked to the World Food Programme, which had made buying arrangements with several of the farmer groups at a price more favourable to the farmers.

> It was the kind of work that I really liked, because it was helping them directly and they were trying to put all their products together and then bring it to the district level and then the World Food Programme would pay them. And a better price than the farmers who go to the middlemen.
>
> (#16, former KIC staff)

The collective bargaining process provided an example of how the women's ability to influence their own situation had been improved with a direct impact on their income. Though structures of inequality still dominated, the women utilized new means and collective strategies to inform their decisions. This corresponded with one of the findings from the 2007 evaluation, which highlighted the way women increasingly were involved in decisions related to the private sphere and the spending of family income: 'Family incomes are increasingly spent on household needs, school fees, medical bills, and most of the surplus is ploughed back into farming activities before alcohol by the husband' (Beijuka 2007: 32).

Despite these positive indicators of change, the daily usage of radio and mobile phones was limited by simple obstacles such as lack of money to buy airtime. Also, many of the women were challenged by lack of ICT skills, as addressed below.

In summary, access to the local systems of communication (community radio, extension workers, middlemen) was seen to have strengthened the farmers' ability to influence their livelihoods, to negotiate as a collective, and to participate in public life. The findings indicated that the farmers perceived their livelihoods as being somewhat improved by the increased access to information and to means of communication. Obviously, access to basic infrastructure remained a problem, but radio shows as well as audio tapes were some of the means used to counter the infrastructural challenges. Regarding WOUGNET's approach to access, emphasis was explicitly placed on using ICTs to provide new information channels and to increase access to information, while access to decision-making processes was less visible as a deliberate strategy. While the latter seemed improved, this appeared more as a positive side-effect than the result of a deliberate focus.

Freedoms

In the context of this case study, the term 'freedoms' refers to the protection of fundamental rights related to public and political life. As previously discussed, there is an increasing focus on freedoms in the online sphere, and on countering various types of censorship. However, in the context of Apac the main concern was not violations of online freedoms, but rather structures of poverty and inequality that impacted negatively on the women's ability to exercise their rights, especially to raise their voice, to own land, and to be politically active. According to the Uganda Participatory Poverty Assessment of 2002, women are still regarded as property by their husbands, thus men have control over women's lives, their access to information, and their participation in politics, social groupings, and training (Bakesha 2008: 143).

> We talk of women's rights here in Kampala but when you go down and up in the villages, then what there exist is what? What my husband tells me to do, that is what I do. If I question him, those are the beatings. I have to submit to everything he tells me to do.
>
> (#13, ISIS)

Concerning participation in political life, the study highlighted some positive indicators of change. First, the women appeared increasingly confident as they gained more practical experience with public appearance, for example being on air, raising issues, posing questions, and so on.

> Like when I call for questions during talk show, now women also say like, hi I am called so-and-so, I am a farmer, a woman farmer from such a sub-country, I want to know about ABCD.
>
> (#25, Radio Apac)

Therefore, the women's increased experience with public communication (in farmer groups, with agricultural experts, or on radio programmes) was seen to have built their confidence both in terms of mastering concrete skills and at a more personal level by building self-esteem. Second, the women farmers had started to aspire to leadership positions at local council (sub-country) level. This engagement with local politics was seen as a result of the increased self-confidence amongst the women.

> If you are not educated and everything you can definitely feel that you are nothing, so I feel that this project has empowered the women because first of all they start talking … so that gives you a bit of confidence-building and then we change into the local politics, they are now going to compete with men and they have actually gone through, so I really think to some extent it has empowered what? The women, though that was not the intention of the project.
>
> (#16, former KIC staff)

> When there were elections most of the women participated in political elections, local elections, and we had a number who came up to the council … yeah more confidence, even value as women because you know our culture is really not very nice … the men really, you know, they make you feel that you are nothing.
>
> (#16, former KIC staff)

However, the presence of women in public and political life, be it as council members or as public voices more generally, was still relatively limited compared to their male counterparts.

Another point, which was also reported in the 2007 evaluation, was the finding that men in Apac increasingly allowed their wives to attend group meetings and to control farm resources such as credit and land. In principle, women may own land, but few do so due to the relatively low income of women.

> Very few women own land, because most of the land is in the male hands because also the income levels of women are low. But you can buy land if you have money, it is within the law.
>
> (#16, former KIC staff)[17]

As the women farmers' income increased, they started buying land, thereby gaining control over the economic resources needed to sustain their livelihood, yet this remained a slow process.

In relation to ICT's potential to facilitate public participation, the study pointed to the way women had become more visible both as participants at community meetings and as voices on the radio. Moreover, the new communicative practices had given women a stronger say in decision making related to the household and the family income. As the women started

---

17 As expressed by a poster from the Uganda Land Alliance in Apac: 'Women are not property, but land is property, which women may own.'

to own more land, associate, negotiate, and participate in political life, existing structures of public and private as male-dominated domains were altered. In this regard the facilitation of increased access to agricultural information may have a longer-term impact than simply being the ability of farmers to communicate via radio and a mobile phone.

In summary, the issues raised in relation to freedoms were by and large related to social structures impacting negatively on women's ability to acknowledge and exercise their rights, and less to state restrictions. The findings spoke to a cultural context in which structural inequality between men and women was seen as an urgent problem related to women's participation in public life. The study indicated that the new means of communication had contributed positively to the women's ability to speak their mind and to participate in the public and political life of the community.

Resources to participate

In the context of this case study, resources to participate is related to the farmers' ability to take part in public life, such as their ability to use technology, express themselves, and collaborate. The study highlighted capacity building as a key priority in the local context, mainly addressed as ICT training.

From the outset, many of the women had never touched a phone or radio, seen a computer, or had access to audio tapes. Training was therefore crucial in order to provide the women with basic skills, as well as to build their confidence. Besides training in specific skills, for example how to use a mobile phone or a radio, the women were encouraged to use the mobile phone to pose questions during radio shows, and to reach extension workers for agricultural advice in order to build their familiarity with the technology. Women who were fast learners assisted as co-trainers of their fellow farmers.

> It's hard to get them to use ICTs like the mobile phone even to make a phone call or to send a message. However, we have singled out a few women who are fast learners and we have made them trainers so they train their fellow women.
> (#16, former KIC staff)

> Like this old woman ... initially when we got on ground she even feared to phone but now the phone is part of her, she can send us a message, she can tell us this is the problem, of course in the local language not in English ... And there are some of them who now can get to the centre and use our computer.
> (#18, KIC staff)

As part of the capacity-building process, meetings were held across the district to explain how the new services would work, for example the QAS. Radio training was also conducted for a couple of women from each parish, including live presentations on the radio. The aim of the training was to develop the women's capacity and understanding of community radio (WOUGNET 2006: 20).

> They do the theory and also they go on air. They teach them like the basics in a five days training what would you first do when you go on the radio, you greet people, you introduce yourself.
>
> (#16, former KIC staff)

In terms of strengthening the farmers' resources for participating in public life, the study highlighted the situations where experiences were shared, such as when the farmers discussed and shared experiences amongst themselves and with other local experts. The radio shows where farmers participated, group demonstration plots, and visits to other farmer groups were emphasized as especially important.

> With the radio and phone we know more what is happening in the other groups.
>
> (#22, local farmer)

The fact that it was local people who shared experiences was stressed as essential in order for the farmers to acknowledge them as experts within the specific context of Apac.

The study pointed to two main conclusions concerning resources to participate. First, training of farmers, in the different forms outlined above, was seen as a crucial component both to provide basic skills and to build the confidence needed to actively use ICT to communicate daily problems and to participate in public spaces. As many farmers lacked basic ICT skills, practical training was needed to familiarize them with the new tools. Second, capacity building within the community largely focused on providing information and strengthening specific skills, and to a lesser extent on making farmers more capable in mobilizing and sharing experiences. However, group demonstration plots, radio shows, and exchange visits between farmer groups were emphasized as important spaces for learning, indicating that despite the strong focus on skills-related training, new spaces for sharing and learning had been facilitated as well.

Conclusion

The study illustrated how a relatively simple application of conventional media may contribute positively to local development and gender equality. It also showed how different platforms were used in a supplementary manner, and suggested a landscape of media diffusion rather than media convergence. Both radio and mobile phones proved to be effective platforms since they were more readily available in the community compared to computers and the internet. The audio form also responded well to the low level of literacy amongst the farmers. Furthermore, the combined use of radio and mobile phones provided the radio shows with an element of interaction and user-defined agendas. Whereas the internet was primarily used by KIC staff and partner organizations to locate and translate information from outside the local context, radio and mobile phones were used to facilitate debate and problem solving within the community. The study presented an example of 'user-generated content' within a platform of conventional media, since the farmers themselves contributed to the agenda setting in the radio programmes, as well as participating in these programmes from time to time. In the context of Apac, the combined use of community radio and mobile phones thus performed some of the interactive, participatory functions that are usually associated with the Web platform. In contrast, the internet was used primarily as a library: a means of locating information, which was then subject to further contextualization before being utilized.

Another finding concerned the discrepancy between the discursive patterns and the social practices with regard to the role of ICT. Whilst WOUGNET stressed the role of various ICTs as information channels used to disseminate information, the study highlighted the participatory spaces facilitated by ICT. When farmers engaged with radio programmes, debated with extension workers, or held discussions amongst themselves, they were communicators rather than information receivers. The majority of examples from the local context thus spoke to the way ICT had facilitated communicative processes amongst the farmers rather than merely providing information transfer.

In relation to the new modalities for public and political life, the findings indicated that the farmers' capacity to influence their own situation had been improved as new avenues for production and bargaining were created. This included deployment of new farming methods, more women in control of economic resources, and collective bargaining for market prices. In addition, with regard to structures of public and private, increased participation of women in public life could be observed, for instance, increased political activity and an increasing number of women voicing issues of concern at community meetings and in local radio shows. However, these positive indicators were not mainly due to ICT use, but appeared as a combined result of strengthening women's confidence and thier ability to raise their voices publicly, encouraging sharing within the groups, and countering gender divides more generally. The positive indicators of change thus seemed to derive from the creation and harnessing of new spaces for experience sharing, decision making, and participation in public life, facilitated by relatively simple ICT structures.

Concerning the analytical framework (access, freedoms, resources to participate), the study pointed to substantial access divides related to lack of infrastructure, lack of access to local systems of communication, and gender inequality. It also illustrated that access to information in particular was a theme highly prioritized by the local actors. With regard to freedoms, the study highlighted some of the cultural factors constraining women's participation in public life, in particular structures of inequality that impacted negatively on the women's ability to exercise their rights. Finally, in relation to resources to participate, the findings stressed the central role of technical skills building in order to benefit from ICT usage, but also pointed to confidence-building as a means of strengthening participation.

4. THE ROLE OF ICT IN AN URBAN SETTING: KAMPALA

Introduction

The second part of the study addressed the way civil society groups had worked with ICT as a tool to empower women and women's organizations in Kampala. Whereas the activities in Apac mainly focused on conventional media, this part of the study to a larger extent included internet-related activities. Furthermore, it reflected some of WOUGNET's initial activities, for example maintaining a mailing list, providing information resources, facilitating forums and advocacy, and interfacing with the international gender and ICT community.

WOUGNET has members throughout the country, however, the majority of their members and partner organizations are located in Kampala, and several of these have used the internet for years. Despite being relatively resourceful and ICT-literate, the organizations operate in a context with considerable constraints such as unstable power supply, unstable network coverage, and high prices for connectivity, thus making it impossible to compare use of the internet to conditions in the developed part of the world. With regard to websites, some of the members have an online presence but lack the necessary skills to update information, whereas many organizations do not have their own website (Beijuka 2007: 13).

The study examined how the civil society groups in Kampala addressed and deployed ICT as a tool for social change using the themes of access, freedoms, and resources to participate to structure the findings. In line with the Apac study, access was addressed as access to infrastructure, access to information, and access to take part in decision-making processes.

Access

Access to infrastructure

In the context of Kampala study, the notion of infrastructure was primarily used in relation to internet infrastructure and network coverage. The findings highlighted the lack of an affordable internet infrastructure as an issue that impacted all parts of Uganda. Until recently, East Africa was the only part of the continent without access to a system of submarine fibre optic cables that brings bandwidth to Africa from the Middle East, Europe, and South Asia. Consequently, internet service providers (ISPs) in Uganda purchased their bandwidth via satellite, which could cost up to five times as much as bandwidth delivered via an undersea cable (OpenNet Initiative, 30 September 2009). Most rural areas were also under-served since they were not commercially viable.

> ICT has become very expensive also because it is dominated by private companies. They look at commercial viability and market-based approach so you find that the rural areas are under-served because of that.
>
> (#12, CEEWA-U)

In July 2009 the first undersea fibre optic cable to bring high-speed internet access to East Africa was launched by African-owned Seacom. Some observers believed this to be the single most important infrastructure investment in East Africa since the construction of the Uganda Railway.[18] Uganda's 2009/2010 government budget included support for expanding current ICT infrastructure, linking most of the country's major towns through 1500 km of optical fibre and providing for connectivity to ease the transition to the East African Submarine Cable System (EASSY) (OpenNet Initiative, 30 September 2009). In 2010 prices for internet connectivity as well as other telecom services started to decrease considerably (Cn.c144.net, 4 January 2011).

In summary, the lack of a national internet infrastructure was a key issue addressed by the organizations in Kampala, particularly the need to secure internet access to all parts of Uganda at an affordable cost.

---

[18] Presentation by Calestous Juma, at the Berkman Center for Internet and Society at Harvard University, 15 October 2009.

Access to information

The majority of the organizations covered by the Kampala study had access to computers and the internet, and hence access to various online resources. For many of the groups online advocacy and networking was somewhat comparable to their counterparts in developed countries. There was, however, a divide between the more professional groups such as the Council for Economic Empowerment for Women of Africa, Uganda Chapter (CEEWA-U), Women's International Cross Cultural Exchange (ISIS), and the East African Sub-regional Support Initiative for the Advancement of Women (EASSI) which had used ICTs for years, and small organizations that only had an online presence via WOUGNET's website.

The study highlighted WOUGNET's mailing list as a key space for sharing information and networking. The information distributed via the mailing list typically concerned various activities and priorities within the local groups and as such facilitated a common space and recollection for gender- and ICT-related advocacy within Uganda, for example providing information on new publications and campaigns, calling for participants or contacts in relation to specific projects and announcing research grants, as well as more personal messages. The mailing list was also mentioned as a good resource for keeping oneself informed about the various advocacy initiatives at national level in relation to gender and ICT.

> Especially the mailing list, we used it a lot to disseminate information and also to get information and we have quite benefited from that list.
>
> (#12, CEEWA-U)

> WOUGNET they have that mailing list and on that platform that is where we share our ideas with women when for example there is a training opportunity.
>
> (#13, ISIS)

> WOUGNET also provides kind of an interconnecting link so to speak so it brings together so many people.
>
> (#14, EASSI)

Moreover, some political discussions had taken place on the mailing list, for example in relation to sensitive topics such as female genital mutilation and women's right to abortion.

> Well, there are some strategic discussions [on the mailing list]. One that really created a lot of interest was the one on female abortion and people's different takes on that. Given our society different cultures different believes they kind of conflict with human rights issues so to speak … I felt that was important to know that even though we are gender-sensitive and we are feminists in one way or another and we do want girl and women's rights promoted, there are several areas that are sensitive. That are not clear-cut in terms of yes or no, whether or not it is a human right.

(#14, EASSI)

The mailing list was primarily spoken of as a space for sharing information rather than as a tool for policy advocacy. In relation to policy advocacy, the civil society coalition (Uganda Women's Caucus on ICT) was emphasized as important. The civil society coalition functioned as an advocacy group in relation to the national ICT policy framework, the Uganda Communication Commission, and during the WSIS process, particularly during the period 2003 to 2005.

> So we have been having one voice, doing policy advocacy as a team. Because as an individual you may achieve less and what we are looking at here is the universal access. How do you make them [ICTs] accessible to everyone, especially the rural communities?
>
> (#12, CEEWA-U)

When questioned about the role of the WOUGNET network, the larger member organizations emphasized the shared space for gender and ICT issues, whereas the smaller organizations stressed the online exposure and access to the network.

> It has helped them so much, when I link them [rural-based micro-organizations] with WOUGNET so they also come and participate in the workshop, they also get communication, they get newsletters, so there is a very good strengthening capacity.
>
> (#10, NVIWODA)[19]

In summary, the groups covered in the study had a strong focus on online resources when reflecting on access to information. Moreover, WOUGNET'S mailing list was iterated as a useful resource for accessing and sharing information pertaining to gender and ICT. Additionally, the smaller organizations emphasized the online exposure and networks to which they gained access via the WOUGNET website.

---

[19] On a more critical note, the 2007 evaluation revealed that many of WOUGNET's members had an information-sharing problem, thus newsletters and invitations to workshops, and so on, tended to end up with the group leaders and were not disseminated further down the organizations (Beijuka 2007: 13). It was also reported that WOUGNET was relatively unknown within Uganda, even among its own members, which may partly be explained by the lack of efficient communication from the chairs who interface with WOUGNET, and further on to their constituencies. Finally, it was reported that limited information on ICT was available for members to exploit easily, and that members would prefer WOUGNET to provide more ICT training (Beijuka 2007: 10, 29).

Access to decision-making processes

As previously mentioned, gender inequality represented a major problem in Uganda, and took many forms, for example uneven access to economic resources such as land and credit, poverty, and domestic violence. Moreover, the representation of women in the political system was emphasized as relatively low, with less than 30 per cent female representation in parliament.

> I would say that if women were more involved in decision making a lot would be improved, bills will be passed and legislation will be in favour of women, but because the women decision making is minimal, then in a sense policies that favour women concerns do not pass to reach women ... In Uganda we are slightly less than 30 per cent.
>
> (#14, EASSI)

Practically all of the groups interviewed addressed this inequality one way or the other and utilized ICT to improve access to information that may strengthen women's decision-making power and their income. One of the local groups that sought to strengthen women's economic power was CEEWA Uganda, which had a number of activities that aimed to make women more economically active, more in control of economic resources, and more able to sustain themselves. This included initiatives in the area of micro-financing, entrepreneurship development, and business training, thereby providing the women with information about, for example, how to gain credit, how to access markets, and how to run a small business.

> We are looking at transformation – how do you transform this grass-root women to a micro-entrepreneur, the so-called economical active women, how do you transform her ... you learn this person how to plan. How to price, how to keep records, how to save, how to manage credits if you want to go into credit, you know. Even the self-discovery, there are those who have potential, but they don't know, so you try to take them to self-discovery and they start up something and you have had quite a number of them who have moved from one level to another level now.
>
> (#12, CEEWA-U)

In relation to CEEWA Uganda's work, the local telecentres were emphasized as spaces for training and knowledge-sharing. The telecentres were, for example, used to train women to find new sources of credit, and to access information on market prices via the internet. Women who received training were subsequently used to train other women. As part of CEEWA Uganda's work with the telecentres, information that was found relevant to the community was made available in local language and audio form.

> We use ICT centres to see how best can we disseminate information to the communities using the centres, and the gap we found there to use the centres was the content actually. The infrastructure is there, but what goes through this infrastructure is it regularly available for this rural woman? Can it be regularly understood by this woman? If you collect content on agriculture and this foreign language, how is it going to benefit this woman? So those are the issues we are now looking at.
>
> (#12, CEEWA-U)[20]

Another example of utilizing ICT to improve access to decision-making processes was the agricultural knowledge fair, organized by Busoga Rural Open Source and Development Initiative (BROSDI).[21] The Knowledge Fair was an event where farmers met and shared their experiences so that others might learn from them. The farmers' experiences were recorded via podcasting, and included topics such as difficulties they face, advice they would want to give others engaged in similar practices, and whether it had made any difference to their livelihoods. Most interviews were conducted in local languages then converted to MP3 format and later uploaded for further distribution.

> It is interesting but true, the generations that can't write … We do podcast, then we do the blogs so they can sit and listen to the voice and learned based on the voice that they listen to.
>
> (#9, BROSDI)

Farmers without internet access received CDs so they could access the material from a stand-alone computer (Basajjabaka 2008).

An additional BROSDI initiative was a citizen journalism project, which focused on capturing and sharing stories as a means of promoting local development. The project started with a survey among the farmers asking them about their specific challenges with regard to accessing agricultural information. The survey revealed that the markets were diminishing and that there was a need to collect the agricultural experiences over past generations. Accordingly, the project started to collect agricultural content that was critical for development in the communities, but that went unnoticed in the mainstream media. The information was translated and distributed using various Web 2.0 technologies such as blogs, Google maps, wikis, online documentation, and chat rooms.

---

[20] The telecentres' use of CD-ROMs to empower women entrepreneurs are covered in Bakesha et al. (2008).

[21] The project addresses male and female farmers equally. For related initiatives such as the Collecting and Exchange of Local Agricultural Content (CELAC) project, see http://www.brosdi.or.ug/, retrieved 25 September 2012.

Additionally the farmers were encouraged to write blogs in the local language, which were then uploaded and translated into English for wider outreach. Farmers with internet access printed out the information and posted it on their noticeboards to make it accessible for people without connectivity.

> So what we did was, we developed a project with the farmers, which is to collect essential agricultural content. But largely it is on the content that the past generations used in agriculture where there were no pesticides, where there was no fertilisers and so on. How did they deal with agriculture, how did they ensure their plantations or whatever they planted was yielded better?
>
> (#9, BROSDI)

The information was collected via group discussions where farmers would share experiences and identify people who were considered experts within a given area. Besides translating and posting the information online, BROSDI provided summaries that were sent via text messages to farmers country-wide.

In relation to the micro-organizations, one of WOUGNET's member organizations, St Bruno Doll-Making Group, had used the WOUGNET online platform to make its enterprise visible to the world. The micro-enterprise offered art and craft services, specializing in doll-making, carried out by rural women from their homes. The online presence had raised the enterprise income significantly via increased foreign exposure and sales, but had also given the owner increased knowledge on how to run a business via studying other micro-enterprises on the internet.

> When we got connected to WOUGNET, they put us on the website, so from that time I have been getting people calling me even from outside Uganda ... it is all through the website, because we are as you see a bit outside Kampala ... Whenever I open [browse] some organizations, I find out their prices and how you can send them and get your money, which is easier, because I know the internet thing, the website, checking and seeing what other people do.
>
> (#15, St Bruno Doll Making Group)

In summary, the Kampala study provided various examples of how ICT has facilitated access to decision-making processes by providing the various groups and individuals with access to local systems of communication. This included relatively simple measures such as the WOUGNET mailing list, and more comprehensive experience-sharing initiatives such as the agricultural knowledge fair and the citizen journalism project. Further, it illustrated how local groups deployed ICT as a resource to improve women's economic power, for example via training in telecentres and via online businesses selling local arts and crafts.

Freedoms

In line with the Apac study, a culture of gender inequality was highlighted by the organizations in Kampala. Internet censorship is a relatively new phenomenon in Uganda. However, some examples of state interference in internet freedoms were highlighted with reference to countries other than Uganda.

> The internet has helped a lot especially in those areas with restrictive environments ... like Egypt where blogging is really restricted ... but the key concern here in Uganda is still the access because I think it is people's right to have access to these tools.
>
> (#12, CEEWA-U)

As illustrated by the preceding quote, Uganda was not spoken of as a particularly restrictive environment with regard to internet communication, whereas the lack of internet access was emphasized as a critical issue. In relation to gender inequality, it was stressed that women, other than a small, educated elite, have little awareness of their rights. As a result many were hesitant to raise their voice, to associate, or to attend public meetings or educational activities.

> It is only the elites, the educated women who know their rights. They might not implement them or practise them, but at least they know that they have rights, but the rural women most of them still don't know, even if they know they have to consult their husbands.
>
> (#16, former KIC staff)

The study indicated that the increased use of ICTs had a positive impact on women's rights in Uganda, particularly in terms of confidence-building and by familiarizing women with raising their voice publicly.

> Training for the ICT, yeah it gives you confidence because most of the women fear to go and get that knowledge ... So when you get trained, at least you get confidence because they allow you to trust your work in computer.
>
> (#15, St Bruno Doll Making Group)

> We trained young girls, most of them had never touched a computer, they did not know what a computer looked like, but we trained them and they were able to speak out, to share their voices with other people.
>
> (#13, ISIS)

In addition, ICT training was seen as an opportunity to bring men and women together and to sensitize men towards the use of ICT for enterprise development.

> Because you know here women sometimes they have to get permission from their husbands to go for a training at the telecentre, the nature of these roles,

> you can't just leave home. So when they ... realize the role of information in their enterprises, they will encourage other men to participate and also allow their wives to participate.
>
> (#12, CEEWA-U)

As indicated by the preceding quote, women's rights are constrained and the attempt to merge gender-divided spaces as part of ICT training illustrated the cultural barriers that had to be countered before women would enjoy the same rights and freedoms as men. The telecentres to some extent represented a space where female participation was accepted on equal terms with their male counterparts, hence a transmission between the private and public sphere.

Regarding ICT's influence on the public debate more generally, there was limited online debate in Uganda. However, there were examples of thematic debates such as a mailing list set up by WOUGNET partner I-Network, which represented some level of public debate and where top officials such as the ICT minister and his officials participated and received feedback on concrete policy initiatives.

> In fact the ministry itself have said that they listen very closely to what is coming out on our mailing list ... because it is a channel for them to get some feedback ... it is a really good way for them to get in touch with what people are feeling and thinking about their policies or their services or their products.
>
> (#1, WN)

> It definitely has changed a lot of debates, a lot of perception on what? On the facilitation, you know, of day-to-day communication and day-to-day living so to speak, a lot have changed ... because now they realize that this is such a powerful tool not just for easy communication, friendly communication, but it is such a powerful tool to send important messages across which in effect in the long term can change policies.
>
> (#14, EASSI)

As illustrated by the above quotes, the mailing list had started to change people's perception of the internet. Besides seeing it as a tool for communication, it was increasingly spoken of as a change factor influencing the way politics were carried out. Whereas the internet was primarily used as an information library in the Apac study, its role as a platform for public communication had started to take off in Kampala.

In relation to public and private dynamics, there were two main findings in the Kampala study. First, ICT was seen to strengthen women's ability to work from home, either directly via an internet connection or indirectly, as illustrated by the example from the St Bruno Doll Making Group, where local women were subcontractors to a micro-enterprise selling art and handicraft via the internet. In a context where travelling even small distances was difficult and expensive, and gender roles kept many women at home, the possibility of working out of your home was seen as something that may benefit women.

> If you are able to work from home as a woman, it is interesting that this question comes to me at this time, because I am thinking of that in my house, having my internet connection … I am a businesswoman as well because I teach entrepreneurship. I can be able to link with my customers as well and also I can be able to communicate with all the women, so I don't miss the link … And for the rural people it is costly, but if they get one point and there is computer there and there is internet connection. Information can spread quite easily. It can.
>
> (#10, NVIWODA)

Second, the online means of networking and gaining visibility were emphasized. One example mentioned was the Association for Progressive Communications (APC), which has its staff and members scattered around the world, and where daily cooperation, networking, and problem solving is almost entirely based online. Despite a relatively small staff and physical office, the organization appears visible and influential in many parts of the world due to its online collaboration and presence. In the physical world the staff may be women working out of their private homes, while in the online sphere they are public nodes, and part of a larger network.

> You know what when people talk about APC, they think that APC is a huge building, but it is a small office so basically you know working the workspace online is really large, but people who don't know ICT can't appreciate it. People can even sit in their home at their dining table when you have connection and talk to everybody and do work … I admire APC because I have gone to their office, it is just a small office, but she communicates to the whole world.
>
> (#2, WN)

In summary, the findings stressed that even in a country with a relatively low internet penetration, the internet was seen as a facilitator of change in a number of areas. In a context where women's ability to participate in public life is restricted, the online public sphere was seen to provide new opportunities for women to connect to professional, political, and social systems of communication.

Resources to Participate

The final theme addressed the means by which the local groups seek to strengthen women's resources to participate in political life. The findings pointed towards ICT training and capacity building as the key efforts conducted by WOUGNET and its partners, targeting women's groups, policymakers, and the media.

The training and capacity-building initiatives took many forms, such as courses in telecentres, ongoing ICT workshops and specific educational programs, training at in-house net cafés, technical support, and providing ICT resources online. Moreover, the area had been a priority since women's organizations such as WOUGNET, CEEWA-U, ISIS, and EASSI started to focus on ICT around 2000 to 2002.

> We decided to set up women's internet cafe because we realized that there was a gender-dictated gap between girls or women and men in Uganda and we decided to create a space for women, where women can come freely and also have a feel of the technology … Most of the women had their first touch on computers here at Isis.
>
> (#13, ISIS)

As use of ICT matured, fewer organizations were providing ICT training. ISIS was still active with the internet cafe and had established an online library with access to training resources. They also used ICT to document women's stories, not least during armed conflicts, and to relay these stories to the global community. CEEWA Uganda continued to train women in ICT for enterprise development. Some of the smaller organizations stressed the role of ICT training in promoting ICT literacy towards children. It was highlighted that the trainers needed to be creative not only in 'translating' ICT terminology into local languages but also in relating it to local concepts, as illustrated by the following quotes:

> This learning, adult learning is so interesting that even if they may not physically be using the computer, they will be able to promote it to their children. So when they talk to their children about it and if the children learn that my mum is 35, 40 or 50 and is able to touch the computer, then it will be enough motivation for the children to also access ICTs.
>
> (#10, NVIWODA)

> [T]hey always use local languages. Like the website the world web, they were teaching us like a spider web, so the way it connects … it is like a spider in our language, which they call, I forgotten the name, but they know the spider, they know how it works, then the mouse they were calling it a rat, which is a 'messy' so they would say now touch your messy … everybody was interested to touch the rat which doesn't bite.
>
> (#15, St Bruno Doll Making Group)

Another area of capacity building had been training and awareness-raising amongst policy makers and journalists. From the official side there was an increasing ICT awareness, and a dedicated ICT Ministry had been established. However, when it came to gender policies and understanding the specific challenges related to gender and ICT, the women's groups reported an ongoing need to sensitize policy makers, and to strengthen cooperation between the two policy areas.

> The problem with the gender people is that they are gender people but they don't understand ICT issues, they only have one element, which is gender, they don't see the connection so we really have to have capacity in ICT.
>
> (#2, WN)

In relation to how ICT had helped to mobilize the women's groups, the findings highlighted the gap between the few that had internet access and the many that did not. The relatively few that were connected increasingly used the internet to find information, share resources, and network more generally. However, for the majority, the mobile phone was still the most accessible medium. Further, it was stressed that for many people the physical meeting or phone call bore more weight than email communication. The importance of seeing the other physically in order to build trust and exchange services and advice was emphasized as a cultural characteristic.

> I think that is our culture, people feel much more when they see somebody physical ... you know our ancient thinking, we still think that we have to be physical. And when you are not physical you are not available.
>
> (#2, WN)

To summarize, ICT capacity building was stressed as crucial amongst the groups covered by the study, and was presented as an activity that had developed considerably over the past years. Capacity building had evolved from basic ICT training to use of collaborative tools such as wikis, blogs, and podcasts. With regard to WOUGNET, its role in terms of ICT capacity building had been more at policy level and less in terms of concrete training targeting the women's organizations.

5. CONCLUSION

The study addressed the role of ICT as an enabler for social change in Uganda and iterated several constraints, such as the lack of basic infrastructure and the small percentage of people who had access to ICTs. The groups covered by the study, however, were convinced that the combined use of various ICTs had contributed to women's empowerment in Uganda. The Apac project and BROSDI's Knowledge Fair were highlighted as examples of the way ICT, in conventional as well as new forms, were used and combined to facilitate communication and sharing of experiences. The initiatives may have affected relatively few people, yet they were perceived to have made a difference. They were seen to slowly enhance women's ability to control their own economic resources, to associate, to seek relevant information, and to speak their mind. As such, they were spoken of as examples of women claiming decision-making powers, both in relation to the private household and in relation to public and political life.

There were some essential differences in the way ICT was used in Apac and Kampala. In the context of Apac, the focus was on the combined use of radio and mobile phones to enable communication within the community.

The emphasis on these media, and not the internet, was primarily due to their local availability, relatively low cost, and audio form. Internet access was limited to a few access points and primarily used by the local organizations to source information, which was then communicated via conventional media platforms. The findings indicated a division of labour between the various ICTs, with the internet playing a minor role, and conventional media performing some of the functionalities that are often ascribed to the internet. In fact, some of the themes associated with Web 2.0, such as user-generated content, collaboration, and information-sharing, could be applied to the communicative space that radio and mobile phones had facilitated in Apac.

In Kampala internet usage played a more dominant role, since many of the organizations covered by the study had internet access and used it on a regular basis. This also implied a higher level of literacy compared to Apac. In Kampala the internet was primarily used to search for information and to communicate more generally, for example to share experiences in written and oral (podcast) form. Another role played by the internet was to provide visibility for smaller organizations and enterprises, and to facilitate public debate via thematic mailing lists. As with the Apac project, the internet was used in combination with other platforms, such as noticeboards, radio, and mobile phones, that were more widely accessible. In this sense the study illustrated how old and new platforms are used to complement one another, remixing some of the roles that are often assigned to the internet as compared with conventional media. The findings pointed to the multiple ways in which various platforms may be combined, even within a context of relatively limited ICT access.

Regarding the public sphere framework, this facilitated a thematic yet explorative approach, where attention was directed towards certain themes. The themes of access and resources to participate resonated well with many of the issues raised by the local groups when reflecting on the role of ICT as an enabler for empowerment. In Apac enhanced access to information was addressed in particular, whereas the Kampala study had a stronger focus on sharing experiences and influencing decision making. However, both locations provided several examples of how ICT was used to strengthen decision-making power. The theme of freedoms directed attention towards a context where gender-based inequality restricted women's exercise of basic rights such as their ability to speak at meetings, organize, control economic resources, and be politically active. Finally, in relation to the cross-cutting theme of public and private, there were some interesting indicators of change, mostly in terms of women increasingly having a public appearance facilitated by ICT usage. The examples included women speaking publicly at community meetings and on radio shows, online exposure of micro-enterprises, and policy advocacy targeting gender and ICT policies. It would be premature to draw strong conclusions on the public and private transmissions based on the study, yet the above examples point to increased public participation by women in Uganda.

Finally, it should be noted that while data was collected and analysed using the public sphere metaphor as the analytical frame of reference, there were several references to the other metaphors, as illustrated by the following quotes:

> I see it also as a medium. It is a very, very powerful tool for advocacy for news and for spreading information very fast.
>
> (#7, I-Network)

> The internet, for me actually I think of it as a road. Yeah and if you can get on you can go anywhere you see.
>
> (#1, WN)

> For me the internet is a creative space, it is time for me to learn something new.
>
> (#14, EASSI)

> I mean when I sit here and I get on the internet I feel part of the globe really, I can see what is happening in Denmark, I can see what is happening, you know. I just feel part of the world.
>
> (#8, I-Network)

The reference to the various metaphors is not surprising since in practice discourses on the internet as a medium, public sphere, infrastructure, and culture are mixed and combined when ICT use is debated, in Uganda and elsewhere. Moreover, it became clear that despite the relevance of themes such as access, freedoms, and resources to participate, the public sphere framework has some limitations, in particular related to its ability to capture issues of poverty, development, and gender inequality.

Leaving aside Uganda at this juncture, we turn next to the study on the German Wikipedia.

9. Wikipedia as a platform for community life and collaboration

1. INTRODUCTION

Over recent years several scholars have referred to Wikipedia as an example of the free culture of the internet due to its open and participatory format (Lessig 2004; Benkler 2006; Sunstein 2006; Zittrain 2009). Scholars have also suggested that the 'success' of Wikipedia testifies to the power of norms such as openness and sharing, and that Wikipedia represents a 'public expression of trust'.[1]

With this in mind, the German Wikipedia community is next examined, specifically Wikipedians from the Berlin-based community.[2] The English Wikipedia is included as a point of reference due to its special status as Wikipedia founder, and since many of the principles and guidelines derive from the English Wikipedia.

Inspired by the culture metaphor, the study focuses on three main themes within the Wikipedia community: first, the values and sense of belonging that make up the community culture (McMillan and Chavis 1986); second, the specific ways in which members of the community organize their contributions towards a common goal, hence the day-to-day collaborative practices of producing Wikipedia articles (London 1995); third, the rules and mechanism used to regulate behaviour within the community (Schultz and Held 2001). In summary, the study examines the norms and practices that constitute a particular online community. The findings represent the reflections of a small group of people compared to the 1.5 million registered users of the German Wikipedia. However,

[1] Wales and Benkler debating at Berkman@10 (10 years Anniversary of the Berkman Center for Internet and Society at Harvard University), 12 June 2008. Available at: http://www.youtube.com/watch?v=ummx6OG1GbM, retrieved 10 July 2012.

[2] The German edition of Wikipedia covers all German-speaking countries, including Austria and Switzerland. Likewise with the English edition, which covers all English-speaking countries.

all of the interviewees have been heavily involved with Wikipedia for several years.

2. WIKIPEDIA

Wikipedia is a multilingual encyclopedia project, launched in 2001 by Jimmy Wales and Larry Sanger, the former editor-in-chief of Nupedia.[3] Wikipedia is part of the Wikimedia Foundation, a non-profit charitable organization based in California. Wikimedia operates several online collaborative projects including Wikipedia, Wiktionary, Wikiquote, Wikibooks, Wikisource, Commons, Wikispecies, Wikinews, Wikiversity, and Meta-Wiki.

Wikipedia is described by Jimmy Wales as 'an effort to create and distribute a free encyclopedia of the highest possible quality to every single person on the planet in their own language'.[4] Wikipedia's articles are written collaboratively by volunteers around the world based on so-called 'Wikis', that is online cooperative platforms.[5] As of June 2013 there are 285 language editions of Wikipedia, and the five largest language editions are, in order of article count, English, German, Dutch, French, and Italian.[6] The majority of the editions, however, have not reached any critical mass. According to Alexa traffic rankings, in June 2013 Wikipedia was ranked as #6 in websites visited worldwide.[7] The English subdomain receives approximately 56.5 per cent of Wikipedia's cumulative traffic, followed by the Spanish, Japanese, and Russian language editions that account for approximately 8, 7 and 6 per cent of the traffic.[8] In terms of size, the number of visitors to Wikipedia far exceeds, for example, that of the *Encyclopedia Britannia*. As of June 2013 Wikipedia contained more

---

[3] Nupedia was an early effort to create a free online English-language encyclopedia with peer-reviewed articles. Wikipedia began as a complementary project for Nupedia, and the two coexisted until Nupedia closed down in 2003, and the articles were incorporated into Wikipedia. For an elaboration on Nupedia see Lih (2009: 32–41). The extent to which Sanger was co-founder is somewhat disputed (Zittrain 2009: 142).

[4] See http://en.wikipedia.org/wiki/Wikipedia#Characteristics, retrieved 10 July 2012.

[5] Wiki technology was designed by Ward Cunningham in 1995 as a tool for collaborative work (Leuf and Cunningham 2001).

[6] See http://meta.wikimedia.org/wiki/List_of_Wikipedias, retrieved 10 July 2012.

[7] See http://www.alexa.com/topsites, retrieved 27 November 2012.

[8] See http://www.alexa.com/siteinfo/wikipedia.org, retrieved 10 July 2012.

than 38 million articles, of which 4.2 million articles are in English. The German edition, being the second largest, contains 1.59 million articles; followed by the Duch version with 1.8 million articles. 'In the English Wikipedia, where activity is nonstop, articles have become an instant snapshot of the state of the world, serving as a continuous working draft of history' (Lih 2009: 7).

In 2004 Wikipedia won the Webby Award, often referred to as the Oscar equivalent for the internet, in the category 'Community', and the Prix Ars Electronica Award in the category 'Digital Communities'.[9]

Wikipedia articles were subject to the GNU Free Documentation License (GFDL) up until June 2009, when the site switched to a creative commons licence. The GFDL was initially designed for software manuals and was found less suitable for online reference works.[10] The creative commons licence implies that the content is freely available for others to use. However, attribution to the original author is required and derivative works must be subject to the same licence.

3. RESEARCH ON WIKIPEDIA

There have been numerous papers, articles, and books written on Wikipedia. Below is a brief introduction to some of this research focusing on the quality of Wikipedia articles, the means of regulation within the community, the incentives for taking part in Wikipedia, and the Wikipedia movement and culture more generally.[11]

---

[9] See http://www.webbyawards.com/ and http://www.aec.at/about/en/, retrieved 2 May 2013.

[10] On 1 December 2007 Jimmy Wales announced that a long period of negotiation between the Free Software Foundation (FSF), Creative Commons, and the Wikimedia Foundation had produced a proposal supported by both the FSF and Creative Commons to modify the Free Documentation License so that the Wikimedia Foundation could migrate the projects to a similar Creative Commons licence. In May 2009 a community vote amongst 17 000 Wikipedians agreed to the licence transfer. See http://wikimediafoundation.org/wiki/Press_releases/Dual_license_vote_May_2009QA, retrieved 10 July 2012.

[11] At Wikimania 2009 Hill presented a research review based on recently published Wikipedia papers, representing ten thematic clusters of research. The themes covered Wikipedia as a data source; quantitative analysis on Wikipedia; topic coverage in Wikipedia; Wikipedia quality; Wikipedian personalities; decentralization in decision making; modelling promotion decisions; rule creation; how Wikipedia might work better; and simple (English) Wikipedia. See Hill 2009.

First, there have been several studies on the quality of Wikipedia articles, as compared to traditional print encyclopedias. Content analysis of a sample of 450 articles in the German Wikipedia to investigate article quality suggests that the higher the relevance and interest of an article, the better is its quality (Brändle 2005). The interest factor is determined by the number of edits and unique authors, traffic, age, and number of back links, whereas the relevance factor is determined by, for example, the number of results delivered by Google. A comparative study of Wikipedia and another collaboratively authored online encyclopedia compared them to traditional print encyclopedias. It found that Wikipedia maintains a standard of contributions almost equivalent to that of printed material, even though it has no central editor. Another conclusion of the study was that the more that control is exercised over the contributions by editors, the more standardized and formal the content becomes (Emigh and Herring 2005). In terms of the topics covered, studies seem to imply that the coverage and quality of articles in Wikipedia are higher with regard to technical topics and lower when it comes to more philosophical entries (Elvebakk 2008). Bellomi and Bonato (2005) have carried out a network analysis of the English Wikipedia to examine potential cultural biases in Wikipedia content. The results suggest a bias towards Western cultures. However, more studies of other language editions would have to be carried out before adopting any conclusions.

The evaluation of Wikipedia articles has been conducted following several different methods. Viégas et al. (2004) have examined the dynamics of creating and editing articles through a history flow visualization tool. Via history flow visualization one may visualize the development of an article and see patterns of, for example, peer review, vandalism-repair, conflict resolution, and so on that occur. Lih (2004) has developed a qualitative tool based on metadata to assess the quality of any given article, whilst Voss (2005) has conducted quantitative assessments, for example the number of edits per author, the total number of authors per article, and the distribution of dead links.

A second cluster of research addresses Wikipedia's means of regulation. A study on Wikipedia's decision-making processes describes Wikipedia as an organization with highly refined policies and norms, anchored in a technological architecture that supports the ideals of consensus building and discussion. The authors describe how governance is becoming increasingly decentralized and how this is predicted by theories of other commons-based systems in the offline world (Forte and Bruckman 2008: 157). Other research on Wikipedia's governing structures has stressed that the community maintains a strong resilience to vandalism and that the fastest growing areas of Wikipedia are devoted to organization, coordination, policy, and process (Viégas et al. 2007). With regard to dispute resolution within

Wikipedia, research suggests that the arbitration system functions not so much to resolve disputes between conflicting Wikipedians, but to weed out problematic users while encouraging productive users back into participating. Strict remedies are rarely used (Hoffman and Mehra 2009).

A third theme is the community culture and the incentives for taking part in Wikipedia. Bryant et al. (2005) use activity theory to study participation in Wikipedia as an adaptable process that changes over time. Their findings suggest a move amongst Wikipedia participants from encyclopedia consumers to encyclopedia creators. Gaved, Heath, and Eisenstadt (2006) propose a typology of wiki users more generally, citing the nature of their involvement or type of contribution. Rafaeli and Arial (2008) find that the collaboration on Wikipedia is enabled more by different motivations for participating than by equalizing rules and norms. They thus see the 'rumors of widespread, even anarchic democracy on Wikipedia' as both premature and wrong, and argue that Wikipedia is less egalitarian than is often presumed (Rafaeli and Arial 2008: 261). In a study of Wikipedia as a knowledge-building community, Rafaeli, Hayat, and Arial (2009) suggest that Wikipedians' motivations are mainly cognitive, affective, and integrative, however also including more selfless motivations such as 'sharing my knowledge' and 'contributing to others' (Rafaeli et al. 2009: 12). Another community study examines how Wikipedia authors write their community into being, thus constructing their self-understanding and self-description as a community (Pentzold 2011). Based on coding of exchanges on the Wikipedia mailing list, Pentzold argues that Wikipedia represents an ethos–action community, which is an ethical community weaving a web of responsibilities between its adherents (Pentzold 2011: 717).

In relation to Wikipedian personalities, a study found that Wikipedia members locate their 'real me' identity on the internet more frequently than non-Wikipedia members. The study revealed differences between Wikipedia members and non-Wikipedia members in agreeableness, openness, and conscientiousness, which were lower for the Wikipedia members (Amichai-Hamburger et al. 2008: 679). Research on the cultural differences in the French, German, Japanese, and Dutch Wikipedias suggests that cultural differences observed in the physical world also exist online (Pfeil et al. 2006). In the study, content analysis was conducted on the 'history' page of the article 'game' within the four Wikipedias. Using Hofstede's cultural dimensions, it was found that in several cases the cultural characteristic of a given country, for example the extent to which the less powerful accept and expect that power is distributed unequally, was reflected in the way Wikipedians would cooperate online.

With regard to the Wikipedia movement, history, and culture in a broader sense, Lih (2009) provides an insider's account in his book *The Wikipedia Revolution – How a Bunch of Nobodies Created the World's*

Greatest Encyclopedia.[12] Other recent books that address the Wikipedia phenomenon include Reagle (2010), Bruns (2009), Zittrain (2009), Benkler (2006), and Sunstein (2006). Finally, there are at least two annual conferences that focus on Wikipedia and continue to provide numerous studies and research related to the content, technical design, and norms and behaviours of Wikipedians across various national settings. One is the Wikimania conference organized by Wikipedia itself;[13] the other is the Wikisym conference, dedicated to wiki and open collaboration research and practice more generally.[14]

The subsequent discussion introduces the German Wikipedia and explores the culture, the practices of collaboration, and the means of self-regulation within the community.

4. THE GERMAN WIKIPEDIA

When Wikipedia was launched, the Germans were well represented in the early development of the English language edition and its articles.

> Several of the early contributors to the German Wikipedia did a lot on the English Wikipedia too and even the idea of, well, doing an encyclopedia with the name of the wiki came from Germany.
>
> (#4)[15]

In March 2001 the German Wikipedia was announced by Jimmy Wales as the first non-English Wikipedia subdomain.[16] One of the earliest snapshots of the home page, dated 21 March 2001, can be seen at the Wayback Machine[17] site.[18]

---

12 Andrew Lih has been active in the Wikipedia community for many years.

13 See http://wikimania2011.wikimedia.org/wiki/Main_Page, retrieved 10 July 2012.

14 See www.wikisym.org, retrieved 10 July 2012.

15 In the following, quotations from interviews are referenced by a number referring to the anonymized list of interviewees in Appendix C.

16 See http://lists.wikimedia.org/pipermail/wikipedia-l/2001-March/000049.html, retrieved 10 July 2012.

17 The Wayback Machine is a 'digital time capsule' created by the Internet Archive and maintained with content from Alexa, allowing users to see archived versions of web pages. Snapshots become available 6 to 24 months after they are archived. However, the frequency of snapshots varies, so not all updates to tracked websites are recorded. For more information see http://en.wikipedia.org/wiki/Wayback_Machine, retrieved 10 July 2012.

18 See http://web.archive.org/web/20010425083506/deutsche.wikipedia.com/wiki.cgi?action=browse&id=HomePage&revision=9, retrieved 10 July 2012.

In 2003 the German community organized the first German Wikipedia meeting in Munich. Many cities followed, and soon a number of regular Wikipedian get-togethers were established around the world. For the German community physical meetings such as monthly '*stammtisch*' (literally 'a table for the regulars') became a common meeting point, usually with 20 to 30 people attending and debating various issues, for instance how people behaved online, how to ban people, and how to protect articles (#3). The community also started to organize city walks to explore and locate new article topics, and to organize workshops around Germany. In 2004 the community established the national chapter of Wikimedia: Wikimedia Germany. The same year the company Directmedia Publishing started producing and distributing hard-copy versions of the German Wikipedia.

The German Wikipedia had a strong rate of growth in the first years, and especially in 2004. Since mid-2006 the level of contributions has been approximately 400 new articles per day and between 6500 and 8500 active Wikipedians[19] per month with a slightly declining curve in 2011 and 2012.[20] In June 2013 the German Wikipedia had a total of 1 678 940 registered users.[21] The exponential growth of new users in 2004 is explained by massive coverage in mainstream media.

> It was a series of fortunate events that put us into the most-read newspaper, the most-read news magazines, TV channels. I think it was a matter of two or three weeks when Wikipedia was extremely prominent on almost every channel and in this time the German Wikipedia language increased 1 per cent per day for almost two weeks and we were completely exhausted … and unable to assemble the coming traffic. I think half of the people I know jumped on Wikipedia in this period of time. So it was an artificial growth, which was unique to the German encyclopedia.
>
> (#5)

Despite the rapid growth of the community in the early years, the study highlighted that many from the 'first generation' are still part of the community.

> In the beginning perhaps one did know the majority personally offline too through these meetings in Berlin … now if you go to a meeting in Wikimedia Deutschland there are still more people every time, but the majority I mean they have been there since the beginning.
>
> (#4)

---

19 An active Wikipedian is defined as someone who contributes five times or more in a month.

20 For statistics related to the German Wikipedia see: http://stats.wikimedia.org/EN/TablesWikipediaDE.htm, retrieved 10 July 2012.

21 See http://meta.wikimedia.org/wiki/List_of_Wikipedias, retrieved 11 June 2013.

In 2005 the German community organized the first global Wikimania conference in Frankfurt with 380 people from over 50 countries in attendance.[22]

> In August 2005, at a modest youth hostel in Frankfurt, Germany, hundreds of writers, students, computer hackers, and ordinary internet users from around the world gathered … There was a curious diversity – they came from different locations, age groups and educational backgrounds – but they all referred to themselves with the same label: Wikipedians. They were there face-to-face for the first-ever Wikimania conference, bound by a common passion to give away their labour, knowledge and know-how.
>
> (Lih 2009: 2–3)

The following year the state of Göttingen and the University Library held a special exhibition documenting the first five years of Wikipedia. In addition, the first two Wikipedia Academies were held in Germany in 2006 and 2007,[23] and in 2008 the German Wikipedia was ranked higher than any other domestic news site within Germany in terms of web traffic.[24] In June 2013 the German Wikipedia ranked seventh amongst most-visited websites in Germany.[25]

The quality of the German Wikipedia has been studied and compared to other encyclopedias several times. In December 2007 the German magazine *Stern* published the results of a research-based comparison between the German Wikipedia and the online version of the 15-volume edition of *Brockhaus Enzyklopädie* (Stern.de, 5 December 2007). The test included 50 articles from each encyclopedia, covering politics, business, sports, science, culture, entertainment, geography, medicine, history, and religion, on the four criteria of accuracy, completeness, timeliness, and clarity. The findings showed that Wikipedia articles were evaluated as being more accurate on average. Wikipedia's coverage was also found to be more complete and up to date. However, *Brockhaus* was judged to be more clearly written, with several Wikipedia articles being criticized for their length and complexity. In January 2011 Sue Gardner, Executive Director of the Wikimedia Foundation, stated that the German Wikipedia is 'the best' language edition.

---

[22] See http://wikimania2005.wikimedia.org/, retrieved 19 September 2012.

[23] Wikipedia Academies are conferences to familiarize the academic world with Wikimedia projects. See http://meta.wikimedia.org/wiki/Wikipedia_Academy, retrieved 10 July 2012.

[24] See http://www.comscore.com/press/release.asp?press=2160, retrieved 10 July 2012.

[25] See http://www.alexa.com/topsites/countries/DE, retrieved 11 June 2013.

> It's accurate, it's comprehensive, it's well maintained, the articles are longer, the articles are well referenced, and so forth. Germany is a wealthy country. People are well educated. People have good broadband access. So the conditions for editing Wikipedia are there. And the fact that German people were able to meet face to face and talk about policies and talk about procedures and so forth because they're geographically located in a relatively small area, for the most part.
>
> (Gardner quoted in On The Media, 14 January 2011)

These characteristics of the German community are further explored below, starting with the community culture.

Community Culture

Wikipedia has a set of declared principles, which has often been emphasized as a crucial normative baseline for the project to succeed: 'These principles may evolve or be refined over time, but they are considered ideals essential to the founding of the Wikimedia project.'[26] The principles are summarized in five pillars that apply to all language editions:[27]

1. Wikipedia is an online encyclopedia (value of neutrality);
2. Wikipedia is written from a neutral point of view (value of neutrality);
3. Wikipedia is free content that anyone can edit, use, modify, and distribute (value of openness and sharing);
4. Editors should interact with each other in a respectful and civil manner (value of trust and dialogue);
5. Wikipedia does not have firm rules (value of dialogue).

Further, is it stressed that Wikipedia is 'more than *just* an encyclopedia, Wikipedia is a community'.[28] When examining the community culture, the study addressed the values that underpin these pillars, such as the value of neutrality, dialogue, trust, openness, and sharing,[29] including the role they played for people deciding to take part in the project.

---

[26] Quote from http://meta.wikimedia.org/wiki/Founding_principles, retrieved 10 July 2012.

[27] See http://en.wikipedia.org/wiki/Wikipedia:Five_pillars, retrieved 10 July 2012.

[28] Quote from http://en.wikipedia.org/wiki/Wikipedia:Wikipedia_is_a_-community, retrieved 9 August 2012.

[29] Love is another value that has been emphasized in relation to Wikipedia: 'Wikipedia is a Shinto shrine; it exists not as an edifice but as an act of love. Like the Ise Shrine, Wikipedia exists because enough people love it and, more importantly, love one another in its context' (Shirky 2008: 141).

The first and second pillar speak to the value of neutrality, which has often been emphasized as the most central community principle.

> Neutral point of view (NPOV) is a fundamental Wikimedia principle and a cornerstone of Wikipedia. All Wikipedia articles and other encyclopedic content must be written from a neutral point of view, representing fairly, and as far as possible without bias, all significant views that have been published by reliable sources. This is non-negotiable and expected of all articles and all editors.[30]

As expressed by Wales, the principle of NPOV means that you have to write for the enemy in order to survive.[31] This implies that articles have to be balanced in presenting various interpretations of a given topic, to an extent where editors who essentially disagree on a specific topic would agree to the content presented. NPOV has been emphasized as the only non-negotiable policy that allows Wikipedians to work together, converging while collaborating (Lih 2009: 113). 'Indeed, the idea that a neutral point of view even exists, and that it can be determined among people who disagree, is an amazingly quaint, perhaps even naive, notion. Yet it is invoked earnestly and often productively in Wikipedia' (Zittrain 2009: 144). In the study the NPOV was described as a community-defined standard on how to write a Wikipedia article. It represents a specific format set out to ensure that a topic is presented according to all reliable sources and arguments.

> I mean, when people hear the neutral point of view, they actually think lots of different things. In fact on Wikipedia it means one specific thing, which is not actually that articles should be written from a neutral point of view, they should be written using this thing called neutral point of view, which is a constrained writing style that Wikipedians have invented ... based on shared values and things like this. That seems to result in text that lots of people can agree on. (#7)

As illustrated by the above quote, neutrality is emphasized as an internal community standard, against which the quality of articles may be judged, rather than a value of neutrality as such. It was also stressed that an article may be biased when first proposed, but the greater the number of editors who work on it, the more neutral it becomes. Further, any national edition is likely to have content biased towards specific national topics.

---

30 Quote from http://en.wikipedia.org/wiki/Wikipedia:Neutral_point_of_view, retrieved 10 July 2012.

31 Wales at Berkman@10, 12 June 2008. Available at: http://www.youtube.com/watch?v=ummx6OG1GbM, retrieved July 10, 2012.

> In the short run Wikipedia can be extremely systematically biased so that the content is not neutral, but it is overwhelming the more content on a specific topic ... people who are specifically childish on concepts has these effects, which gives them some sort of balance ... for example geographic articles in the German language are usually focused on areas that we have in German-speaking community and the same should be about the Danish or Dutch, maybe not about the English.
>
> (#5)

The norm of neutrality has been linked to the non-commercial character of Wikipedia, as a guarantee for arguments based on reason rather than commercial agendas (Lih 2009: 11). The strong anti-commercial focus of Wikipedia became evident in 2002 when it was debated whether Wikipedia should open up for commercial income. The suggestion of introducing commercial advertisements on Wikipedia raised great concerns over the risk of future censorship and commercialization by Bomis Inc, which was Wikipedia's original host. It also led to the 'Spanish revolt', where most of the Spanish Wikipedia community left within a few weeks to establish Enciclopedia Libre.[32] The study found that the anti-commercial norm is a crucial element of the Wikipedia culture.

> The day Wikipedia gets forked there will be another one that will take the data somewhere else ... I mean you can ask anyone at the foundation and they will tell you 'no way'.
>
> (#7)

Whereas the norm of neutrality addresses the way articles are written, the fourth and fifth pillars address cooperation within Wikipedia, based on dialogue and trust. As a norm for this trustful dialogue, a principle of good faith has been stipulated in the guidelines for Wikipedia editors:

> It is the assumption that editors' edits and comments are made in good faith. Most people try to help the project, not hurt it. If this were false, a project like Wikipedia would be doomed from the beginning ... When disagreement occurs, try to the best of your ability to explain and resolve the problem, not cause more conflict, and so give others the opportunity to reply in kind.[33]

As illustrated by the above quote, Wikipedians are encouraged to trust one another as sensible human beings, and to use dialogue to reach agreement via trustful communication rather than to suspect bad motives from fellow

---

[32] See http://en.wikipedia.org/wiki/History_of_Wikipedia and http://en.wikipedia.org/wiki/Enciclopedia_Libre, retrieved 10 July 2012.

[33] Quote from http://en.wikipedia.org/wiki/Wikipedia:Assume_good_faith, retrieved 10 July 2012.

editors. In consequence, conflict resolution should be used only as a last resort. In relation to dialogue and trust within the German Wikipedia, the findings stressed that the debate amongst the German community is harsh, whereas the English counterpart is characterized more by a 'be-nice' and 'wiki-love' culture (#1).

> [T]his is the official version by Jimmy Whales [wiki-love]. He spreads, you know, he always speaks about how and I think that is not the case. I think that the principal of the German Wikipedia is … there is a lot of arguments a lot of dispute and so and really it is not just dispute, it is really discussion and sometime it is really offensive, people offend each other very easily on the discussion page, which can sometimes be a problem because this is public and you can always see that this and that person has a very offensive way of discussing with other people, so this is an interesting aspect I think. The discussion is really very harsh; if you read discussion pages you almost never get a feeling of harmony and love. It is just the opposite.
>
> (#4)

There is thus some discrepancy between the declared principles of a kind and trustful dialogue, and the actual form of debating and disagreeing within the German community. It was stressed that the harsh tone of discussion might be a Western characteristic rather than a German characteristic per se.

The third pillar, openness and sharing, is related to the technical platform and legal licence of Wikipedia. The findings highlighted that openness and sharing is seen as integral to Wikipedia at both the technical and legal level. On a technical level, openness and sharing is anchored in the software design of wikis as the Wikipedia platform is open for anyone to enter, with relatively few security restrictions. Wikipedia does not require its contributors to submit their names or provide other information to establish their identity, and most articles in Wikipedia may be edited anonymously. On a legal level the licensing model makes any contribution available for others to use, ensuring that the contributions belong to the broader public and not to any individual or company. In this regard the legal licence represents a codification of sharing. Further, it was stressed that sharing and feedback are key factors for contributing, as further addressed below.

> Yeah that is the thing I mean [to share] and individuals that want to share and want to have feedback.
>
> (#4)

Scholars have argued that the German 'hacking culture' provided a natural normative outset for Wikipedia involvement, not least because of the familiarity with the open-source culture (Lih 2009:147).

Summing up on the five pillars, neutrality was perceived as an editorial standard more than a value as such. As for the values of dialogue and trust, there was some discrepancy between the declared norms and the relatively harsh dialogue unfolding within the German community. With regard to openness and sharing, these values are inherent in the licensing model and the technical platform. However, to what extent they apply to the social practices will be further explored below, starting with the incentives for becoming part of the community.

When Wikipedia started in Germany, many Wikipedians perceived it as being for idealists, and several were sceptical as to whether it could work in 'the real world'. The community consisted of only a handful of people at that time, and the content in the German edition was scarce and with lots of mistakes. However, the community quickly started to gain momentum, to meet physically, and to celebrate each time a certain number of articles was reached. In 2004, when the German chapter of Wikimedia was founded, it comprised a small but dedicated community where most people knew each other.

> I discovered Wikipedia in 2003 so I was one of the first people in Germany I think to discover Wikipedia … we met in a bar somewhere here in Berlin and there were some seven people or something like that. So it is a really small crowd of strange people at that time … some interesting nerdy people so … I liked them quite a lot … everybody thought that Wikipedia was something for idealists that would not work in the real world you know … every month it got bigger and bigger and then we had parties when there was another 10 000 articles on the German Wikipedia, for every 10 000 articles we had a party. And it was every two or three months or so then more often and … we stopped partying at 10 000 and had parties at 100 000. And that was I think in 2004, it turned out that things would really work and lots of people joined us, there was lots of press coverage.
>
> (#4)

> English Wikipedia had a huge advantage in the beginning because they had the momentum of the Nupedia project. In Germany nobody knew about Nupedia so it was just a very small community, so I thought it was really important to have some press articles about the project and so, yeah, this was my first involvement on an organizational level. And then in 2004 we founded the German chapter, the Wikimedia Deutschland Verein … in the beginning I think there were like 300 articles or pages there, and the articles were like one sentence and so on. In some parts it is also big articles about certain social theories or the Hollywood of the twenties and so on, so very strange weighting of the content. So yeah, I started being active in the community, which meant like five people or so.
>
> (#6)

Regarding incentives for participation, the findings highlighted that several people from the first Wikipedia generation were there for ideological reasons. Many perceived Wikipedia as a proponent for a new kind of enlightenment, building on Habermas's ideal of rational–critical conversations and the power of the better argument. Moreover, as the content in the German edition was limited, it was relatively visible and rewarding within the community to contribute new articles.

> Simply out of curiosity I just had a look at the content and it was pretty and quite easy to figure some obvious mistakes and to finish sentences with the right words and so. Just open-ended and never finished and I quickly forgot about Wikipedia and half a year later I rediscovered it, and to my surprise I found that the content had actually improved from the moment I had left Wikipedia … In June 2004 we did found Wikimedia in Berlin. Jimmy Wales was there, he was on a European tour, I think for the first time in his life. it was amazing for us and for him, a great weekend in Berlin, and I became member of the board of Wikimedia in Germany.
>
> (#5)

As the community continued to grow, so did the various reasons for participating in Wikipedia. Therefore the following categorization of motivations may oversimplify what might be much broader in complexity. It is also important to bear in mind that people usually have a variety of reasons for taking part in any social act, with some being more explicit than others. The following four themes, however, were iterated in the study.

The first theme was related to ideological reasons, explained as a support for the principles on which Wikipedia is built, and a willingness to help make the world a better place based on the principles of free knowledge.

> So I think in the beginning you needed some kind of '*weltverbesserungs antrieb*' to make the world a better place … I think the first generation of contributors mainly did it because of ideological reasons. I think many people of the first generation saw it as a way of developing a new kind of enlightenment, so I think if I am talking about my own motivation, I think this is the main reason why I was so hooked in the beginning.
>
> (#6)

Most of those interviewed mentioned the ideological outset as a motivating factor when becoming involved with Wikipedia. Yet the ideological motivation was mostly presented in combination with some of the other incentives outlined below.

The second theme addressed the ability to express oneself and get reactions within a specific area of interest. For many contributors Wikipedia seems to be about one or more particular interests, and the possibility of exercising that specific interest while interacting with like-minded people. The importance of being read, and receiving a reaction in response to your writing, was frequently stressed, precisely because it implies an active and largely qualified reaction to some of the issues with which the contributor is occupied. One of the Wikipedians compared this reaction to a digital hug:

> [E]specially those [the very active Wikipedians] are very much motivated by getting feedback from other community members and they are getting some digital hugs and so on.
>
> (#6)

> That was really the thing that fascinated me from the beginning, when I started to work on Wikipedia, I just could not wait for the reaction. I wrote something and I could not get away from the computer, because if I was away I was waiting for people to comment or to change my things and to react to it. And I was really keen on that, still I am keen on that reaction, it is even better now, when I write some text sentence and there will be a reaction or not it depends.
>
> (#4)

A third and closely related theme concerned the visibility that the site represents. Not only do contributors receive reactions from people interested in the same topics, but their writings also become visible to a wider audience. Visibility was stressed as a key motivating factor in contributing to Wikipedia, albeit an anonymous form of visibility. It was described as being recognized in front of a wider audience for the contributions made, but without the usual link to physical identity, name, and status. Some of the Wikipedians described these two factors, interaction and visibility, as a way out of loneliness.

> I still think that this is the main reason why people contribute to Wikipedia rather than to other projects, because there is that high visibility and an immediate reaction. That is what we call it: a reaction. Because it is not that people comment, it is really reaction because people interact on the text and that is the fascinating thing … visibility of what you do. I think it is not so much what you as a person do because the normal thing still with Wikipedia is that we work with a pseudonym name, so it is not your real personality and very many people even hide their real personality … I think it is not so much that people want to get fame for themselves as persons in real life … I think it is simply that what you do is seen by lots of people who interact with you and you start interacting with them. So perhaps it is a way out of loneliness … That is perhaps a way of seeing it.
>
> (#4)

Fourth, community involvement was mentioned as an important incentive for taking part in Wikipedia. Whereas the ideological focus was mentioned as a reason for joining Wikipedia, the sense of being part of a group of like-minded people working towards a common goal was emphasized time and again. As illustrated by the quote below, there was a clear distinction between the community and public life as such, with the latter receiving less attention.

> It is a bit irritating how important it is for them to be recognized inside the community and how unimportant it is for many people to know about millions of readers that are out there … but the thing that people realizes when some community member leaves a comment on your discussion page and says you have written a great article, there just two things I did not understand and so on and so forth, I have some sources here that may be interesting for you … this is the feedback that people see and motivate them much more than just some numbers of where you don't have faces but you count them.
>
> (#6)

Finally, besides the reasons discussed above, some contributors simply liked the writing and editing process, including solving various problems that occur during the process. Every Wikipedian who participated in the study expressed pride at being part of the community.

The findings also addressed the level of policy awareness and the degree to which the participants perceived themselves as part of a political movement vis-à-vis a community of writers. In general the findings indicated limited political awareness, hence the community seemed more concerned with solving various problems related to editing standards as compared to influencing internet politics. However, involvement in Wikipedia was seen to augment political awareness.

> [T]here are very many Wikipedians who are deeply involved in Wikipedia and don't know that much about politics. On the other hand if I take a look at myself I became much more aware of the political dimension of the internet thanks to Wikipedia.
>
> (#4)

> I am surprised sometimes how seldom this ideological perspective on the project is discussed within the community, I mean people they are discussing how to structure certain texts and which kind of writing style we want to follow and so on, and they can discuss it like for kilometres of text and never end, but it is very seldom that you see a discussion about how we want to change the world in such perspectives.
>
> (#6)

With regard to the English language edition, the findings indicated that the German edition was strongly influenced by English Wikipedia in the early years. However, it was seen as increasingly independent and with a stronger focus on the quality of the final product rather than the wiki process. Also, there are stricter rules for deciding if an article should be allowed and the use of scholarly sources is more strongly encouraged, as addressed in the next section.

Summing up, the German Wikipedia community by and large reflected Wikipedia's founding principles and values. It did, however, differ in certain aspects. The most notable difference was related to the dialogue between editors, which was described as relatively harsh compared to the norm of a trustful dialogue based on good faith. There was also some discrepancy between the focus on the quality of the final product, the encyclopedia, in contrast to the wiki process, which is elaborated below. In relation to participation, the sense of being part of a larger vision, with which one normatively agrees, as well as the reward of exchange and feedback from people with similar interests, was seen as an important incentive to contribute. The contributors were aware of, and supported, the founding vision of Wikipedia. Yet in their daily practices they seemed less occupied with the normative outset – to set knowledge free – and more oriented towards writing and exchanging views in a dialogue with other community members. Responses to one's own writings by other Wikipedians with similar interests was mentioned as one of the strongest incentives for participation. In this regard the norm of sharing seemed particularly important for participation in the Wikipedia community.

Collaboration

The theme of collaboration addresses the practices that constitute cooperation within Wikipedia, including how the above-mentioned values are reflected in these practices. The first part of this section addresses the topic more generally, whereas the second part addresses the German community specifically.

Collaboration within Wikipedia is essentially about co-production in which groups of people voluntarily cooperate on a common product, with each article being the result of a collective process. In practice, the daily activity of creating and editing Wikipedia articles is carried out in smaller units, gathered around specific fields of interests.

> So, if you work on a particular article, and you do it over a long period of time, then you end up working with a smaller group, I mean that's just sort of the way that things work. So, if I'm editing the vegetarianism article, right, there is the veganism article, it's the same sort of people that edit these two articles, really, I mean so you get to know them, if you work on that article.
>
> (#7)

The collaborative model is anchored in the internet's open and decentralized architecture, which in principle allows for participation by anyone with an internet connection. The decentralized collaboration on a shared resource would thus not be possible within the context of conventional media. With regard to values, the collective process requires openness and sharing in the sense that any contribution must be open for other people to comment on and further refine.

The editing system was described as 'last editor rule', referring to the fact that the last edit represents the current and public version of any given article (#1). At the same time, each article has a 'history' page reflecting the editing history of that particular text and a 'talk' page representing a meta-space for debate related to the article. Another editing tool is the 'watch list', which is a list of articles that the editor has decided to monitor for changes. As an example, one of the Wikipedians had a watch list with 2500 articles that he followed, which amounted to approximately 200 daily edits, reflecting approximately two working hours (#3). Wikipedia has often been compared to Usenet, which was one of the first online forums for topical debates, with similar open access for everyone to participate and share views. However, whereas Usenet was directed towards debate, and thus the merits of certain arguments, Wikipedia is directed towards improvement of a common product. 'We are working together on statements of what is known (what constitutes free human knowledge) about various subjects ... It is difficult to write the perfect article single-handedly, but it becomes easier when working together.'[34]

When working on articles, editors create a public record of every word added, deleted, or modified. Writing on Wikipedia is therefore a public act, and editors are identified publicly as the author of the changes they perform. Due to the public character, anyone has the ability to observe the work and social interaction of others. Despite the fact that everything is open for public inspection, there is also room for the private domain. While the technical platform facilitates a public format, it also allows Wikipedians to work from their private domain, for example their home, while participating in the public space that the platform represents.

One of the essentials of the collaboration is the production of cumulative knowledge, whereby people gradually improve each other's work and, in this way, create a totality that no one could accomplish alone. In practice this is achieved via 'stubs', which are preliminary article drafts. Stubs are referred to as signals for help (Lih 2009: 97), whereby editors call for community assistance to improve a specific article in progress. As explained below, stubs are not allowed in the German edition, thus collaborative work on new articles starts at a higher bar. Concerning the contributors' willingness to improve the common product, the study stressed that

[34] Quote from http://en.wikipedia.org/wiki/Wikipedia:Replies_to_common_objections, retrieved 12 July 2012.

some articles are more popular than others and therefore subject to more attention from editors. In other words peer assistance to improve articles may not always occur, just as some articles may receive a disproportionate amount of attention simply because the theme is a hot topic.

> So if a page becomes more popular, the chances that someone else will improve the article just because it is popular are going to increase.
>
> (#5)

Another characteristic is the voluntary character of the collaboration. Due to the voluntary nature of the work there is no guarantee that people will respond to the writing done by any given editor. However, if people were not generally willing to respond, Wikipedia would cease to exist.

> There is a proverb thing like 'people are voting with their feet', so they decide where to work, so if they are there, it contains the answer. I think.
>
> (#5)

The growth of the German Wikipedia over the past ten years indicates that a considerable number of people are willing to contribute, without any claim of ownership or monetary compensation. As a way of encouraging various contributions that are seen as essential to the German edition, the community has since 2005 had a reward mechanism that is a page where users may offer rewards for completion of Wikipedia-related tasks.[35] The reward mechanism is an example of soft intervention in the voluntary process.

One of the consequences of collaboration based on sharing rather than authorship is the necessity to include challenging points of views. Unlike websites here authors have complete control over content and where it is difficult or impossible to debate the arguments presented, Wikipedia articles are by nature open for diverging arguments. In addition, Wikipedians have to accept critical editing of their contributions. 'In the best case, cranks who are unable to accept critical editing of their writing will find they have no platform and leave; those willing to present their interests in less-biased ways become valuable contributors.'[36]

However, the findings also indicated that despite an emphasis on sharing, there was an expectation of 'payback' from people who have benefited from Wikipedia. It was argued that by now many people have benefited

---

[35] See http://de.wikipedia.org/wiki/Wikipedia:Auftragsarbeiten, retrieved August 3, 2012.

[36] Quote from http://en.wikipedia.org/wiki/Wikipedia:Replies_to_common_objections, retrieved 3 August 2012.

from Wikipedia for a longer period of time, hence these people have a moral obligation to start giving something back to the common pool of knowledge.

> Now that you have taken benefits from the existence from Wikipedia so long reading articles, and now that you have become an expert on some topic, don't you feel obliged to give something back? So if someone is a student and use Wikipedia for his work … the moment he turns into an expert whatever it means, then he should be able to ask, well now it would be a good time to improve Wikipedia.
>
> (#5)

The quote indicates that it was seen as fair, at least by some Wikipedians, for people who have benefited from that public resource to contribute knowledge back to it. Despite the voluntary character of Wikipedia, there was thus some expectation of 'payback' from the Wikipedia community towards its users.

In relation to disagreements between editors, the community offers several spaces that facilitate disagreement and provide for meta-debate. These spaces include the above-mentioned 'talk pages', the 'articles for deletion' forum that is a space in which articles proposed for deletion are debated, and a number of mailing lists. In relation to the daily editing of articles, the term 'edit war' is used to describe the conflicts that unfold around the collaboration on specific articles. In an edit war contributors disagree on the substance of a given topic and typically keep reverting the page to a version they approve of, or mark the page as one that ought to be deleted. According to Wikipedia, the community practises 'something along the lines of vigilant justice'.[37] The term vigilant justice implies that any community member has various means of combating edit wars or more severe vandalism, for example by reverting the page to a previous version and suggesting that vandals be added to the 'vandalism in progress' page. As a means of creating openness around the conflicts, the article history was stressed as an essential feature in making the differences in opinions transparent, and illustrating the conflicting viewpoints in the various versions. However, as stressed by one interviewee, there are many cases in which it is difficult to resolve which argument should prevail in the article in question. 'There is still no really good method to deal with two qualified opinions (#1)'.

---

[37] Quote from http://ang.wikipedia.org/wiki/Wikipedia:Dealing_with_vandalism, retrieved 4 December 2012.

Another finding concerned the community approach towards the end-product vis-à-vis the collaborative process. The English-speaking community was perceived as largely oriented towards the process – the open and inclusive way of cooperating on a common text, referred to as the 'wiki way' – whereas the German community to a greater extent focuses on the end-product. The Germans aim at producing the best encyclopedia ever, even at the cost of less openness in the process. They described themselves as more pragmatic towards the wiki platform, and its specific way of collaboration.

> We are not here because we want to use the wiki and have fun about it, but we want to have an encyclopedia which is bigger and better than any encyclopedia that has been there before ... they say it is not the '*reine Lehre*', the original idea of the wiki or so. But I would say and I think many people in the German community also would say the wiki is just a tool and if we have another tool which is better to write an encyclopedia, we will use that, yeah, and we are not bound to use the wiki for ever.
>
> (#6)

The divergent opinions on whether emphasis should be on the process or the product can be traced back to the start of Wikipedia, and was reflected in the controversies between the Wikipedia community and co-founder Larry Sanger. Sanger argued for quality insurance via installing a layer of academic experts with special authority, and by eliminating anonymous editing (Lih 2009: 211). This model was never approved by the community, and in response Sanger left Wikipedia, and in 2006 established Citizendium, which combines anonymous editors with layers of experts.[38]

In order to enhance the quality of Wikipedia, the German community has deployed a system of 'stable versions'.[39] According to this, certain users may mark article versions as reviewed, indicating that the text contains no obvious vandalism. The idea of these revisions is to indicate that a given text has been validated by Wikipedians according to standards of quality such as spelling and factual accuracy, allowing for work-in-progress on a given article 'behind the scene', while presenting the validated version to the public. The German community was the first to introduce stable versions in 2008, and paid developers to deploy it on the German Wikipedia.

> [T]his is a development that started in the German Wikipedia, the software was paid by the German chapter and there were several community members which

---

38 See http://en.citizendium.org/wiki/CZ:About, retrieved 12 July 2012.

39 See http://de.wikipedia.org/wiki/Hilfe:Gesichtete_und_gepr%C3%BCfte_Versionen, retrieved 12 July 2012.

> tried to push this, and what I can read now even in the English Wikipedia there is a much more sceptical discussion about this stable version feature. They are discussing if they want to implement it and if this is against wiki way and so on, and in the German Wikipedia people are much more pragmatic in saying okay, we want to have a certain standard quality, so we need to have the tools to do this.
>
> (#6)[40]

The issue of article relevance is also disputed in the German community, and was spoken of as the 'excludist versus includist' approach. The discourse on this relates to the German community's emphasis on the quality of the final product, rather than allowing anyone to contribute in a more inclusive manner.

> There are two groups, and this is I think very typical again of the German Wikipedia and not so much visible in the other Wikipedias, although it is present everywhere ... the includists and the excludists. The excludists want to take out things because they think they are not relevant ... and the includists want to put everything in ... and there is a lot of discussion about relevance and ... perhaps such discussion is a good thing because those who want to keep the article have to improve it, so the discussion can foster the article.
>
> (#4)

As a final indicator of the German focus on quality, the German guidelines classify scholarly sources as inherently more reliable than non-academic sources, and articles on 'indisputably notable subjects' may be deleted if they are deemed too short.[41] Consequently, it has been decided to eliminate stubs from the German Wikipedia and, unlike many other Wikipedias, the German edition does not contain large collections of bot-generated geographical stubs or similar articles. 'While the norm in many Wikipedias is to encourage the creation of incomplete stub articles as starting articles, the Germans see it differently. To them, having no article at all is better than a very bad article' (Lih 2009: 148).

Another feature of the German community is the extensive use of discussions within the community. The findings stressed that the voluntary character of the work in principle provides unlimited time to discuss, contrary to organizations with commercial agendas.

---

[40] The English Wikipedia has introduced an assessment scale against which the quality of articles is judged, and other language editions have adopted similar policies. The highest rank in the English Wikipedia is 'featured article', which 'provides thorough, well-written coverage of their topic, supported by many references to peer-reviewed publications'. See http://en.wikipedia.org/wiki/Wikipedia:Featured_article_criteria, retrieved 12 July 2012.

[41] See http://en.wikipedia.org/wiki/German_wikipedia, retrieved 12 July 2012.

> We are free to discuss things forever as long as we don't have really big juridical problems, there is nothing that forces us to be in a hurry. So this is a very comfortable position that we are in.
>
> (#6)

> For example there is this discussion about relevance. Then there is a wikipage for relevance, or *relevanz* in German, listing all the principles there are, and it is a really long list and nobody reads it at all. It is awful and there has been a lot of discussion about all these points, every point that pops up on the list is discussed.
>
> (#4)

As a final characteristic of collaboration within the German community a variety of offline activities were mentioned, for example study tours to other Wikipedia communities nationally and abroad, city walks to explore potential Wikipedia articles, and various projects that link Wikipedia articles with physical sites. As an example, meeting with the Balkan Wikipedia community was emphasized as a dialogue that created understanding of how Wikipedia may serve to help reconcile various ethnic groups in post-conflict areas (#3). The audio recording for a specific bus line was also described as a fun and informal way to explore new uses of Wikipedia together with other Wikipedians.

> There was a few Wikipedians in Berlin that had a project going on to involve recording an audio book for the bus line. I think it was bus line 100, which was the famous tourist line. I think that the route of this bus is extremely well planned to cross any monuments or point of interest in the city centre, so what they did was that they took the timing and the schedule of the bus and then made a recording based on Wikipedia articles on the items that they crossed in the bus line, so that you could sit in the bus and hear Wikipedia articles on the things that you see outside, assuming that the bus is on time. And that was fun. I mean there was no formal corporation with the bus company, there was no announcement, it was just a few weekends out of the plan making it possible.
>
> (#5)

In summary, Wikipedia is based on collaborative processes, where numerous individuals contribute to the final encyclopedia, organized in subgroups around specific articles. The collaborative model is based on shared resources and is voluntary, as no employment structure is involved. Any individual has the freedom to contribute or not, just as the community identifies and deploys the norms and structures, guiding the collaborative practices. Some of the specifics of the German Wikipedia community relate to a strong focus on the quality of the final product vis-à-vis the wiki process, hence a system of stable versions has been deployed to enhance article quality. In addition, long-lasting discussions between community members was emphasized as a characteristic of the German community's way of cooperating. In relation to values, the focus on the quality of the

German encyclopedia implies that the community has defined limits to its openness, such as restrictions on which articles to include.

Self-regulation

The final theme, self-regulation, refers to the rules and procedures that regulate behaviour within the community. The regulatory model of Wikipedia has been described as a light regulatory touch coupled with an openness to flexible public involvement, including a focus on earnest discussion, neutral dispute resolution, and a 'core of people prepared to model an ethos, which others can follow' (Zittrain 2009: 146). Others have characterized Wikipedia as collaboration by numerous people with minimum oversight (Lih 2009: 8). In relation to the German Wikipedia, however, it entails more hierarchy compared to the English edition (Lih 2009: 148).

Wikipedia presents itself as a deliberative democracy where discussion amongst community members, rather than votes, is used as the primary means to reach agreement. 'Basically, whenever you feel like it, you can try to start a vote on a talk page, but people will probably not participate in it if they think discussion has not yet been exhausted as a way to resolve conflicts of opinion.'[42]

Despite the claim for a light regulatory model, a remarkable amount of written guidelines, policies, official positions, and mechanisms to counter various community problems are in place, not least if compared with conventional grass-roots organizations. The study indicated that although the German community is more regulated than its English-speaking counterpart, Wikipedia was not seen as a bureaucracy but rather as a mixture of community anarchy and community rules. Some of these rules and mechanisms are addressed in more detail below, including the role of Jimmy Wales, the Wikimedia Foundation, the German chapter, the various positions installed as part of the community rule, and the potential conflict between Wikipedia and external regulation pertaining to copyright and defamation.

Jimmy Wales, the so-called 'constitutional monarch' of the English-speaking Wikipedia, was described as someone who appears to have much weight in the international community due to his special role as Wikipedia founder. It was emphasized that Wales is aware of his special position and takes an accordingly diplomatic stand in discussions.

---

[42] Quote from http://meta.wikimedia.org/wiki/Wikipedia_power_structure, retrieved 12 July 2012.

> He [Jimmy Wales] is still active in large debates. He is aware of his reputation. If he speaks out on some issue people, will take notice for this statement, so which makes his statements in many ways usually more balanced diplomatic than they could be … he is an authority thanks to this role in starting the whole Wikipedia.
>
> (#5)

Wales is chairman emeritus of the Wikimedia Board of Trustees, which is the ultimate corporate authority in the Wikimedia Foundation. However, despite Wales's status and recognition, it was stressed that his monarchical power is inherently dependent on the consent of the community. With regard to the Wikimedia Foundation, its role was described as mainly fundraising and long-term strategy, with limited involvement in the daily life of the community. It was also stressed that although members of the Foundation may theoretically pull the switch if they completely disagree with the way the community is evolving, dialogue is in fact the way of solving various problems within the community.

> I mean they could pay people to write stuff and so but it would not work, so I think the only way that is there besides just shutting the whole thing down is to communicate and this is what is happening.
>
> (#6)

As an example of the dialogue between the foundation and the community, an email from chief executive officer (CEO) Sue Gardner was mentioned, in which she engaged the community in problem solving despite the fact that this is a very time-consuming process.

> Sue Gardner the CEO of the Wikimedia Foundation just like three weeks ago wrote a long email about biographies of Wikimedia … And said okay … I see these problems first, second, third … and she is really trying to have an open discussion of how to solve these … And I think the only way to solve these is to communicate with as many people as possible because they are so many people out there and which are very intelligent … You need to have a really big ego to say I am standing at the top. I know how to solve all these problems … Of course the problem with this process is IT TAKES TIME.
>
> (#6)

Wikimedia Germany, the national chapter of the foundation, was described as an administrative body dealing with issues such as fundraising, finances, and contracts. Board members of Wikimedia Germany often hold positions within the community; however, the findings indicated that the Wikipedians prefer to keep the community positions independent of the board.

> I think it is better to keep it apart, because it is the idea that the community can work by itself without any instructions like association of a board.
>
> (#4)

As emphasized in the above quote, the perception was that everything begins and ends with the community, thus this is the legitimate basis for defining and applying the rules guiding the daily practices within Wikipedia. The community was seen to continuously implement norms and rules as its members edit and debate articles.

> Policies are not developed in a [national] chapter, the policies are developed in communities … the community can not force somebody to do this, the German chapter can take money and pay somebody to do it and there the chapter comes into play and say, okay, the community wants this and that, we will try to make it happen, but it is not a chapter who is pushing this because it does not work this way, it works the other way around.
>
> (#6)

Similarly, it was stressed that most rules develop out of discussions within the community, rather than by some central mechanism. However, rules need to be supported by the majority in order to be accepted. The German community was perceived to have a relatively large number of rules. Yet, as the rules may be ignored, they were not seen as indicative of a bureaucracy.

> There are more rules. There are lots of rules and actually that maybe another reason why I think they don't differ that much [the English and German editions] because I have somehow lost oversight of all those rules. I mean people always ignore them, but it is better to know some of the rules. That is a point, it is more rule-governed than bureaucratic because … I think you can still ignore them to a certain degree.
>
> (#4)

The point that rules may be ignored refers to a specific norm within Wikipedia, the 'ignore rules' norm, which is not literally an encouragement to ignore rules, but rather a reminder that rules should not interfere with work on Wikipedia if they seem senseless. It is thus an encouragement to critical assessment if a rule seems to contradict a reasonable way of solving a problem.

> If there is a rule that does not make any sense to you, please don't let this rule get in the way of your work! If you have the choice between not doing and sticking to the rule, and doing something and ignoring the rule, just do it anyway and deal with the consequences, and if the rules is indeed stupid then, well then you shouldn't have anything to worry about … this corrective is highly efficient to prove structures to be … ineffective because it helps people to get along with structures that have no longer any [value]. It is officially you can simply ignore any regulation if you feel it is stupid.
>
> (#5)

The community rules are mostly bundled in guidelines and policies.[43] With regard to content policies, the principles of 'Neutral Point Of View' (NPOV), 'Verifiability', and 'No Original Research' are the main standards. As previously mentioned, the NPOV implies that all Wikipedia content must represent significant views fairly, proportionately, and without bias. The Verifiability policy states that 'material challenged or likely to be challenged, and all quotations, must be attributed to a reliable, published source'.[44] The policy of No Original Research stresses that Wikipedia does not publish original thought, thus all material must be attributable to a reliable, published source.[45] As previously discussed, the process of quality control is highly prioritized within the German community. However, the community also exhibits examples of less restrictive content regulation compared to the English edition. It is, for example, allowed to upload local images without any pointer to Wikimedia Commons.[46] The use of local image upload became German policy when some images that were acceptable according to the German rules were deleted on Wikimedia Commons, and as such is an example of German content regulation that is more liberal than the common Wikipmedia standard.

In addition to various guidelines and polices there is also a 'Wikiquette' that exemplifies how Wikipedians should act towards one another. This includes an encouragement to 'treat others as you would have them treat you, even if they are new'; 'be polite, please'; 'be civil'; 'work towards agreement'; 'argue facts, not personalities', and so forth.[47] The Wikiquette underscores a professional and dialogue-oriented approach to fellow Wikipedians and represents more concrete guidelines for co-worker interaction compared to many conventional organizations. As previously mentioned, the German community was seen to deploy a relatively harsh tone, especially if compared with the Wikiquette.

With regard to hierarchy, the community distinguishes between 'authors new to Wikipedia' and 'editors in good standing'. Only those who make

---

43 See the overview provided at: http://en.wikipedia.org/wiki/Wikipedia:List_of_policies_and_guidelines, retrieved 9 August 2012.

44 Quote from http://en.wikipedia.org/wiki/Wikipedia:Verifiability, retrieved 12 July 2012.

45 See http://en.wikipedia.org/wiki/Wikipedia:No_original_research, retrieved 12 July 2012.

46 See http://en.wikipedia.org/wiki/German_wikipedia, retrieved 12 July 2012.

47 Quotes from http://en.wikipedia.org/wiki/Wikipedia:Etiquette, retrieved 10 November 2012. There is also a Wikiquette alert page, where users may report Wikiquette issues, available at http://en.wikipedia.org/wiki/Wikipedia:Wikiquette_alerts, retrieved 12 November 2012.

enough edits to be considered active Wikipedians may participate whenever there is a vote within the community. As stressed by one of the interviewees, some make many edits to obtain this status (#7).[48] Further, the community has defined three levels of positions – administrator, bureaucrat, and steward – that editors in good standing may apply for.

Administrators have the technical ability to delete and undelete pages, block and unblock users and IP addresses, protect and unprotect pages, and edit the interface, however only on the local wiki where they are appointed.[49] In the early years being appointed administrator was 'no big deal (James quoted in Lih 2009: 95). However, as the community grew, the processes around adminship formalized into a voting system with procedures for adminship nominations and approval. The study indicated that the German procedure around adminship is increasingly complex, with many votes and many internal conflicts.

Bureaucrats, the second group of Wikipedia officials, are users with the technical ability to promote other users to administrator or bureaucrat, to grant and revoke a user's bot flag, and to rename a user.

> There is the bureaucrats … if you draw an organizational chart they are on top of it, but the truth is that they only got so much control because they don't really use it. They just use it in a way that … some just logical-thinking person would use it, and if they would misuse it suddenly their power would be gone. So it is. Of course you can say they are on top of the hierarchy, but the truth is that they are only there as long as they are doing what the collected will of the community wants, so I would not really call this a hierarchy. I think the hierarchy that is there is much more informal is much more like okay this and this person has been active since 2003 and have written several dozen of excellent articles and has been active in certain discussions and people agree that the things that this person says are very thoughtful and so on, and this is what makes a important person in the community.
>
> (#6)

As articulated by the quote, the position of bureaucrat was not seen to imply power per se, but is indicative of community trust and respect for the work conducted by that particular person. The top level of Wikipedia officials is the steward. Stewards are users with complete access to the wiki interface on all Wikimedia wikis, including the ability to change any and all user rights and groups. Stewards are tasked with technical implementation

---

48 A study on the criteria for promotion within English-speaking Wikipedia (to become administrator, for example) suggests that there is a 10 per cent increase in likelihood of administrator approval for every 3800 edits the individual has conducted (Burke and Kraut 2008).

49 See http://de.wikipedia.org/wiki/Wikipedia:Administratoren, retrieved 12 July 2012.

of community decisions, dealing with emergencies, and intervening against cross-wiki vandalism. They are elected roughly annually by the global Wikimedia community, and appointed from the elected candidates by the Board of Trustees. Steward candidates need a support/oppose ratio of at least 80 per cent with at least 30 supporting users.[50] They thus represent 'extremely trusted users' (Lih 2009: 179).

Concerning the hierarchical structure outlined above, the study iterated that the real power derives from the community's trust towards a certain person, rather than from formal appointments. However, it was also argued that it is part of the culture to state that being an administrator, a bureaucrat, or a steward does not put one in a position of superiority. Hence there is a sense of downplaying the role of these positions when in reality most Wikipedians are proud of being appointed to, for example, an administrator position, just as there is community status associated with these appointments.

> Every administrator has the fact that they are administrator on their user page. I mean I have never met an admin who didn't ... If you are getting into an argument with someone, it doesn't mean that you are going to win, but at least it's a proxy for the fact that a group of people have considered your contribution and validated them.
>
> (#7)

The emphasis on the community as 'king' of Wikipedia was stressed time and again, hence power first and foremost relates to community recognition and respect, which is earned via the edits and arguments presented in the daily work in the community.

Other community tools related to problem notification and problem-solving include the administrator notice board[51] and the Wikipedia counter-vandalism unit.[52] As outlined above, Wikipedia relies on its own community to identify and correct various problems that arise in relation to specific articles or users. While the open Wikipedia design provides easy access to vandalize pages, it also provides a public track of the acts of vandalism, and easy access to rectify the articles in question. The role of Wikipedia's rules and guidelines has been compared to the essence of law, thus something beyond arbitrary exercise of force: 'couched in neutral terms for the purpose of social acceptability' (Zittrain 2009: 144).

---

[50] See http://meta.wikimedia.org/wiki/Stewards, retrieved 12 July 2012.

[51] See http://en.wikipedia.org/wiki/Wikipedia:Administrators%27_noticeboard, retrieved 12 July 2012.

[52] See http://en.wikipedia.org/wiki/Wikipedia:Counter-Vandalism_Unit, retrieved 12 July 2012.

> Enforcement on Wikipedia is similar to other social interactions. If an editor violates the community standards described in policies and guidelines, other editors can persuade the person to adhere to acceptable norms of conduct, over time resorting to more forceful means, such as administrator and steward actions … This means that individual editors (including you) enforce and apply policies and guidelines. In cases where it is clear that a user is acting against policy (or against a guideline in a way that conflicts with policy), especially if they are doing so intentionally and persistently, that user may be temporarily or indefinitely blocked from editing by an administrator.[53]

As a final resort for disputes, the community has installed an Arbitration Committee, which is a panel of editors responsible for conducting arbitration with the authority to impose binding solutions to disputes between editors.[54] Rulings enforced through the Arbitration Committee may result in a lifetime exclusion from Wikipedia and blocking by IP address or user name (#1).[55] The German community established an Arbitration Committee in 2007 in order to ensure a more legal process towards conflicts.

> We don't want decisions by mob rule, but more focus on judicial evidence. (#1)

The arbitration mechanism was stressed as the main example of bureaucracy within the German community, however one that is seen as legitimate.

Concerning regulation that has an impact on Wikipedia, copyright and defamation laws in particular were highlighted. The current licence, Creative Commons Attribution Share-Alike, implies that all Wikipedia content is freely available for others to use,[56] providing that there is attribution to the original author[57] and requiring derivative works to be subject to the same licence. In relation to copyright infringements,

---

53 Quote from http://en.wikipedia.org/wiki/Wikipedia:Policies_and_guidelines, retrieved 12 July 2012.

54 See http://en.wikipedia.org/wiki/Wikipedia:Arbitration_policy, retrieved 12 July 2012.

55 As previously mentioned, research on the Arbitration Committee has found that strict remedies were rarely used and that the Committee tried to encourage productive Wikipedians back into participating (Hoffman and Mehra 2009).

56 English Wikipedia provides a few exemptions to the free content licence that allow for use of copyrighted material, including when it is considered fair use under US copyright law. In the German edition there are no fair use provisions since this is not part of European copyright law. See http://en.wikipedia.org/wiki/Wikipedia:Non-free_content, retrieved 12 July 2012.

57 Since no authorship is claimed on Wikipedia, the attribution to original author refers to Wikipedia articles, rather than to specific editors.

the study indicated that this has not been a significant problem. In fact, the issue of journalists using Wikipedia content without crediting the source has been a greater problem than Wikipedia infringing on copyrights.

> Well, when I started we assumed that Wikipedia is extremely vulnerable to copyright violations, that anyone could capture violations and take restricted material ... and then we have to take extra care about preventing this from happening, and it turned out that the greater risk is that people are using Wikipedia content without sticking to the licence, so it seems to be newspapers.
>
> (#5)

There have been relatively few cases concerning defamation. However, incidents such as the Seigenthaler case had a negative influence on Wikipedia's public reputation.[58] As a result of the case, the quality requirements for biographies of living persons were strengthened, and registration became mandatory in order to create these articles. The Seigenthaler case illustrated that Wikipedia is perceived be an 'interactive computer service' rather than a publication with a chief editor. Accordingly only the author of any given Wikipedia article, and not Wikipedia itself, may be held liable for the article in question (Myers 2006). This speaks to Wikipedia as a public platform in which the individual is responsible for his or her own expressions, rather than framing it as a publication with a central editor.

A final point concerns means of influence in the community. In terms of influencing policy, solving conflicts, and forming friendships, the study pointed to the importance of having physically met other community members.

> In terms of influencing policy it is much more important on the Wikimedia level than on the Wikipedia level ... I think of course it is important too for conflict resolution, so if you nearly get angry about a certain person, then you are able to see him the next week at a *stammtisch*, then it stops.
>
> (#6)

> Where there is some sort of anonymity people may change their attitudes and their behaviour quite a lot. And they don't do if they know the other person. So I think it is important to know people in person if you want to be influential – is perhaps the wrong word – but if you want to argue for certain points ... it is good to know people.
>
> (#4)

---

[58] In this case, Seigenthaler made a story out of his own bibliographic article on Wikipedia, in which he was accused of being part of the Kennedy assassinations (Lih 2009: 191–2).

As stressed in the above quotations, conflicts may escalate online not least where people have not met physically. In contrast, having met someone physically was seen to balance potential disagreement. The German *stammtisch* tradition was mentioned as an important facilitator for physical meetings, since it provides a space where Wikipedians meet and discuss various issues within the community on an ongoing basis.

In summary, the Wikipedia community is self-organizing and with self-appointed public positions. Despite a relatively high number of rules and policies, the practical barrier to entering the community and starting to contribute is low. Furthermore, everyone in principle has access to participation in the government of Wikipedia after having earned some credits within the community. Therefore access to power is generally available, however premised on being online and of having achieved a certain level of recognition within the community. The community was stressed as king of Wikipedia, hence official positions first and foremost indicate that the individual has earned respect within the community via the quality of his/her edits and arguments. With regard to potential conflicts between the German Wikipedia and copyright regulation, this has not been a major issue, and a limited number of cases have arisen in which Wikipedia was accused of breaching copyright law. On the contrary, there have been cases where content from the German Wikipedia was used in newspaper articles without acknowledging Wikipedia as the source.

With reference to Luhmann, Wikipedia may be described as a communicative system that operates according to specific communicative codes, for example contribution/non-contribution. In relation to public life, the boundary between the community and the general public consists of the willingness/non-willingness to take part in Wikipedia's system of communication, thus to make active contributions to the common resource. Participating in Wikipedia's system of communication implies adhering to the norms that define communications within the system, for instance to follow community-defined standards on editing. With regard to the various subsystems, for example the Arbitration Committee and administrator position, these represent mechanisms by which the system handles an increasing amount of complexity, as Wikipedia has expanded since 2001.

Wikipedia and Public Life

This final section presents a few observations concerning the role of Wikipedia in relation to public life.

The findings have indicated that Wikipedia was first and foremost seen as a community gathered around a common purpose, rather than an expression of public life. While Wikipedia contributes to the making and remaking of common goods, the active contributors represent a purposeful community rather than 'random members of the public' (Zittrain 2009: 145). As illustrated by Wikipedia statistics, the majority of German Wikipedia articles are written by a relatively limited group of active contributors.[59]

> I think 1.0 per cent of the registered users of Wikipedia did contribute, I think 50 per cent or 60 per cent, and this is the calculation, this is flawed, yes there is a corkscrew of Wikipedia.
>
> (#5)

When asserting the role of Wikipedia with respect to public life, it is thus important to distinguish between the vast number of people using Wikipedia and the people who actually produce it. While Wikipedia is a public platform open for anyone, the study found a strong sense of community amongst those interviewed seemed strong, just as they expressed pride in being part of this particular community.

When addressing Wikipedia in relation to public life, the Wikipedians mostly focused on Wikipedia's impact on public life, for instance the way Wikipedia has democratized the public information domain and has established itself as one of the key sources of public domain information. Moreover, the fact that Wikipedia is not written by an expert community was seen as valuable to the general public.

> Wikipedia is really changing the general public access to information. Wikipedia has a kind of, an information monopoly. If it's not in Wikipedia it's not existing.
>
> (#3)

Seen from a global perspective, the majority of contributions derive from the developed countries, whereas contributions to Wikipedia from the developing part of the world are limited by lack of connectivity, many minority languages, and a small number of editors.

In line with this, Wikipedia was described as a 'club of the privileged'.

> The idea of a world in which everyone has access to some qualified knowledge is still there and it is important. And at the same time we have to acknowledge that to a certain degree Wikipedia was primarily a tool for rich people, by rich people to tell rich people, someone who could afford access to the internet.
>
> (#5)

Obviously, the conditions for peer-production have essential differences in a developing compared to a developed context, as it requires a certain

---

59 See http://stats.wikimedia.org/EN/ChartsWikipediaDE.htm, retrieved 5 November 2012.

standard of living to be able to dedicate resources to a voluntary project with no financial compensation. Yet Wikipedia was perceived to have a positive human rights impact, especially for the right to freedom of information. This was attributed to Wikipedia's expansion of the public domain of information, and the way it facilitates information search, although mostly in majority languages.

5. CONCLUSION

The study has examined how people engage with the German edition of Wikipedia, and understand and make sense of Wikipedia as an online community. The study has iterated interactions with fellow Wikipedians as one of the strongest incentives for taking part in Wikipedia. While the majority were well aware of the normative goal of Wikipedia, that is to set knowledge free, their daily practices seemed less occupied with the general public, and more oriented towards their own areas of interests, ongoing debates within the community, and fellow Wikipedians. Furthermore, the means of gaining visibility in front of a larger crowd, while remaining anonymous, was seen as fascinating in its insight. This points to a relatively strong internal focus, for example on article quality, compared to an external focus such as the value of Wikipedia for its users, or for countries with a less developed domain of public information.

The norms of openness and sharing were visible in relation to the technical platform, the legal licence, and the cooperative practices. As Wikipedia articles are produced in cooperation between smaller groups of editors, sharing of one's own contributions is a premise for taking part, and was emphasized as a key motivating factor for contributing. Compared to other voluntary associations, the community norms of openness and sharing may not differ essentially; however, the technical platform provides different means for realizing these norms. Likewise, the wiki platform facilitates a collective and creative space that is essentially different from non-mediated cooperation.

In addition to the norms of openness and sharing, the German community had a strong academic focus, stressing that Wikipedia is first and foremost an encyclopedia, and should comply with the highest quality standards. The German focus on the product was stressed as somewhat different from the English Wikipedia, where the wiki process was perceived as more important. Various mechanisms to ensure quality control have been installed, providing some limits to openness within the German community.

The norm of dialogue was manifested in the numerous debates amongst German Wikipedians in online as well as physical spaces. In addition, the many physical meetings were emphasized as an important feature of the community, not least since they may counter conflicts that would otherwise escalate online. As the community has grown, an increasing number of rules and mechanisms have been deployed to reduce complexity. However, the interviewees did not perceive Wikipedia as being bureaucratic, but described it as a 'rule-governed anarchy'. The community favoured debate as a means to solving conflicts, and in many ways submitted to the power of the better argument.

In relation to public life, the German Wikipedia was seen as a purposeful community that is occupied with creating an encyclopedia, rather than an expression of public life as such. However, Wikipedia's contribution to the public domain of knowledge was stressed as important, hence its ability to empower public life by expanding the available sources of public and multilingual information.

Concerning the analytical framework, the themes of community culture and collaborative practices resonated well with many of the issues raised by the Wikipedians when asked to reflect on the social practices and norms of the community, including why they had become involved with Wikipedia. The theme of self-regulation addressed the various means of regulating behaviour within the community, and the complex system of policies and positions that have evolved, while maintaining some space for community anarchy. While data was analysed using the themes from the culture metaphor, there were several references to the other metaphors in the study, in particular the public sphere and medium metaphor. As mentioned in the Uganda study, this is not surprising since the metaphors in practice are mixed and combined. This interrelation and the potential conflict between the different metaphors is addressed in the final chapter.

10. Conclusion

1. FRAMING THE NET

The focus on human rights protection in the internet era has risen considerably since 2010. Important moments include the endorsement of Frank La Rue's report by the UN Human Rights Council in June 2011 and the adoption of the resolution on the protection of human rights on the internet at the UN Human Rights Council in July 2012. At the Internet Governance Forum in Baku in November 2012, more than 25 of the approximately 100 workshops directly or indirectly referred to human rights,[1] and in December 2012 the European Parliament endorsed its first Digital Freedom Strategy.[2] Moreover, the revolutions in North Africa and the Middle East have contributed to a more general awareness of the way the internet is related to human rights and social change.

The protection of human rights in an internet era is a broad topic that covers a diverse range of issues such as the right to express opinions online, the right to search for information without restrictions, the right to mobilize in online communities, the right to have one's personal data protected, the right not to be discriminated against in access to public infrastructure, and so forth. Likewise, characterizing the current status of human rights protection is complex and involves both positive and negative tendencies. On a positive note, there is a growing number of empirical examples from around the world that speak to the way ICT may enable individuals' enjoyment of human rights, covering not only freedom of expression and freedom of assembly but also the right to health and the right to education, amongst others. At policy level, internet freedoms are now addressed by, for example, the UN Human Rights Council, the OSCE, the OECD, the Council of Europe, and the European Commission. In the civil society sphere there is also a growing community advocating human rights

[1] The programme is available at: http://www.intgovforum.org/cms/2012/IGF%20Schedule/IGF%202012%20schedule.pdf, retrieved 10 December 2012.

[2] The presentation of the digital freedom strategy by Marietje Shaake MEP on 11 December 2012 is available at: http://www.youtube.com/watch?v=5Q37llqvCY4, retrieved 6 January 2013.

protection in the internet era, most notably global networks such as APC and the Coalition on Internet Rights and Principles. There is also a rising human rights awareness amongst companies, not least due to the UN Guiding Principles on Business and Human Rights from 2011 and the follow-up initiatives at UN and EU level.

Against these positive observations, we can draw out countless empirical examples of how ICT is used by state and private parties to censor, monitor, retain, and exchange data about the individual, threatening not only the right to privacy, but essentially the very essence of free and open societies. In line with this, personal data is increasingly used for commercial purposes without the required safeguards and with limited means of enforcing privacy and data protection standards towards companies. In addition, industry self-regulation is by and large promoted, for example within the EU, with adverse human rights impacts for freedom of information and the rule of law. Finally, there has been limited political will to work towards a global standard for data protection and to critically examine existing intellectual property regulation in relation to human rights.

This book has organized the analysis of these human rights challenges around four metaphors – infrastructure; public sphere; medium; culture – while recognizing that many competing metaphors exist. As previously argued, most policy discourses are not explicit or even conscious about the metaphors they draw upon. However, the various framings have implications for the policy choices made.

The infrastructure metaphor speaks to the internet as a global public resource; a virtual highway consisting of, for example, internet protocols and standards. Associated human rights issues include the challenge of ensuring that a private corporation manages a global infrastructure in accordance with international human rights law, and that non-US citizens have means of redress. The public sphere metaphor focuses on the internet as a space for public debate and opinion making; a realm for political life. Related human rights issues include the debate on internet access as a fundamental right, the protection of internet freedoms, and the means of participation in the online sphere. The medium metaphor speaks of the internet as a new kind of medium: the most recent newcomer in the media family. Associated human rights issues concern the various means of restricting content on the internet with adverse impact on freedom of information, and the conflict between publicly available information in relation to privacy. Finally, the culture metaphor addresses the cultural practices on the internet, in particular those associated with the free culture movement. Related human rights issues include the interrelation between intellectual property law and human rights, and the challenge of protecting privacy in online public spaces.

This book suggests that greater awareness of the metaphors entailed in specific policy discourses may inform a more critical take on internet-related policy making. Whereas it is relatively uncontroversial for the state to praise rights and freedoms in the online sphere – especially abroad – this might not be reflected in national internet policies. Denmark, for instance, has been praised as a digital front-runner with a high level of internet penetration and online public services, yet controversies related to blocking of content without due process, privatized law enforcement, privacy protection of internet users, retention of communication data, and so forth remain unresolved. In this regard the metaphors highlight a variety of human rights issues pertaining to different aspects of internet use. Moreover, they speak to different expectations related to social change, as further addressed below.

2. ICT AS A TOOL FOR SOCIAL CHANGE

The four metaphors entail different assumptions related to the internet's potential to facilitate social change. The infrastructure metaphor speaks to the universal and non-discriminatory infrastructure that the internet represents. The public sphere metaphor refers to the new modalities for public and political life. The media metaphor is concerned with the democratization of publishing and broadcasting, whilst the culture metaphor speaks to the potential of a more participatory culture.

In the Uganda and Wikipedia case studies some of these assumptions were examined in more detail. In either case, the involved actors have a declared aim of providing substantive changes to the current conditions in their respective context. In Uganda the call for social change concerned the local groups' declared goal of using ICT to empower women, whereas Wikipedia strives to provide free knowledge in all languages of the world.

The Uganda study stressed that the combined use of various ICT platforms had facilitated debate, problem solving and collaboration, despite a lack of basic infrastructure. Whereas many of the local initiatives focused on information delivery, the increased use of ICT was seen to enable women to access decision-making processes, rather than just improving the individual's access to information. In Kampala, experiences were increasingly shared via a combination of mailing lists, podcasts, mobile phones, and conventional media. Furthermore, ICT was seen to facilitate a merger between gender-divided spaces, for example at farmers' meetings in Apac and at telecentres in Kampala. The findings indicated that ICT served as an enabling factor with regard to women's means of mobilizing and exercising their rights, merely by strengthening their means of communication.

On a methodological level, the public sphere framework highlighted some overall themes related to public participation. The themes of access to infrastructure, access to information, and resources to participate resonated particularly well with the concerns of the local groups, yet had to be unfolded during the analysis. The theme of freedoms was addressed more indirectly, as was access to participation in decision-making processes. As previously mentioned, the study could have been conducted with any of the metaphors, which would have given a different focus to the analysis. The infrastructure metaphor could have spoken to the development of a technical internet infrastructure in Uganda, including the role of the state and private parties within this process. The medium metaphor might highlight the role of the internet in contrast to conventional media, for example in terms of making available local content, whereas the culture metaphor might address the online collaboration between the members of WOUGNET.

The Wikipedia study pointed to a purposeful and dedicated community that had implemented values of openness and sharing at the technical, legal, and practical level. Yet there were also limits to this openness, for example to ensure article quality. The findings revealed that the community was mainly focused on standards and practices within the community, as compared to the value of Wikipedia for its users. In line with this, interaction with like-minded peers was mentioned as one of the strongest incentives for participation. Despite a limited focus on Wikipedia's normative goal, the study showed that the founding and normative idea of Wikipedia was important for the people who took part. As such, the community members' sense of belonging was closely linked to the founding values of the project. Moreover, the expectation was that a shift in these norms, for example to introduce commercial advertisements on Wikipedia, would imply that members would leave the community. Finally, Wikipedia was seen to have a positive impact on human rights, particularly on freedom of information, by enhancing the individuals' ability to freely access multilingual information.

With regard to the analytical framework, the themes of community culture, collaboration, and self-regulation resonated well with the issues that the Wikipedians were concerned to address As such, 'fitting' the analytical notions with the empirical data was a more straightforward exercise compared to the Uganda study. The analytical framework, however, provided limited guidance when unpacking each theme analytically. As with the Uganda study, any one of the metaphors could have been used, which would in turn have led to different themes and priorities. The infrastructure metaphor might have focused on Wikipedia as a public infrastructure connecting local, regional, and international resources. The medium metaphor could speak to the role Wikipedia plays as an alternative content provider, both in terms of its lexica articles, news items, and other types of content. As for the public sphere metaphor, it could explore Wikipedia as a public space, addressing barriers to access and participation within this space.

3. FUTURE CHALLENGES

In this final section I will outline some cross-cutting perspectives and future challenges for human rights protection in the internet era.

The first perspective draws on the debate of the information society and the claim that the internet represents a structural match to modern society. As argued by Luhmann/Qvortrup, current societies are increasingly complex because so many social actions have become communicatively accessible. In this highly complex society, the internet provides for an unseen number of structural couplings, thus an opportunity to relate to an indefinite number of communications, while also providing for mechanisms to select only a few of these communications. Moreover, in the information society access to the means of communication is intimately linked to power. In line with these two perspectives, access to the internet is increasingly discussed as a fundamental right related to societal participation and to power, as illustrated by the debate at the UN Human Rights Council in 2011 and 2012.

Second, as argued by Castells, the information society implies new powers assigned to those who control access and barriers to the systems of communication. Whereas the public/private construction plays out differently in the four metaphors, the increasing power of private parties is a cross-cutting tendency. The infrastructure framing speaks to the role of a private corporation, ICANN. The public sphere and the medium framing both address the role of internet service providers, whereas the culture framing speaks to public life unfolding within a commercial platform. Therefore, private parties increasingly control various aspects of internet use, thereby challenging the human rights protection afforded to the individual. Moreover, states increasingly involve internet companies in law enforcement on the internet, with ACTA as a recent example. In summary, while access to the internet is increasingly debated as a fundamental right, the power to control internet communication is increasingly in the hands of private parties with a commercial agenda.

A third point relates to the way discourse shapes policy. A particular framing of a topic renders some policy responses more obvious than others. If we think of the internet, or a specific part of the internet, as a publication, the idea of an editor seems natural. Likewise with internet archives and editorial standards for content. However, if one considers it a public space, similar to a park or a public plaza, the idea of an editor seems contextually inappropriate, just as the recording of all conversations in a public plaza for many people would be associated with a surveillance society. In this sense, clarifying the discursive framing is vital for understanding and challenging the various policy responses, and for addressing the kind of culture we wish to promote.

If the aim is to promote internet regulation based on human rights, this requires that internet-related policy and practices are examined from the baseline of human rights. Current developments suggest a global move towards internet regulation disproportionately balanced towards the need for law enforcement rather than the rights and freedoms stipulated in human rights law. Whereas authoritarian states have long tried to censor and monitor public life on the internet, democratic countries increasingly propose legislation that enables tracking and control of online behaviour. The UK Prime Minister David Cameron, for example, in August 2011 suggested that social media should monitor and ban trouble-makers involved with the London riots (Halliday, 11 August 2011). The proposal was met with severe public criticism and was eventually withdrawn. Recently, however, this has been followed up by a UK draft communications bill that will enable tracking of emails and internet use by the police and intelligence agencies.[3] The proposal is echoed by similar anti-terrorism and data retention regulation across Europe, and is just one out of many examples that point to increased state control of the online realm, as justified by law enforcement purposes. This is not to suggest that such purposes are illegitimate. However, any policy proposal that interferes with fundamental rights and freedoms, must be examined for human rights compliance. Such an examination should evaluate whether the proposed measure is justified and proportionate to the aim it serves, and ensure that it is the least invasive measure to serve a clearly specified and lawful purpose. Regulation that does not comply with these standards contradicts the requirements integral to human rights law. Moreover, codifying such proposals into law diminishes rather than promotes a human rights culture on the internet.

---

[3] The bill is available at: http://www.official-documents.gov.uk/document/cm83/8359/8359.pdf, retrieved 15 November 2012.

One major future challenge is thus to enable a transition towards internet policy and practice based on human rights standards. This may entail, among many other things, the following research agendas.

First, the existing internet regulation should be examined for human rights compliance should be examined. This would include an assessment of whether current regulation at national, regional, and international level complies with and promotes the standards stipulated in international human rights law. It may also include the development of benchmarks for human rights assessment to be integrated into the law-making process. In the past a great deal of internet-related legislation has passed below the human rights radar; thus the provision of benchmarks to policy makers and various groups active in this field might improve decision making and highlight where proposed regulations might violate human rights.

Second, the role of national human rights institutions (NHRIs) with regard to internet policies should be addressed. The NHRIs represent a global network of human rights researchers and practitioners cooperating on thematic issues both regionally and globally. As previously mentioned, the NHRIs have not to any large extent taken on board the internet-related policy topics. However, they represent a local, regional, and global node of expertise that should be leveraged to inform national internet discourse and law-making from a human rights perspective.

Third, the human rights obligations of private parties should be elaborated, in particular internet companies and internet service providers. The human rights responsibility of companies is an important research and practice field, not least with regard to the ICT sector. The UN Guiding Principles for Business and Human Rights have set a common and widely-agreed-upon standard. The guiding principles are supported by follow-up initiatives such as the EU guidelines for the ICT sector, as well as various industry-specific initiatives. The role and responsibility of private companies is a crucial component in the transition towards an internet based on human rights. Whereas norms and standards for ICT companies have started to develop, for example in the realm of the Global Network Initiative, further research, analysis and awareness-raising lie ahead. This could include, for example, the development of human rights due diligence indicators for various types of ICT companies; research on the human rights responsibility of companies that are integral to the functioning of democracy, such as search engines; research on the human rights responsibility of companies that provide major social infrastructures such as social media; the privacy and data protection obligations of internet companies and how to audit these; and analysis of the human rights and due process obligations of private companies when engaged with law enforcement. With the state as the primary duty bearer to protect the individual's rights and freedoms, it must be clearly specified how specific human rights are protected when control over public infrastructure and public life are in the hands of companies.

Appendix A: Summary of internet metaphors

	Infrastructure	Public sphere	Medium	Culture
Notions	'Global information highway', 'public utility', 'backbone'	'Space', 'conversation', 'participation'	'Content', 'audience', 'literacy', 'archive'	'Free culture', 'cyber culture', 'community'
Potential for social change	Universal and non-discriminatory access	New modalities for public and political life	Democratization of publishing and broadcasting	The potential for a more participatory culture
Public/ private framing	The liberal model: the internet as a privately run service	The republican model: the internet as a space for public deliberation	The public-as-open model: the internet as an open medium	The sociability model: the internet as social/cultural practices
Key policy themes	Coordination of internet resources Governance of internet resources	Access Internet freedoms Participation	Harmful and illegal content Protection of youth audiences Internet archives	Free culture Collaboration Self-regulation
Policy controversies	Technical coordination versus public policy US control over a global resource	The role and powers of private parties in the online sphere	Various means of content regulation	Online practices of sharing versus IP rights
Human rights issues	Rule of law Protection of user data in WHOIS Potential censorship of domain name strings	Access as a fundamental right Gatekeepers in the online sphere Protection of internet freedoms The right to participate	Content regulation and freedom of expression Publicly available information and the right to privacy	The impact of IP rights on human rights Protection of privacy in online public spaces

Appendix B: List of interviewees (Uganda)

Staff of WOUGNET (#1, #2, #3, #4, #5, #6)

Representatives of I-Network, WOUGNET partner (#7, #8)

Representative of Busoga Rural Open Source and Development Initiative (BROSDI), WOUGNET partner (#9)

Representative of Ntulume Village Women's Development Association/ NVIWODA, WOUGNET member (#10)

Representatives of Counsel for Economic Empowerment for Women of Africa, Uganda Chapter/CEEWA-U, WOUGNET member (#11, #12)

Representative of Women's International Cross Cultural Exchange/ISIS-WICCE, WOUGNET member (#13)

Representative of East African Sub-regional Support Initiative for the Advancement of Women/EASSI, WOUGNET member (#14)

Representative of St Bruno Doll Making Group, WOUGNET member (#15)

Former KIC staff/Representative of Mamas Group, former WOUGNET/ Apac staff (#16)

Staff at Kubera Information Centre/KIC (#17, #18)

Representative of Volunteer Efforts for Development Concerns/VEDCO (#19)

Agricultural Officer, Apac (#20)

Representative of Women and Children Advocacy Network/WACANE (#21)

Representatives of St Luke Farmers Women's Group (#22, #23, #24). I met with a group of approximately twelve of the local women farmers; however, only three conversations were translated.

Representatives of Radio Apac (#25, #26)

Administrative officer, Apac (#27)

Representative of International Humanist Institute for Cooperation with Developing Countries/HIVOS (#28)

Journalist from Kampala conducting a video on the Apac project (#29). Notes only.

Appendix C: List of interviewees (Wikipedia)

Deputy Director of Wikimedia Foundation, previously active in the German community, #1

Representative of Directmedia Publishing (German Wikipedia DVD) #2

German Wikipedian #3

German Wikipedian, former board member of Wikimedia Germany #4

German Wikipedian, project manager for Wikimedia Germany #5

German Wikipedian, former chairman of Wikimedia Germany #6

Member of Wikimedia Advisory Board, USA #7

In addition:

Jimmy Wales, Wikipedia founder, Keynote Speech at Republica Conference 2009

Wikipedians at the Wikipedia Developer Forum, Berlin, 2009

Bibliography

Aarseth, E. (2003). We all want to change the world: the ideology of innovation in digital media. *Digital Media Revisited*. Eds G. Liestøl, A. Morrison and T. Rasmussen. Cambridge, MA: MIT Press, 415–39.

Abbate, J. (1999). *Inventing the Internet*. Cambridge, MA: MIT Press.

Accuosto, P. and N. Johnson (2004). *Financing the Information Society in the South: A Global Public Goods Perspective*. Montevideo: Association for Progressive Communications (APC).

Adalsteinsson, R. and P. Thórhallson (1999). Article 27. *The Universal Declaration of Human Rights: a Common Standard of Achievement*. Eds G. Alfredsson and A. Eide. The Hague: Martinus Nijhoff, 575–96.

Akdeniz, Y. (4 March 2011). 'Fighting political internet censorship in Turkey: one site won back, 10 000 to go.' Retrieved 12 November 2012, from http://www.indexoncensorship.org/2011/03/fighting-political-internet-censorship-in-turkey-one-site-won-back-10000-to-go/.

Akdeniz, Y. for the OSCE Representative on Freedom of the Media (8 July 2011). *Freedom of Expression on the Internet. Study of Legal Provisions and Practices Related to Freedom of Expression, the Free Flow of Information and Media Pluralism on the Internet in OSCE Participating States*. Vienna: OSCE.

Ambrosi, A., V. Peugeot, et al., eds (2005). *Word Matters – Multilingual Perspectives on Information Societies*. Caen: C&F Editions.

Amichai-Hamburger, Y., N. Lamdan, et al. (2008). 'Personality characteristics of Wikipedia members.' *Cyberpsychology* 11(6): 679–81.

Anheier, H. K. and L. Carlson (2002). *Civil Society: What It Is, and How to Measure It*. CCS Briefing. London: LSE.

APC, Council of Europe, et al. (June 2010). *Code of Good Practice on Information, Participation and Transparency in Internet Governance*. Retrieved 28 August 2011, from http://www.apc.org/en/node/9507/.

APC and HIVOS (2011). *Global Information Society Watch 2011 – Internet Rights and Democratisation*. Johannesburg: APC and HIVOS.

Arendt, H. (1958). *The Human Condition*. Chicago: University of Chicago Press.

Ariès, P. (1962). *Centuries of Childhood: a Social History of Family Life*. New York: Vintage.

Article 29 Data Protection Working Party (13 June 2003). Opinion 2/2003 on the application of the data protection principles to the Whois directories. Brussels: The European Commission.

Article 29 Data Protection Working Party (25 March 2006). Opinion 3/2006 on the data retention directive. Brussels: EC Justice.

Article 29 Data Protection Working Party (22 June 2009). Opinion 5/2009 on online social networking. Brussels: EC Justice.

Bakesha, S., A. Nakafeero, et al. (2008). ICTs as agents of change: a case of grassroots women entrepreneurs in Uganda. *African Women and ICTs*. Eds I. Buskens and A. Webb. London: Zed Books, 143–53.

Balkin, J. M. (2004). 'Digital speech and democratic culture: a theory of freedom of expression for the information society.' *New York University Law Review* 79(1): 1–55.

Balkin, J. M. (2009). *The Future of Free Expression in a Digital Age*. Faculty Scholarship Series. Paper 223. Retrieved 8 May 2013, from http://digitalcommons.law.yale.edu/fss_papers/223.

Banda, F., O. F. Mudhai, et al. (2009). Introduction: new media and democracy in Africa – a critical interjection. *African Media and the Digital Public Sphere*. Eds F. Banda, O. F. Mudhai and W. J. Tettey. New York: Palgrave Macmillan.

Banisar, D. (2006). The right to information in the age of information. *Human Rights in the Global Information Society*. Ed. R. F. Jørgensen. Boston, MA: MIT Press, 73–89.

Barnett, C. (2003). *Culture and Democracy – Media, Space and Representation*. Edinburgh: Edinburgh University Press.

Basajjabaka, A. (21 November 2008). 'Podcasting a good case for Africa.' Retrieved 28 August 2011, from http://www.bellanet.org/content/podcasting-good-case-africa.

Bauman, Z. (1995). *Life in Fragments: Essays in Postmodern Morality*. Oxford and Cambridge, MA: Blackwell.

Baxter, P. and S. Jack (2008). 'Qualitative case study methodology: study design and implementation for novice researchers.' *The Qualitative Report* 13(4): 544–59.

BBC News (13 January 2010). 'Google "may pull out of China after Gmail cyber attack".' Retrieved 12 July 2011, from http://news.bbc.co.uk/2/hi/8455712.stm.

Bechmann Petersen, A. (2006). *Mediediffusion*. Paper from the Center for Internet Research (CIF), Aarhus University.

Beijuka, J. K. (2007). *Mid-term Evaluation of WOUGNET 2005–2007 ICT Program*. Kampala: Women of Uganda Network.

Bell, D. (1973). *The Coming of Post-industrial Society: a Venture in Social Forecasting*. New York: Basic Books.

Bell, D. (2001). *An Introduction to Cybercultures*. London: Routledge.
Bellomi, F. and R. Bonato (2005). *Network Analysis for Wikipedia*. Wikimania, Frankfurt, Germany.
Benhabib, S. and D. Cornell (1987). *Feminism as Critique: on the Politics of Gender*. Minneapolis: University of Minnesota Press.
Benkler, Y. (2006). *The Wealth of Networks – How Social Production Transforms Markets and Freedom*. New Haven, CT: Yale University Press.
Benkler, Y. and H. Nissenbaum (2006). 'Commons-based peer production and virtue.' *The Journal of Political Philosophy* 14(4): 394–419.
Benn, S. I. and G. F. Gaus (1983). *Public and Private in Social Life*. London: Croom Helm.
Benoit-Barné, C. (1999). The formation of publics in a mediated world. *Public Participation and Information Technologies*. Eds F. de Abreau and J. de Meo. Lisbon: Citidep.
Benoit-Barné, C. (2007). 'Socio-technical deliberation about free and open source software: accounting for the status of artifacts in public life.' *Quarterly Journal of Speech* 93(2): 211–35.
Berkman Center for Internet and Society (2009). 'Next generation connectivity: a review of broadband Internet transitions and policy from around the world with Yochai Benkler as principal investigator.' Retrieved 23 April 2013, from http://cyber.law.harvard.edu/pubrelease/broadband/.
Berkman Center for Internet and Society (20 October 2010). 'Accountability and transparency at ICANN: an independent review.' Retrieved 2 September 2011, from http://cyber.law.harvard.edu/pubrelease/icann/.
Best, M. L., E. J. Wilson, et al., eds (2004). *The World Summit in Reflection: A Deliberative Dialogue on the WSIS*. Information Technologies and International Development. Cambridge, MA: MIT Press.
BigThink (6 July 2010). 'What will privacy be like in ten years?' Retrieved 12 October 2012, from http://bigthink.com/ideas/20756.
Bildt, C. (10 June 2011). *Freedom of Expression on the Internet Cross-regional Statement*. Human Rights Council 17th session, Geneva.
Binger, A. (2003). *Global Public Goods and Potential Mechanisms for Financing Availability*. Fifth Session of the Committee for Development Policy. New York.
Bjerke, F. (2006). The social and powerful computer. *Digital Governance://Networked Societies*. Eds H. K. Hansen and J. Hoff. Copenhagen: Samfundslitteratur Press/NORDICOM, 173–200.
Blavin, J. H. and I. G. Cohen (2002). 'Gore, Gibson, and Goldsmith: the evolution of Internet metaphors in law and commentary.' *Harvard Journal of Law and Technology* 16: 265–86.

Blume, P., European Parliament, et al. (2001). *Nordic Data Protection Law*. Copenhagen: DJØF.

Bobbio, N. (1989). *Democracy and Dictatorship: the Nature and Limits of State Power*. Minneapolis: University of Minnesota Press.

Bohman, J. (2004). Expanding dialogue: the Internet, the public sphere and prospects for transnational democracy. *After Habermas*. Eds N. Crossley and J. M. Roberts. Oxford: Blackwell, 131–48.

Borah, P. (2011). 'Conceptual issues in framing theory: a systematic examination of a decade's literature.' *Journal of Communication* 61(2): 246–63.

Bourdieu, P. and R. Johnson (1993). *The Field of Cultural Production: Essays on Art and Literature*. Cambridge: Polity Press.

Bowker, G. C., K. Baker, et al. (2010). Towards information infrastructure studies: ways of knowing in a networked environment. *The International Handbook of Internet Research*. Eds J. Hunsinger, L. Klastrup and M. Allen. Dordrecht and London: Springer.

boyd, d. (2007). 'Social network sites: public, private, or what?' Retrieved 28 August 2011, from http://kt.flexiblelearning.net.au/tkt2007/edition-13/social-network-sites-public-private-or-what/.

boyd, d. (2008). *Taken Out of Context: American Teen Sociality in Networked Publics*. Berkeley: University of California, School of Information, PhD thesis.

boyd, d. (25 January 2010). 'Public by default, private when necessary.' *DMLcentral Blog*. Retrieved 28 August 2011, from http://dmlcentral.net/blog/archive/1/2010.

boyd, d. (13 March 2010). *Making Sense of Privacy and Publicity*. Keynote Speech, SXSW, Austin, Texas.

boyd, d. and N. B. Ellison (2007). 'Social network sites: definition, history, and scholarship.' *Journal of Computer-Mediated Communication* 13(1): 210–30.

boyd, d. and A. Marwick (2011). *Social Steganography: Privacy in Networked Publics*. Paper presented at the International Communications Association, 28 May. ICA, Boston.

Brändle, A. (2005). *Too Many Cooks Don't Spoil the Broth*. Wikimania, Frankfurt, Germany.

Brin, D. (1998). *The Transparent Society*. New York: Perseus Books.

Brown, I. (2010). 'Internet self-regulation and fundamental rights.' *Index on Censorship* 1: 98–106.

Bruhn Jensen, K. (2008). Media. *International Encyclopedia of Communication*. Ed. W. Donsbach. Oxford: Blackwell.

Bruns, A. (2009). *Blogs, Wikipedia, Second Life, and Beyond. From Production to Produsage*. New York: Peter Lang Publishing.

Bryant, S. L., A. Forte, et al. (2005). *Becoming Wikipedian: Transformation of Participation in a Collaborative Online Encyclopedia*. Sanibel Island, Florida, USA: ACM.

Burch, S. (2002). 'Latin American social movements take on the Net.' *Development* 45(4): 35–40.

Burch, S. (2005). Information society and knowledge society. *Word Matters: Multicultural Perspectives on Information Societies*. Eds A. Ambrosi, V. Peugeot and D. Pimienta. Caen: C&F Editions, 49–72.

Burke, M. and R. Kraut (2008). *Mopping Up: Modelling Wikipedia Promotion Decisions*. Conference on Computer Supported Cooperative Work, San Diego, California.

Calhoun, C., ed. (1992). *Habermas and the Public Sphere*. Cambridge, MA: MIT Press.

Calhoun, C. (1993). 'Civil society and the public sphere.' *Public Culture* 5(2): 267–80.

Callahan, C., M. Gercke, et al. (2009). *Internet Blocking. Balancing Cybercrime Responses in Democratic Societies*. Report prepared with funding from the Open Society Institute.

Cardon, D. (2010). *La démocratie Internet: promesses et limites*. Paris: Seuil.

Cardon, D. and C. Aguiton (2007). *The Strength of Weak Cooperation: an Attempt to Understand the Meaning of Web 2.0*. MPRA Paper. Munich.

Castells, M. (1996). *The Rise of the Network Society*. Oxford: Blackwell.

Castells, M. (1997). *The Power of Identity*. Oxford: Blackwell.

Castells, M. (2001). *The Internet Galaxy*. Oxford: Oxford University Press.

Castells, M. (2009). *Communication Power*. Oxford and New York: Oxford University Press.

Cerf, V. G. (28 October 2004). 'Internet Governance, Draft 1.3.' Retrieved 28 August 2011, from http://www.icann.org/en/presentations/cerf-internet-publication-28oct04.pdf.

Cerf, V. G. (4 January 2012). 'Internet Access Is Not a Human Right.' *New York Times*. New York.

Civil Society – TUAC (16 June 2008). 'The Seoul Declaration to the OECD Ministerial Conference on the Future of the Internet Economy.' Retrieved 28 August 2011, from http://thepublicvoice.org/events/seoul08/.

Clinton, H. R. (21 January 2010). 'Remarks on Internet Freedom.' Retrieved 6 September 2011, from http://www.state.gov/secretary/rm/2010/01/135519.htm.

Cn.c144.net (4 January 2011). 'Uganda: Year of Extremes for the Telecoms Sector.' Retrieved 8 September 2011, from http://www.cn-c114.net/575/a573681.html.

Coleman, S., ed. (2003). *The e-Connected World: Risks and Opportunities*. Montreal: McGill-Queen's University Press.

Coleman, S. and J. Blumler (2009). *The Internet and Democratic Citizenship. Theory, Practice and Policy*. New York: Cambridge University Press.

Columbia Encyclopedia (2008). 'Columbia Encyclopedia, 6th edn, 2012 Online Supplement.' Retrieved 2 May 2013, from http://www.encyclopedia.com/topic/culture.aspx#3.

Comninos, A. (June 2011). *Freedom of Peaceful Assembly and Freedom of Association and the Internet*. Issue Paper, APC.

Cornwall, A., J. Gaventa, et al. (2001). *From Users and Choosers to Makers and Shapers: Repositioning Participation in Social Policy*. Brighton: IDS.

Council of Europe (1998). *Gender Mainstreaming, Conceptual Framework, Methodology, and Presentation of Good Practices*. Strasbourg: CoE.

Council of Europe (2006). *Blogged Submission to the Internet Governance Forum (30 October to 2 November)*. Strasbourg: CoE.

Council of Europe (2007). *Recommendation CM/Rec(2007)16 of the Committee of Ministers to Member States on Measures to Promote the Public Service Value of the Internet.* Strasbourg: CoE.

Council of Europe (2008). *Recommendation CM/Rec(2008)6 of the Committee of Ministers to Member States on Measures to Promote the Respect for Freedom of Expression and Information with Regard to Internet Filters.* Strasbourg: CoE.

Council of Europe (2009). *Recommendation CM/Rec(2009)5 of the Committee of Ministers to Member States on Measures to Protect Children against Harmful Content and Behaviour and to Promote their Active Participation in the New Information and Communications Environment*. Strasbourg: CoE.

Council of Europe (October 2010). *Recent Achievements of the Media and Information Society Division (October 2010)*. Strasbourg: CoE.

Council of Europe (2011). *Draft Recommendation on a New Notion of Media, Including the Draft Appendix Setting out Criteria for Identifying Media and Guidance for a Graduated and Differentiated Response*. Strasbourg: CoE.

Council of Europe (4 April 2012). *Recommendation CM/Rec(2012)3 of the Committee of Ministers to Member States on the Protection of Human Rights with Regard to Search Engines*. Strasbourg: CoE.

Crawford, S. (1983). 'The origin and development of a concept: the information society.' *Bulletin of the Medical Library Association* 71(4): 380–85.

Crawford, S. (10 October 2005). 'Why Communications Law?' *Susan Crawford Blog*. Retrieved 2 May 2013, from http://scrawford.net/why-communications-law/.

CRIS Campaign (September 2005). *Assessing Communication Rights: A Handbook*. Ed. S. Ó. Siochrú .

CSISAC (28 June 2011). 'CSISAC Statement on OECD Communique on Internet Policymaking Principles 28 June 2011.' Retrieved 28 August 2011, from http://csisac.org/CSISAC_Statement_on_OECD_Communique_06292011_FINAL_COMMENTS.pdf.

Dahlberg, L. (2007). 'Rethinking the fragmentation of the cyberpublic: from consensus to contestation.' *New Media and Society* 9(5): 827–47.

Daley, S. (9 August 2011). 'On Its Own, Europe Backs Web Privacy Fights.' Retrieved 14 August 2011, from http://www.nytimes.com/2011/08/10/world/europe/10spain.html?_r=1.

Deibert, R. (1997). *Parchment, Printing and Hypermedia*. New York: Columbia University Press.

Deibert, R. (2002). *The Politics of Internet Design. Securing the Foundations for Global Civil Society Networks*. Toronto.

Deibert, R., J. Palfrey, et al. (2010). *Access Controlled: the Shaping of Power, Rights, and Rule in Cyberspace*. Cambridge, MA: MIT Press.

Deibert, R. J. Palfrey, et al., eds (2008). *Access Denied: the Practice and Policy of Global Internet Filtering*. Cambridge, MA: MIT Press.

Demchak, C. C., P. Dombrowski, et al. (2011). *Rise of a Cybered Westphalian Age*. Ft Belvoir: Defense Technical Information Center.

DeNardis, L. (2012). 'Hidden levers of internet control.' *Information, Communication and Society* 15(5): 720–38.

Dictionary.com (2011). 'Regulation.' Retrieved 10 July 2011, from http://dictionary.reference.com/browse/regulation.

Dijck, J. Van and D. Nieborg (2009). 'Wikinomics and its discontents: a critical analysis of Web 2.0 business manifestos.' *New Media and Society* 11(5): 855–74.

Dijk, P. van, F. van Hoof, et al., eds (2006). *Theory and Practice of the European Convention on Human Rights*. Antwerp and Oxford: Intersentia.

Donk, W. van de, B. D. Loader, et al., eds (2004). *Cyberprotest, New Media, Citizens and Social Movements*. London: Routledge.

Drake, W. J. (2004). Reframing internet governance discourse: fifteen baseline propositions. *Internet Governance: a Grand Collaboration*. Ed. D. MacLean. New York: UN Information and Communication Technologies Task Force, 122–61.

Drake, W. J., ed. (2005). *Reforming Internet Governance: Perspectives from the Working Group on Internet Governance*. ICT Task Force

Series 12. New York: United Nations Information and Communication Technologies Task Force.

Drake, W. J. and R. F. Jørgensen (2006). Introduction. *Human Rights in the Global Information Society*. Boston, MA: MIT Press, 1–49.

Dutton, W. H. and M. Peltu (November 2005). *The Emerging Internet Governance Mosaic: Connecting the Pieces.* Forum Discussion Paper No. 5. Forum held at the Oxford Internet Institute (OII) in May 2005. Oxford: Oxford Internet Institute.

Dutton, W. H. and M. Peltu (2010). The new politics of the internet. Multi-stakeholder policy-making and the internet technocracy. *The Routledge Handbook of Internet Politics*. Eds A. Chadwick and P. N. Howard. Oxford: Routledge, 384–400.

Dynamic Coalition on Internet Rights and Principles (2010). 'Draft Charter of Rights and Principles on the Internet.' Retrieved 12 July 2011, from http://internetrightsandprinciples.org/.

Eade, D. (1997). *Capacity-Building. An Approach to People-Centered Development*. Oxfam UK and Ireland.

Earl, J. and K. Kimport (2011). *Digitally Enabled Social Change: Activism in the Internet Age*. Cambridge, MA: MIT Press.

Edwards, S. (10 January 2012). 'Is Internet Access a Human Right?' Amnesty International: *Human Rights Now Blog*. Retrieved 12 October 2012, from http://blog.amnestyusa.org/middle-east/is-internet-access-a-human-right/.

Eecke, Patrick Van and M. Truyens (November 2009). *EU Study on the New Rules for a New Age. Legal Analysis of a Single Market for the Information Society*. Brussels: DLA Piper.

Elias, N. (1982/1939). *The Civilizing Process*. New York: Pantheon Books.

Elvebakk, B. (2008). 'Philosophy democratized? A comparison between Wikipedia and two other web-based philosophy resources.' *First Monday* 13(2).

Emigh, W. and S. C. Herring (2005). *Collaborative Authoring on the Web: a Genre Analysis of Online Encyclopedias*. Proceedings of the Thirty-Eighth Hawaii International Conference on System Sciences.

Engelen, A. van (6 December 2007). 'Facebook's Intrusive Ad Strategy Rejected by Advertisers.' Retrieved 28 August 2011, from http://www.digitaljournal.com/article/247033.

Esterhuysen, A. (2007). 'APC Opening Speech at IGF in Rio.' Retrieved 11 July 2011, from www.ipjustice.org/Audio/Anriette-IGF2007.MP3.

European Commission (2008a). *EC Background Report on Cross Media Rating and Classification, and Age Verification Solutions*. Safer Internet Forum 25–26 September 2008. Luxembourg.

European Commission (2008b). *Multiannual Community Programme on Protecting Children Using the Internet and other Communication Technologies*. 16 December 2008. Brussels: European Commission.
European Commission (2009). *EU Safer Internet Programme (2009–2013), COM (2009)8301)*. Brussels: European Commission.
European Commission (2011a). *Combating the Sexual Abuse and Sexual Exploitation of Children and Child Pornography (2011/92/EU)*. Brussels: European Commission.
European Commission (2011b). 'Draft Recommendations for Public–Private Cooperation to Counter the Dissemination of Illegal Content within the European Union.' Retrieved 10 July 2011, from http://www.edri.org/files/Draft_Recommendations.pdf.
European Commission (2011c). 'Safer Internet Program: Self Regulation.' Retrieved 7 July 2011, from http://ec.europa.eu/information_society/activities/sip/self_reg/index_en.htm.
European Commission (20 June 2011). *Answer from Cecilia Malmstöm on behalf of the EC (E-004996/2011)*. Brussels: European Commission.
European Commission (2012). *European Strategy for a Better Internet for Children (COM/2012/0196 final)*. Brussels: European Commission.
European Court of Human Rights (2011). *Factsheet – New Technologies*. Strasbourg: European Court of Human Rights.
European Data Protection Supervisor (31 May 2011). *Opinion of the European Data Protection Supervisor on the Evaluation Report from the Commission to the Council and the European Parliament on the Data Retention Directive (Directive 2006/24/EC)*. Brussels: European Commission.
Federal Trade Commission (20 December 2007). *FTC Staff Proposes Online Behavioral Advertising Privacy Principles.* Washington DC: FTC.
Filmer-Wilson, E. (2005). 'The human rights-based approach to development: the right to water.' *Netherlands Quarterly of Human Rights* 23(2): 213–42.
Finnemann, N. O. (2005). *Internettet i mediehistorisk perspektiv*. Copenhagen: Forlaget Samfundslitteratur.
Flichy, P. (2007). *The Internet Imaginaire*. Cambridge, MA: MIT Press.
Florini, A. M., ed. (2000). *The Third Force – The Rise of Transnational Civil Society*. Washington DC: Carnegie Endowment for International Peace/Japan Center for International Exchange.
Flyverbom, M. (2006). *Making the Global Information Society Governable: on the Governmentality of Multi-stakeholder Networks*. Frederiksberg: Copenhagen Business School, PhD School in Economics and Business Administration: Samfundslitteratur. PhD thesis.

Ford, S. and M. Gammon (2007). *Space and Place: the New Playground of 21st Century Life.* Internet Research 8.0 – Let's Play! Annual Conference of the Association of Internet Researchers, 17–20 October, Vancouver.
Forte, A. and A. Bruckman (2008). *Scaling Consensus: Increasing Decentralization in Wikipedia Governance.* Proceedings of the 41st Annual International Conference on System Sciences.
Fraser, N. (1997). *Justice Interruptus.* London: Routledge.
Frischmann, B. M. (2012). *Infrastructure: The Social Value of Shared Resources.* New York: Oxford University Press.
Gal, S. (2002). 'A semiotics of the public/private distinction.' *Differences: A Journal of Feminist Cultural Studies* 13(1): 77–95.
Gandy, O. H. and K. N. Farral (2010). The political economy of property in cyberspace. *The Routledge Handbook of Internet Politics.* Eds A. Chadwick and P. N. Howard. London and New York: Routledge.
Garnham, N. (1992). The media and the public sphere. *Habermas and the Public Sphere.* Ed. C. Calhoun. Cambridge, MA: MIT Press, 359–76.
Garnham, N. (2000). *Emancipation, the Media, and Modernity.* Oxford: Oxford University Press.
Garnham, N. (2004/1998). Information society theory as ideology. *The Information Society Reader.* Eds F. Webster and R. Blom. London: Routledge, 165–83.
Gauntlett, D. (2004). Web studies: what's new. *Web.Studies.* Eds D. Gauntlett and R. Horsley. London: Arnold, 3–23.
Gauntlett, D. (2009). 'Media Studies 2.0: a response.' *Interactions: Studies in Communication and Culture* 1(1): 147–57.
Gauntlett, D. (2011/2007). 'Media Studies 2.0.' Retrieved 12 July 2011, from http://www.theory.org.uk/mediastudies2.htm.
Gaved, M., T. Heath, et al. (2006). *Wikis of Locality: Insights from the Open Guides.* Proceedings of the 2006 International Symposium on Wikis, Odense, Denmark.
Gavison, R. (1983). Information Control: Availability and Exclusion. *Public and Private in Social Life.* S. I. Benn and G. F. Gaus. London: Croom Helm and New York: St Martin's Press, 113–34.
Geertz, C. (1973). Thick description: toward an interpretive theory of culture. *The Interpretation of Cultures: Selected Essays.* Ed. C. Geertz. New York: Basic Books, 3–30.
Gibson, W. (1984). *Neuromancer.* New York: Ace Books.
Giddens, A. (1984). *The Constitution of Society.* Cambridge: Polity Press.
Giddens, A. (1990). *The Consequences of Modernity.* Cambridge: Polity Press.
Goode, L. (2005). *Jürgen Habermas – Democracy and the Public Sphere.* London: Pluto Press.

Government of Uganda (13 February 2003). *Uganda's Working Document For The Second Preparatory Meeting For The World Summit On The Information Society (WSIS)*. Geneva: WSIS.

Graham, G. (1999). *The Internet – A Philosophical Inquiry*. London: Routledge.

Grassmuck, V. (2004). *Freie Software. Zwischen Privat- und Gemeineigentum*. Bonn: Bundeszentrale für politische Bildung.

Grassmuck, V. (2009). 'The World Is Going Flat(-Rate).' *IP Watch*. Retrieved 10 July 2011, from http://www.ip-watch.org/weblog/2009/05/11/the-world-is-going-flat-rate/.

Gray, M. L. (2009). *Out in the Country: Youth, Media, and Queer Visibility in Rural America*. New York: New York University Press.

Gurak, L. (2004). Internet studies in the 21st century. *Web.Studies*. Eds D. Gauntlett and R. Horsley. London: Arnold, 25–33.

Habermas, J. (1989). *The Structural Transformation of the Public Sphere*. Trans. Thomas Burger and Frederick Lawrence. Cambridge, MA: MIT Press.

Habermas, J. (1991–1992). *The Theory of Communicative Action, Volumes I-II*. Trans. Thomas McCarthy. Cambridge: Blackwell.

Habermas, J. (1996). *Between Facts and Norms*. Trans. William Rehg. Cambridge: Polity Press.

Habermas, J. (2006). 'Political communication in media society: does democracy still enjoy an epistemic dimension? The impact of normative theory on empirical research.' *Communication Theory* 16(4): 411–26.

Halliday, J. (11 August 2011). 'David Cameron Considers Banning Suspected Rioters from Social Media.' Retrieved 23 April 2013, from http://www.guardian.co.uk/media/2011/aug/11/david-cameron-rioters-social-media.

Hamelink, C. J. (1995). The democratic ideal and its enemies. *The Democratization of Communication*. Ed. P. Lee. Cardiff: University of Wales Press.

Hamelink, C. J. (2000). *The Ethics of Cyberspace*. London: Sage Publications.

Hamelink, C. J. (2002). 'Social development, information and knowledge: whatever happened to communication?' *Development* 45: 5–9.

Hansen, E. (2011). *Mobile Distributed Public Spheres*. Crossing Boundaries Conference, Berkeley, 17–18 March 2011.

Hansen, H. K. and J. Hoff (2006). *Digital Governance://Networked Societies: Creating Authority, Community and Identity in a Globalized World*. Frederiksberg: Samfundslitteratur.

Hauser, G. A. (1999). *Vernacular Voices: the Rhetoric of Publics and Public Spheres*. Columbia: University of South Carolina Press.

Hayek, F. A. von (1945). *The Use of Knowledge in Society*. Menlo Park, CA: Institute for Humane Studies.

Heacock, R. (18 April 2011). 'Ugandan Government Asks ISPs to Block Facebook, Twitter.' *OpenNet Initiative*. Retrieved 28 August 2011, from http://opennet.net/blog/2011/04/ugandan-government-asks-isps-block-facebook-twitter.

Heinrich Böll Foundation, ed. (2003). *Visions in Process*. Berlin: Henrich Böll Foundation.

Heinrich Böll Foundation, ed. (2005). *Visions in Process II*. Berlin: Henrich Böll Foundation.

Helfer, L. R. (2007). 'International rights approaches to intellectual property – toward a human rights framework for intellectual property.' *U.C. Davis Law Review* 40(3).

Hick, S., E. F. Halpin, et al. (2000). *Human Rights and the Internet*. New York: St Martin's Press.

Hill, B. M. (2009). *305/Notes*. Proceedings of Wikimania 2009, Buenos Aires, Argentina.

Hindman, M. S. (2009). *The Myth of Digital Democracy*. Princeton: Princeton University Press.

Hjarvard, S. (2009). 'Samfundets medialisering.' *Nordicom-Information* 1–2(31): 5–35.

Hoboken, J. van (2011). *Search Engine Freedom. On the Implications of the Right to Freedom of Expression for the Governance of Web Search*. Amsterdam: University of Amsterdam. PhD thesis.

Hoff, J. (2004). *Danmark som informationssamfund: muligheder og barrierer for politik og demokrati*. Århus: Aarhus Universitetsforlag.

Hoff, J. (2006). The shaping of digital political communication. *Digital Governance://Networked Society*. Eds H. K. Hansen and J. Hoff. Copenhagen: Samfundslitteratur Press, 261–300.

Hoff, J. and F. Bjerke (2004). Politics, power, and democracy in the information society. *Denmark as Information Society. Opportunities and Barriers for Politics and Democracy*. Århus: Århus University Press, 22–70.

Hoff, J. and K. Storgaard (2005). Indledning. *Informationsteknologi og demokratisk innovation – borgerdeltagelse, politisk kommunikation og offentlig styring*. Eds J. Hoff and K. Storgaard. Frederiksberg: Samfundslitteratur, 11–57.

Hoff, J., H. K. Hansen, et al. (2006). Introduction. *Digital Governance:// Networked Society*. Eds H. K. Hansen and J. Hoff. Copenhagen: Samfundslitteratur Press/NORDICOM, 9–43.

Hoffman, D. A. and S. Mehra (2009). 'Wikitruth through Wikiorder.' *Emory Law Journal*, 59: 151–210.

Hofmann, J. (2007). 'Internet Corporation for Assigned Names and Numbers (ICANN).' *Global Information Society Watch*: 39–47.

Hofstede, G. H. (1991). *Cultures and Organizations: Software of the Mind.* London and New York: McGraw-Hill.

Hogge, B. (May 2009). *Winning the Web – Stories of Grassroots Campaigning for Access to Knowledge in the Networked Digital Age.* New York: Open Society Institute.

Hood, J. (19 September 2009). 'Facebook Turns Off Beacon.' *ConsumerAffairs.com.* Retrieved 28 August 2011, from http://www.consumeraffairs.com/news04/2009/09/facebook_beacon.html.

Horner, L., Hawtin, D., et al. (June 2010). *Information and Communication Technologies and Human Rights*. Brussels: European Parliament.

Hosein, G. (2006). Privacy as Freedom. *Human Rights in the Global Information Society*. Ed. R. F. Jørgensen. Cambridge, MA: MIT Press, 121–47.

Huberman, M. and M. Miles (1994). Data management and analysis methods. *Qualitative Data Analysis*. Eds M. Huberman and M. Miles. Thousand Oaks, CA: Sage Publications, 428–44.

Hughes, T. P. (1987). Evolution of large technological systems. *The Social Construction of Technological Systems: New Directions in the Sociology and History of Technology*. Eds W. E. Bijker, T. P. Hughes and T. J. Pinch. Cambridge, MA and London: MIT Press, 51–83.

Hutchby, I. (2001). *Conversation and Technology: from the Telephone to the Internet*. Cambridge, UK and Malden, MA: Polity Press.

Hyde, L. (2007). *The Gift: Creativity and the Artist in the Modern World.* New York: Vintage Books.

ICANN (21 November 1998). Articles of Incorporation of Internet Corporation for Assigned Names and Numbers. Retrieved 25 August 2011, from http://www.icann.org/en/general/articles.htm.

ICANN (Version of 4 June 2012). 'gTLD Applicant Guidebook.' Retrieved 24 August 2012, from http://newgtlds.icann.org/en/applicants/agb/guidebook-full-04jun12-en.pdf.

Innis, H. A. (1977). *The Bias of Communications*. Toronto: Toronto University Press.

International Data Protection and Privacy Commissioners (2007). Resolution on Development of International Standards. 29th Conference, Montreal, 26–28 September.

International Telecommunication Union (2011). *The World in 2011 – ICT Facts and Figures*. Geneva: ITU.

Internet Governance Forum (2009). *Chairman's Summary*. Fourth Meeting of the Internet Governance Forum (IGF), Sharm El Sheikh.

Internet World Stats (2012). 'Uganda.' Retrieved 3 December 2012, from http://www.internetworldstats.com/af/ug.htm.

Jacobs, J. (1961). *The Death and Life of Great American Cities*. New York: Random House.

Jacobsen, A. F., ed. (2008). *Human Rights Monitoring*. Leiden: Martinus Nijhoff Publishers.

Jenkins, H. (2001). 'Convergence, I Diverge.' *Technology Review*, 28 August 2011. Retrieved 23 April 2013, from http://www.technologyreview.com/business/12434/.

Jenkins, H. (2006). *Convergence Culture: Where Old and New Media Collide*. New York: New York University Press.

Johnson, D. R. and D. G. Post (1997). And how shall the Net be governed? A meditation on the relative virtues of decentralised, emergent law. *Coordinating the Internet*. Eds B. Kahin and J. H. Keller. Cambridge, MA: MIT Press.

Jørgensen, R. F., ed. (2006). *Human Rights in the Global Information Society*. Cambridge, MA: MIT Press.

Kaddu, S. B. (2007). *Information and Communication Technologies (ICTs) Contribution to the Provision of Agricultural Information to the Rural Women in Selected districts of Uganda.* Kampala: Makere University. PhD thesis.

Kaul, I., I. Grunberg, et al. (1999). *Global Public Goods: International Cooperation in the twenty-first Century*. New York: Oxford University Press.

Keane, J. (1999). *On Communicative Abundance*. London: University of Westminster Press.

Keane, J. (2003). *Global Civil Society?* Cambridge: Cambridge University Press.

Kimby, C. K. (2006). Communicating the breast cancer experience on the internet – shaping the patient identity. *Digital Governance://Networked Society*. Eds H. K. Hansen and J. Hoff. Copenhagen: Samfundslitteratur Press, 210–27.

Kirkpatrick, M. (9 January 2010). 'Facebook's Zuckerberg says the age of privacy is over.' *ReadWriteWeb.* Retrieved 10 July 2011, from http://www.readwriteweb.com/archives/facebooks_zuckerberg_says_the_age_of_privacy_is_ov.php.

Klein, H. (2005). *ICANN Reform: Establishing the Rule of Law*. A policy analysis prepared for The World Summit on the Information Society (WSIS), Tunis, 16–18 November 2005.

Klein, H. (2006). The right to political participation and the information society. *Human Rights in the Global Information Society*. Ed. R. F. Jørgensen. Boston, MA: MIT Press, 185–96.

Kleinwachter, W. (2004). Beyond ICANN v. ITU: Will WSIS open new territory for internet governance? *Internet Governance: a Grand Collaboration*. Ed. D. MacLean. New York: UN Information and Communication Technologies Task Force, 31–52.

Knowledge Ecology International (9 May 2005). 'Treaty On Access To Knowledge (Draft).' Retrieved 2 September 2011, from http://www.cptech.org/a2k/a2k_treaty_may9.pdf.

Koch, I. E. (2005). 'Dichotomies, trichotomies or waves of duties?' *Human Rights Law Review* 5(1): 81–103.

Koktvedgaard, M. (1996). *Lærebog i immaterialret: Ophavsret, patentret, brugsmodeller, mønsterret, varemærkeret*. Copenhagen: Jurist- og Økonomforbundets Forlag.

Korey, W. (1998). 'NGOs: fifty years of advocating human rights.' *Issues of Democracy* 3(3): 42–50.

Kortteinen, J., K. Myntti, et al. (1999). Article 19. *The Universal Declaration of Human Rights: A Common Standard of Achievement*. Eds G. Alfredsson and A. Eide. The Hague: Martinus Nijhoff, 392–415.

Kreiss, D., M. Finn, et al. (2011). 'The limits of peer production: some reminders from Max Weber for the network society.' *New Media and Society* 13(2): 243–59.

Krippendorff, K. (1993). 'Major metaphors of communication and some constructivist reflections on their use.' *Cybernetics and Human Knowing* 2(1): 3–25.

Kurbalija, J. (2010). *An Introduction to Internet Governance*. Msida, Malta: Diplo Foundation.

Laidlaw, E. B. (2012). *Internet Gatekeepers, Human Rights, and Corporate Social Responsibility*. London: London School of Economics and Political Science. PhD thesis.

Lakoff, G. and M. Johnson (1980). *Metaphors We Live By*. Chicago: University of Chicago Press.

Lanier, J. (2010). *You Are not a Gadget: a Manifesto*. New York: Alfred A. Knopf.

La Rue, F. (2011). *Report of the Special Rapporteur on the Promotion and Protection of the Right to Freedom of Opinion and Expression. Frank La Rue.* United Nations General Assembly, Human Rights Council.

Lee, H. (2007). *Negotiating the public/private boundary and informal public life in Cyberspace: a case study of 'Cyworld' in Korea*. Internet Research 8.0 – Let's Play! Annual Conference of the Association of Internet Researchers, 17–20 October, Vancouver.

Lessig, L. (1999). *Code and other Laws of Cyberspace*. New York: Basic Books.

Lessig, L. (2001). *The Future of Ideas: the Fate of the Commons in a Connected World*. New York: Random House.

Lessig, L. (2004). *Free Culture: How Big Media Uses Technology and the Law to Lock Down Culture and Control Creativity*. New York: Penguin Press.

Lessig, L. (2008). *Remix: Making Art and Commerce Thrive in the Hybrid Economy*. New York: Penguin Press.

Leuf, B. and W. Cunningham (2001). *The Wiki Way: Collaboration and Sharing on the Internet*. Readings, MA: Addison-Wesley.

Lewis, C. (2006). The right of assembly and freedom of association in the information age. *Human Rights in the Global Information Society*. Ed. R. F. Jørgensen. Boston, MA: MIT Press, 151–83.

Liddicoat, J. (March 2012). *Internet Rights Are Human Rights – Freedom of Expression, Freedom of Association and Democracy: New Issues and Threats*. Issue Paper, APC.

Liestol, G., A. Morrison, et al. (2004). *Digital Media Revisited: Theoretical and Conceptual Innovations in Digital Domains*. Cambridge, MA: MIT Press.

Ligabo, A. (17 December 2004). *Civil and Political Rights, Including the Question of Freedom of Expression: The Right to Freedom of Opinion and Expression.* Report of the Special Rapporteur, Ambeyi Ligabo. New York: United Nations Economic and Social Council, Commission on Human Rights.

Lih, A. (2004). *Wikipedia as Participatory Journalism: Reliable Sources? Metrics for Evaluating Collaborative Media as a News Resource.* 5th International Symposium on Online Journalism, Hong Kong.

Lih, A. (2009). *The Wikipedia Revolution: How a Bunch of Nobodies Created the World's Greatest Encyclopedia*. New York: Hyperion.

Lipnack, J. and J. Stamps (1997). *Virtual Teams: Reaching across Space, Time, and Organizations with Technology*. New York: Wiley.

Lipson, M. (2008). *Situating the Values of the Networked Communications Environment within the International Human Rights Framework.* Paper for the Freedom of Expression Project, London, April.

Loader, B. and D. Mercea (2011). 'Networking democracy?' *Information, Communication and Society* 14(6): 757–69.

London, S. (1995). 'Collaboration and Community.' Retrieved 12 July 2011, from http://www.scottlondon.com/reports/ppcc.html.

Lovink, G. and S. Zehle (2005). *Incommunicado Reader*. Amsterdam: Institute of Network Cultures.

Luhmann, N. (1986). The autopoesis of social systems. *Sociocybernetic Paradoxes.* Eds F. Greyer and J. van der Zouwen. London: Sage Publications.

Luhmann, N. (1992). 'What is communication?' *Communication Theory* 2(3): 251–9.

Luhmann, N. (2000). *The Reality of the Mass Media*. Trans. Kathleen Cross. Stanford, CA: Stanford University Press.

Lyon, D. (1988). *The Information Society: Issues and Illusions*. Oxford: Polity Press.

MacKinnon, R. (3 January 2008). 'Yahoo!, the Shi Tao Case, and Lessons for Corporate Social Responsibility.' *Rconversation*. Retrieved 14 July 2011, from http://rconversation.blogs.com/rconversation/2008/01/yahoo-the-shi-t.html.

MacKinnon, R. (2012). *Consent of the Networked: the World-wide Struggle for Internet Freedom*. New York: Basic Books.

MacLean, D. (2004a). Herding Schrödinger's Cats: Some conceptual tools for thinking about internet governance. *Internet Governance: a Grand Collaboration*. Ed. D. MacLean. New York: UN Information and Communication Technologies Task Force, 73–99.

MacLean, D., ed. (2004b). *Internet Governance: A Grand Collaboration*. New York: United Nations Information and Communication Technologies Task Force.

Mahoney, H. (5 April 2011). 'EU Abandoning Internet Policing to Private Companies.' *EU Observer*. Retrieved 2 September 2011, from http://euobserver.com/893/32044.

Mäkinen, M. (2006). 'Digital empowerment as a process for enhancing citizens' participation.' *E-Learning* 3(3): 381–95.

Mansell, R. (2009). 'The Information Society and ICT Policy: a Critique of the Mainstream Vision and an Alternative Research Framework.' Retrieved 2 September 2011, from http://eprints.lse.ac.uk/24990/1/The_Information_Society_and_ICT_Policy_(LSERO).pdf.

Marzouki, M. and R. F. Joergensen (2004). 'A human rights assessment of the World Summit on the Information Society.' *Information Technologies and International Development* 1(3): 86–8.

Mathur, P. (2005). 'Neither cited nor foundational: Niklas Luhmann's ecological communication: a critical exegesis and some theoretical suggestions for the future of a field.' *The Communication Review* 8(3): 329–62.

McAdam, D. (1999). Conceptal origins, current problems, future directions. *Comparative Perspectives on Social Movements: Political Opportunities, Mobilizing Structures, and Cultural Framings*. Eds D. McAdam, J. D. McCarthy and M. N. Zald. Cambridge: Cambridge University Press, 23–40.

McLuhan, M. (2002/1964). *Understanding Media*. London: Routledge.

McMillan, D. W. and D. M. Chavis (1986). 'Sense of community: a definition and theory.' *Journal of Community Psychology* 14(1): 6–23.

McNamee, Joe (EDRI) (2011). *The Slide from 'Self-regulation' to Corporate Censorship*. Brussels: EDRI.

Merrin, W. (2009). 'Media Studies 2.0.' *Interactions: Studies in Communication and Culture* 1(1): 17–34.

Meyrowitz, J. (1985). *No Sense of Place: the Impact of Electronic Media on Social Behavior*. New York: Oxford University Press.

Miller, D. and D. Slater (2000). *The Internet: an Ethnographic Approach*. Oxford and New York: Berg.

Ministry of Information Technology and Research (2000). *Realigning to a Network Society: IT and Telecommunications – Policy Report to Folketinget*. Copenhagen: Ministry of Information Technology and Research.

Morozov, E. (2011). *The Net Delusion: the Dark Side of Internet Freedom*. New York: PublicAffairs.

Morris, J. (2007). *MySpace.com: Political Economy and Social Network Sites*. Canadian Communication Associations annual conference, Saskatoon, Saskatchewan.

Mueller, M. L. (2002). *Ruling the Root*. Cambridge, MA: MIT Press.

Mueller, M. L. (2009). *ICANN, Inc.: Accountability and Participation in the Governance of Critical Internet Resources*. Syracuse: Syracuse University School of Information Studies. Internet Governance Project (IGP).

Mueller, M. L. (2010). *Networks and States: the Global Politics of Internet Governance*. Cambridge, MA: MIT Press.

Mueller, M. L., B. Kuerbis, et al. (2007). 'Democratizing global communication? Global civil society and the campaign for communication rights in the information society.' *International Journal of Communication* (1): 267–96.

Mueller, M.L., B. Kuerbis, et al. (2009). *Comments of the Internet Governance Project on the ICANN Transition*. Syracuse: Syracuse University School of Information Studies. Internet Governance Project (IGP).

Myers, K. S. (2006). 'Wikimmunity: fitting the Communications Decency Act to Wikipedia.' *Harvard Journal Of Law and Technology* 20(1): 163–208.

Naughton, J. (23 January 2011). 'Yet Another Facebook Revolution: Why Are We So Surprised?'. Retrieved 12 July 2011, from http://www.guardian.co.uk/technology/2011/jan/23/social-networking-rules-ok.

Netarkivet.dk (June 2005). 'Pligtaflevering af dansk materiale, offentliggjort på Internettet fra 1. juli 2005.' Retrieved 2 September 2011, from http://netarchive.dk/publikationer/vejledning.pdf.

Newman, J. (17–19 January 2012). 'SOPA and PIPA: Just the Facts.' *PCWorld*. Retrieved 10 November 2012, from http://www.pcworld.com/article/248298/sopa_and_pipa_just_the_facts.html.

Nissenbaum, H. (2007). Privacy in context. *Goodbye Privacy – Ars Electronica 2007*. Eds G. Stocker and C. Schöpf. Ostfildern-Ruit: Hatje Cantz Verlag, 39–44.

Norberto Gomes de Andrade (2010). 'Technology and metaphors: from cyberspace to ambient intelligence.' *Observatorio (OBS*) Journal* 4(1): 121–46.

Norris, P. (2001). *Digital Divide: Civic Engagement, Information Poverty, and the Internet Worldwide*. Cambridge and New York: Cambridge University Press.

OECD (1980). *OECD Guidelines on the Protection of Privacy and the Transborder Flows of Personal Data*. Paris: OECD.

OECD (2011a). *OECD Communiqué on Principles for Internet Policy-Making, Adopted at the OECD High Level Meeting on the Internet Economy June 28–29*. Paris: OECD.

OECD (2011b). *Communications Outlook 2011*, retrieved 20 August 2012, from http://www.keepeek.com/Digital-Asset-Management/oecd/science-and-technology/oecd-communications-outlook-2011_comms_outlook-2011-en.

OECD (Working Party on Information Security and Privacy) (2011c). *The Evolving Privacy Landscape: 30 Years after the OECD Privacy Guidelines*. Paris: OECD.

Office of the Privacy Commissioner of Canada (25 August 2009). 'Letter from OPC to CIPPIC Outlining its Resolution with Facebook.' Retrieved 2 May 2013, from http://www.priv.gc.ca/media/nr-c/2009/let_090827_E.asp.

Office of the United Nations High Commissioner For Human Rights (2006). *Frequently Asked Questions on a Human Rights-based Approach to Development Cooperation*. Geneva: United Nations.

Okello, D. (2007). 'Empowering Women through ICT: Enhancing Access to Information by Rural Women.' Retrieved 12 July 2011, from http://www.egovmonitor.com/node/14541.

Oldenburg, R. (1989). *The Great Good Place: Cafés, Coffee Shops, Community Centers, Beauty Parlors, General Stores, Bars, Hangouts, and How They Get You through the Day*. New York: Paragon House.

Oldenburg, R. (2001). *Celebrating the Third Place: Inspiring Stories about the 'Great Good Places' at the Heart of our Communities*. New York: Marlowe & Co.

Olsen, L., O. Rieper, et al. (2006). E-participation in local governance in Denmark. *Digital Governance://Networked Societies – Creating Authority, Community, and Identity in a Globalized World*. Eds H. Krause and J. Hoff. Copenhagen: Samfundslitteratur Press, 301–27.

On The Media (14 January 2011). '10 Years of Wikipedia: Transcript.' *On the Media*. Retrieved 2 September 2011, from http://www.onthemedia.org/2011/jan/14/10-years-of-wikipedia/transcript/.

OpenNet Initiative (30 September 2009). 'Uganda.' Retrieved 12 July 2011, from http://opennet.net/research/profiles/uganda.

O'Reilly, T. (2005). 'What is Web 2.0: Design Patterns and Business Models for the Next Generation of Software.' Retrieved 2 September 2011, from http://www.oreillynet.com/pub/a/oreilly/tim/news/2005/09/30/what-is-web-20.html.

Orgad, S. (2006). 'The cultural dimensions of online communication: a study of breast cancer patients' internet spaces.' *New Media and Society* 8(6): 877–99.

Ó Siochrú, S. (2004). 'Will the real WSIS please stand up? The historic encounter of the information society and the communication society.' *Gazette* 66(3/4): 203–24.

Ó Siochrú, S. and A. Alegre (2005). Communication rights. *Word Matters*. Eds A. Ambrosi and V. Peugeot. Caen: C & F Editions, 475–502.

Paccagnella, L. (1997). 'Getting the seats of your pants dirty: a methodology for ethnographic research on virtual communities.' *Journal of Computer-Mediated Communication* 3(1).

Palfrey, J. G. and U. Gasser (2008). *Born Digital: Understanding the First Generation of Digital Natives*. New York: Basic Books.

Papacharissi, Z. (2002). 'The virtual sphere.' *New Media and Society* 4(1): 9–27.

Papacharissi, Z. (2010). *A Private Sphere: Democracy in a Digital Age*. Cambridge, UK and Malden, MA: Polity.

Parayil, G. (2005). 'The digital divide and increasing returns: contradictions of informational capitalism.' *The Information Society: An International Journal* 21(1): 41–51.

Pariser, E. (2011). *The Filter Bubble: What the Internet is Hiding from You*. New York: Penguin Press.

Patry, W. F. (2009). *Moral Panics and the Copyright Wars*. New York: Oxford University Press.

Pelkonen J. and other members of the Assembly (27 June 2012). *The Right to Internet Access (Doc. 12985)*. Strasbourg: Council of Europe.

Pentzold, C. (2011). 'Imagining the Wikipedia community: what do Wikipedia authors mean when they write about their "community"?' *New Media and Society* 13(5): 704–21.

Peters, B. G. (2001). *The Future of Governing*. Lawrence: University Press of Kansas.

Peters, B. G. (2006). *American Public Policy: Promise and Performance*. Washington DC: Congressional Quarterly Press.

Pfeil, U., P. Zaphiris, et al. (2006). 'Cultural differences in collaborative authoring of Wikipedia.' *Journal of Computer-Mediated Communication* 12(1): 88–113.

Pieterse, J. N. (2006). 'Digital capitalism and development: the unbearable lightness of ICT4D.' *Incommunicado Reader.* Amsterdam: Institute of Network Cultures: 11–29.

Pollicino, O. and M. Bassini (2011). *Internet Law in the Era of Transition Law*. Florence: European University Institute.

Preece, J. and D. Maloney-Krichmar (2006). 'Online communities: design, theory, and practice.' *Journal of Computer-Mediated Communication* 10(4): 1–13.

Privacy International (9 June 2007). *A Race to the Bottom: Privacy Ranking of Internet Service Companies*. London: Privacy International.

Privacy International (5 November 2007). 'Regarding the Acquisition of Doubleclick by Google. Letter to EU Commissioner Neelie Kroes.' Retrieved 12 July 2011, from http://www.privacyinternational.org/issues/compliance/lettertocommissionerkroes.pdf.

Privacy International, Electronic Privacy Information Center, et al. (2010). 'European Privacy and Human Rights (EPHR) 2010.' Retrieved 12 July 2010, from https://www.privacyinternational.org/ephr.

Public Voice (3 November 2009). 'The Madrid Privacy Declaration – Global Privacy Standards for a Global World.' Retrieved 2 September 2011, from http://thepublicvoice.org/madrid-declaration/.

Qvortrup, L. (2003). *The Hypercomplex Society*. New York: P. Lang.

Raboy, M. and J. Schtern (2005). The Internet as a global public good: towards a Canadian position on Internet governance for phase II of WSIS. *Paving the Road to Tunis/WSIS II.* Ed. P. Dugré. Ottawa: Canadian Commission for UNESCO, 126–32.

Rafaeli, S., T. Hyatt, et al. (2008). Online motivational factors: incentives for participation and contribution in Wikipedia. *Psychological Aspects of Cyberspace: Theory, Research, Applications*. Ed A. Barak. Cambridge: Cambridge University Press, 243–67.

Rafaeli, S., T. Hayat, et al. (2009). Knowledge building and motivations in Wikipedia: participation as 'Ba'. *Cyberculture and New Media*. Ed. F. J. Ricardo. New York: Rodopi, 52–69.

Rasmussen, T. (2000). *Social Theory and Communication Technology*. Aldershot: Ashgate.

Rasmussen, T. (2003). On Distributed Society. *Digital Media Revisited: Theoretical and Conceptual Innovation in Digital Domains*. Eds G. Liestøl, A. Morrison and T. Rasmussen. Cambridge, MA: MIT Press, 443–67.

Rasmussen, T. (2007). *Kampen om Internett*. Oslo: Pax.

Rasmussen, T. (2008). 'The Internet and differentiation in the political public sphere.' *Nordicom Review* 2008(2): 73–83.

Ratzan, L. (2000). 'Making sense of the Web: a metaphorical approach.' *Information Research* 6(1).

Raymond, E. S. (2001). *The Cathedral and the Bazaar*. Cambridge, MA: O'Reilly Media.

Raynes-Goldie, K. (2012). *Privacy in the Age of Facebook: Discourse, Architecture, Consequences*. Perth, Australia: Curtin University. PhD thesis.

Reagle, J. M. (2010). *Good Faith Collaboration: the Culture of Wikipedia*. Cambridge, MA: MIT Press.

Rehof, L. A. (1999). Article 12. *The Universal Declaration of Human Rights: a Common Standard of Achievement*. Eds G. Alfredsson and A. Eide. The Hague: Martinus Nijhoff, 251–64.

Reid, E. (1999). *Hierarchy and Power: Social Control in Cyberspace*. London and New York: Routledge.

Rheingold, H. (1993). *The Virtual Community: Homesteading on the Electronic Frontier*. Reading, MA: Addison-Wesley.

Rheingold, H. (1999). A slice of life in my virtual community. *High Noon on the Electronic Frontier: Conceptual Issues in Cyberspace*. Ed. P. Ludlow. Cambridge, MA: MIT Press.

Ribes, D. and K. S. Baker (2007). *Modes of Social Science Engagement in Community Infrastructure Design.* Proceedings of Third International Conference on Communities and Technology. London: Springer.

Rifbjerg, S. (13 May 2011). 'Digital megafon.' *Weekendavisen*. Copenhagen.

Rigspolitiet (2006). Rigspolitiet, Samarbejdsaftale, 30 January 2006. Copenhagen.

Robbins, B. (1993). Introduction: the public and the phantom. *The Phantom Public*. Ed. B. Robbins. Minneapolis: University of Minnesota Press, vii–xxvi.

Rosaldo, M. and L. Lamphere (1974). *Women, Culture and Society*. Stanford: Stanford University Press.

Rosas, A. (1999). Article 21. *The Universal Declaration of Human Rights: A Common Standard of Achievement*. Eds. G. Alfredsson and A. Eide. The Hague: Martinus Nijhoff, 431–51.

Rössler, B. (2007). The value of privacy. *Goodbye Privacy – Ars Electronica 2007*. Eds G. Stocker and C. Schöpf. Ostfildern-Ruit: Hatje Cantz Verlag, 39–44.

Rytter, N. (9 March 2010). 'Undersøgelse: Netadgang er en menneskeret.' Retrieved 2 September 2011, from http://politiken.dk/tjek/digitalt/article919243.ece.

Sartor, G. and M. de Azevedo Cunha (2010). 'The Italian Google-case: privacy, freedom of speech and responsibility of providers for user-generated contents.' *International Journal of Law and Information Technology* 18(4): 356–78.

Scheinin, M. (1999). Article 20. *The Universal Declaration of Human Rights: A Common Standard of Achievement*. Eds G. Alfredsson and A. Eide. The Hague, Martinus Nijhoff, 417–29.

Scheinin, M. (2009). *Report of the Special Rapporteur on the Promotion and Protection of Human Rights and Fundamental Freedoms while Countering Terrorism. Martin Scheinin*. United Nations General Assembly, Human Rights Council.

Schulz, W. and T. Held (2001). *Regulated Self-Regulation as a Form of Modern Government*. Study Commissioned by the German Federal Commissioner for Cultural and Media Affairs, Interim Report. Hamburg, Germany.

SearchCIO (2011). 'ICT (information and communications technology – or technologies).' Retrieved 10 July 2011, from http://searchcio-midmarket.techtarget.com/definition/ICT.

Searls, D. (2010). 'The Net: Free Infrastructure for Speech, Enterprise and Assembly.' Retrieved 10 July 2011, from http://blogs.law.harvard.edu/doc/2010/01/13/the-net-free-infrastructure-for-speech-enterprise-and-assembly/

Sennett, R. and E. Zola (1976). *The Fall of Public Man*. New York: W. W. Norton.

Servaes, J., N. Carpentier, et al. (2006). *Towards a Sustainable Information Society: Deconstructing WSIS*. Bristol and Portland, OR: Intellect.

Shannon, C. E. and W. Weaver (1949). *The Mathematical Theory of Communication*. Urbana: University of Illinois Press.

Shirky, C. (2008). *Here Comes Everybody: the Power of Organizing without Organizations*. New York: Penguin Press.

Silver, D. (2000). Looking backwards, looking forward: cyberculture studies. *Web.studies: Rewiring Media Studies for the Digital Age*. Ed. D. Gauntlett. London: Arnold, 19–30.

Slevin, J. (2000). *The Internet and Society*. Malden, MA: Polity.

Smith, L. G. (1983). *Impact Assessment and Sustainable Recourse Management*. Harlow: Longman.

Smith, M. A. and P. Kollock (1999). *Communities in Cyberspace*. London: Routledge.

Snyder, D. (2007). 'The NSA's "General Warrants": How the Founding Fathers Fought an Eighteenth-century Version of the President's Illegal Domestic Spying.' Retrieved 2 September 2011, from http://www.eff.org/files/filenode/att/generalwarrantsmemo.pdf.

Socha, B. and B. Eber-Schmid (2012). 'What is new media?' Retrieved 10 November 2012, from http://www.newmedia.org/what-is-new-media.html.

Souter, D., ed. (2009). *The APC ICT Policy Handbook, 2nd edition*, Association for Progressive Communications.

Souter, D. (March 2012). *Human Rights and the Internet: A Review of Perceptions in Human Rights Agencies*. London: APC.

Spar, D. (1999). The public face of cyberspace. *Global Public Goods: International Cooperation in the twenty-first century*. Eds I. Kaul, I. Grunberg and M. A. Stern. New York: Oxford University Press.

Stalder, F. (2005). *Open Cultures and the Nature of Networks*. Novi Sad, Serbia: Futura publikacije.

Stalder, F. (2007). Our new public life, 2.0. *Goodbye Privacy*. Eds G. Stocker and C. Schöpf. Ostfildern: Hatje Cantz Verlag.

Stallman, R. M. (2002). *Free Software, Free Society: Selected Essays of Richard M. Stallman*. Boston, MA: Free Software Foundation.

Stefik, M. (1996). *Internet Dreams: Archetypes, Myths, and Metaphors*. Cambridge, MA: MIT Press.

Stern, de (5 December 2007). 'Wikipedia schlägt Brockhaus.' Retrieved 28 August 2011, from http://www.stern.de/digital/online/stern-test-wikipedia-schlaegt-brockhaus-604423.html.

Stone, A. R. (1991). Will the real body please stand up? Boundary stories about virtual cultures. *Cyberspace*. Ed. M. Benekikt. Cambridge, MA: MIT Press, 81–118.

Sunstein, C. R. (2006). *Infotopia: How Many Minds Produce Knowledge*. Oxford: Oxford University Press.

Sveningsson, M. E. (2005). Ungdomars köns- og identitetsarbete på Internet. *Kulturstudier i Sverige. National Forskerkonferens*. Eds B. Axelsson and J. Fornäs. Norrköping, Sweden: Linköping University Press.

Sveningsson, M. E. (2009). Question Three: How do various notions of privacy influence decisions in qualitative internet research? *Internet Inquiry: Conversations about Method*. Eds A. N. Markham and N. K. Baym. Thousand Oaks, CA: Sage Publications, 69–93.

Tække, J. (2006). *Mediesociografi*. Copenhagen, IT-University Copenhagen/ Innovative Communication (InC). PhD thesis.

Tambini, D., D. Leonardi, et al. (2008). *Codifying Cyberspace: Communications Self-regulation in the Age of Internet Convergence*. London and New York: Routledge.

Taylor, T. L. (2006). *Play Between Worlds: Exploring Online Game Culture*. Cambridge, MA: MIT Press.

Thagaard, T. (2004). *Systematic Approaches and Empathy. An Introduction to Qualitative Methods*. Copenhagen: Akademisk Forlag.

The White House (23 February 2012). *Consumer Data Privacy in a Networked World: A Framework for Protecting Privacy and Promoting Innovation in the Global Digital Economy*. Washington, DC: The White House.

Thompson, J. B. (1995). *The Media and Modernity: a Social Theory of the Media*. Cambridge: Polity Press.

Thorhauge, C. and P. Bjerge (2004). *It-boblen: da internettet rykkede vores verden*. Copenhagen: Børsen.

Tocqueville, A. de (1955/1856). *The Old Regime and the French Revolution*. Maine: Anchor.

Tönnies, F. (1887/1955). *Community and Association (Gemeinschaft und Gesellschaft)*. London: Routledge and Kegan Paul.

Tripp, A. M. (2010). *Museveni's Uganda: Paradoxes of Power in a Hybrid Regime*. Boulder, CO: Rienner.

Turkel, G. (1992). *Dividing Public and Private: Law, Politics, and Social Theory*. Westport, CT: Praeger.

Turkle, S. (1995). *Life on the Screen: Identity in the Age of the Internet*. New York: Simon & Schuster.

Uganda Human Rights Commission (2010). *The 13th Annual Report 2010*. Kampala: Uganda Human Rights Commission.

UNDP (1999). *Human Development Report 1999*. New York: Oxford University Press.

UNDP (2001). *A Human Rights-based Approach to Development Programming in UNDP – Adding the Missing Link*. Geneva: UNDP.

UNESCO (1976). *Recommendation on Participation by the People at Large in Cultural Life and their Contribution to It*. The General Conference of UNESCO meeting in Nairobi from 26 October to 30 November 1976. UNESCO.

UNESCO (2008). *UNESCO Medium-Term Strategy 2008–2013*. Paris: UNESCO.

United Nations (1997). Compilation of General Comments and General Recommendations adopted by Human Rights Treaty Bodies: Note by the Secretariat, 15 August 1997, 49–54.

United Nations (3 February 2011). 'Governments Must Pay More Attention to People's Voices – UN Experts.' Retrieved 25 August 2011, from http://www.humanrights-defenders.org/2011/02/governments-must-pay-more-attention-to-people%E2%80%99s-voices-%E2%80%93-un-experts/.

United Nations and Committee on Economic Social and Cultural Rights (2005). *General Comment No. 17: The Right of Everyone to Benefit from the Protection of the Moral and Material Interests Resulting from any Scientific, Literary or Artistic Production of which He Is the Author*. Geneva: United Nations.

United Nations General Assembly (31 January 2002). *Resolution Adopted by the General Assembly 56/183. World Summit on the Information Society*. New York: United Nations.

United Nations Human Rights Committee (8 April 1988). *General Comment No. 16: The Right to Respect of Privacy, Family, Home and Correspondence, and Protection of Honour and Reputation*. Geneva: OHCHR.

United Nations Human Rights Committee (12 July 1996). *General Comment No. 25: The Right to Participate in Public Affairs, Voting Rights and the Right of Equal Access to Public Service (Art. 25). CCPR/C/21/Rev.1/Add.7*. Geneva: OHCHR.

United Nations Human Rights Committee (12 September 2011). *General Comment No. 34 on Article 19: Freedoms of Opinion and Expression*. Geneva: United Nations.

United Nations Human Rights Council (21 March 2011). *Report of the Special Representative of the Secretary-General on the Issue of Human Rights and Transnational Corporations and other Business Enterprises. John Ruggie.* Guiding Principles on Business and Human Rights: Implementing the United Nations 'Protect, Respect and Remedy' Framework. New York: United Nations.

United Nations Human Rights Council (5 July 2012). *The Promotion, Protection and Enjoyment of Human Rights on the Internet*. A/HRC/20/L.13. Geneva.

United States Department of Commerce (5 June 1998). 'Statement of Policy on the Management of Internet Names and Addresses.' Retrieved 2 September 2011, from http://www.ntia.doc.gov/ntiahome/domainname/6_5_98dns.htm.

United States Department of Commerce and ICANN (30 September 2009). 'Affirmation of Commitments by the United States Department of Commerce and the Internet Corporation for Assigned Names and Numbers.' Retrieved 2 September 2011, from http://www.icann.org/en/documents/affirmation-of-commitments-30sep09-en.htm.

United States Department of State (2011). 'Background note: Uganda.' Retrieved 9 September 2011, from http://www.state.gov/r/pa/ei/bgn/2963.htm.

UPI (28 May 2011). 'Mubarak Fined for Internet Shutdown.' *UPI.com*. Retrieved 2 September 2011, from http://www.upi.com/Top_News/World-News/2011/05/28/Mubarak-fined-for-Internet-shutdown/UPI-28301306604342/.

Viégas, F., M. Wattenberg, et al. (2007). *Talk Before You Type: Coordination in Wikipedia*. 40th Annual Hawaii International Conference on System Sciences. HICSS 2007.

Viégas, F., et al. (2004). *Studying Cooperation and Conflict between Authors with History Flow Visualizations.* SIGCHI 2004.

Viskovatoff, A. (1999). 'Foundations of Niklas Luhmann's Theory of Social Systems.' *Philosophy of the Social Sciences* 29(4): 481–516.

Vitaliev, D. (2007). *Digital Security and Privacy for Human Rights Defenders*. Dublin: FrontLine.

Voss, J. (2005). *Measuring Wikipedia*. 10th International Conference of the International Society for Scientometrics and Infometrics, Stockholm.

Wagner, B. (July 2012). *After the Arab Spring: New Paths for Human Rights and the Internet in European Foreign Policy*. Strasbourg: European Parliament.

Webster, F. (2006). *Theories of the Information Society*. London: Routledge.

Weintraub, J. (1997). The theory and politics of the public/private distinction. *Public and Private in Thought and Practice*. Eds J. Weintraub and K. Kumar. Chicago: The University of Chicago Press, 1–42.

Westerwelle, G. (27 May 2011). 'Die Freiheit im Netz.' *Frankfurter Rundschau*. Retrieved 14 July 2011, from http://www.fr-online.de/politik/meinung/die-freiheit-im-netz/-/1472602/8496970/-/.

Wildermuth, N. (2010). Empowerment: the real challenge of digital inclusion. *Digital Content Creation: Creativity, Competence, Critique*. Eds K. Schrøder and K. Drotner. New York: Peter Lang, 267–86.

Winston, M. (2007). 'Human rights as moral rebellion and social construction.' *Journal of Human Rights* 6(3): 279–305.

Wolfe, A. (1997). Public and private in theory and practice: some implications of an uncertain boundary. *Public and Private in Thought and Practice: Perspectives on a Grand Dichotomy*. Eds J. A. Weintraub and K. Kumar. Chicago: University of Chicago Press.

Working Group on Internet Governance (2005). *Report of the Working Group on Internet Governance*. Geneva: United Nations.

World Summit on the Information Society (2003). *Declaration of Principles*. Geneva: WSIS.

World Summit on the Information Society (2005). *Tunis Agenda for the Information Society*. Tunis: WSIS.

WOUGNET (2006). *Annual Report 2006*. Kampala: Women of Uganda Network.

WOUGNET (October 2009). 'Newsletter.' Retrieved 10 July 2010, from www.wougnet.org.

WSIS Civil Society Plenary (2003). *Shaping Information Societies for Human Needs. Civil Society Declaration to the World Summit on the Information Society*. Geneva: WSIS.

Yin, R. K. (2009). *Case Study Research: Design and Methods*. Thousand Oaks, CA: Sage.

Yu, P. K. (2008). Challenges to the development of a human-rights framework for intellectual property. *Intellectual Property and Human Right*. Ed. P. L. C. C. Torremans. Alphen aan den Rijn: Kluwer Law International, 77–100.

Zittrain, J. (2009). *The Future of the Internet – and How to Stop It*. New Haven, CT: Yale University Press.

Cases

Abrams v. *United States*, 250 U.S. 616 (1919)
Ahmet Yıldırım v. *Turkey*, 18 December 2012, ECtHR
Amann v. *Switzerland*, 16 February 2000, ECtHR
Copland v. *The United Kingdom*, 3 April 2007, ECtHR
Handyside v. *The United Kingdom*, 7 December 1976, ECtHR
Kruslin v. *France*, 24 April 1990, ECtHR
Perrin v. *The United Kingdom*, 18 October 2005, ECtHR
Reno et al. v. *American Civil Liberties Union et al.*, 26 June 1997, US Supreme Court
SABAM v. *Scarlet Extended*, 24 November 2011, The Court of Justice of the European Union
United States v. *American Library Association*, 23 June 2003, US Supreme Court

EU Legislation

Directive on Data Protection (95/46 EC), 24 October 1995
Directive on E-Commerce (2000/31/EC), 8 June 2000
Directive on Copyright (2001/29/EC), 22 May 2001
Directive on Data Retention (2006/24/EC), 15 March 2006
Directive on Universal Service (2002/22/EC), amended 25 November 2009
Directive on Combating Sexual Abuse (2011/93/EU), 13 December 2011

International Covenants and Treaties

Charter of the Organization of American States 1948
Universal Declaration of Human Rights 1948
European Convention on Human Rights 1950
Convention on the Elimination of All Forms of Racial Discrimination 1965
International Covenant on Civil and Political Rights 1966
International Covenant on Economic, Social and Cultural Rights 1966
American Convention on Human Rights 1969
Convention on the Elimination of All Forms of Discrimination Against Women 1979
African Charter of Human Rights and Peoples' Rights 1981
Convention on the Protection of Individuals with Regard to Automatic Processing of Personal Data 1981

Convention Against Torture and Other Cruel, Inhuman or Degrading Treatment or Punishment 1984
Convention on the Rights of the Child 1989
Arab Charter on Human Rights 1994
WIPO Copyright Treaty 1996
Charter of Fundamental Rights of the European Union 2007
Convention on Cybercrime 2001
Treaty of Lisbon 2009

Glossary

Civil society Refers to the sphere of institutions, organizations and individuals located between the family, the state, and the market, in which people associate voluntarily to advance common interests (Anheier and Carlson 2002).

Commons Indicates a shared resource that is not owned privately but available to all members of a community (Stalder 2005).

Community Refers to a feeling that members have of belonging, a feeling that members matter to one another and to the group, and a shared faith that members' needs will be met through commitment to be together (McMillan and Chavis 1986).

Culture Addresses the integrated system of socially acquired values, beliefs, and rules of conduct that delimit the range of accepted behaviours in any given society (Columbia Encyclopedia 2008).

Empowerment Refers to a process whereby individuals gain strength, confidence, and vision to work for positive changes in their lives (Eade 1997).

Framing Addresses the construction of meaning, for example via metaphors, catchphrases, and visual images (Borah 2011).

Global public goods Refers to a benefit-providing utility that, in principle, is available to the global population (Binger 2003).

Information and communication technology (ICT) An umbrella term that includes any communication device or application, encompassing: radio, television, cellular phones, computers and network hardware and software, satellite systems and so on, as well as the various services and applications associated with them (SearchCIO 2011).

Information Society Refers to the political, economic, scientific, and social changes related to globalization and communication infrastructure. The term is often used to characterize the post-industrial era (Bell 1973).

Infrastructure The underlying foundation or basic framework of a system or organization (Frischmann 2012).

Internet Refers to a global information and communication system that is linked together via the TCP/IP protocol (Federal Networking Council Resolution 1995).

Media Refers to the range of tools that humans have used throughout history to communicate with each other about a shared reality (Bruhn Jensen 2008).

Mediated publicness Refers to a publicness, which is not linked to individuals' sharing of a common locale, but is linked to transmission of actions via the media (Thompson 1995).

Metaphor Refers to associational frameworks, enabling us to understand and experience one kind of thing in terms of another (Lakoff and Johnson 1980).

Opportunity Structure The factors that limit or empower collective actors, such as the group's access to political institutions (McAdam 1999).

Power Refers to the relational capacity that enables a social actor to influence asymmetrically the decisions of other social actor(s) in ways that favour the empowered actor's will, interests, and values (Castells 2009).

Public policy Refers to government activities, whether acting directly or through agents, that have an influence on the life of citizens (Peters 2001).

Public sphere A state-independent realm used to shape public issues (Habermas 1989).

Regulation Refers to a law, rule, or other order prescribed by authority, especially to regulate conduct (Dictionary.com 2011).

Self-regulation Refers to a process whereby private actors agree to rules regulating their activities, defined and enacted via codes of conduct (Schulz and Held 2001).

Index

access to information 40, 92, 147, 155, 169, 213
access to infrastructure 105, 154, 168
access to Knowledge (A2K) 47–8, 137
African Charter of Human Rights and Peoples' Rights 36
Amnesty International 44, 97
Anti-Counterfeiting Trade Agreement (ACTA) 48, 135
anti-terror 44, 61, 221
Arab Charter on Human rights 36
Arab Spring 44, 56, 85
Arab League Human Rights Committee 36
ARTICLE 19, 44–6
Association of Internet Researchers (AoIR) 123
Association for Progressive Communications (APC) 45, 105, 151–2, 176

Barlow, J. P. *see* Declaration of the Independence of Cyberspace
Benkler, Y. 81, 85, 122, 131–2, 181
biometrics 44
blogs 54, 84, 111, 172–3
business 33, 56–8, 95, 140, 171

Castells, M. 18–19, 23–4
Charter of Fundamental Rights of the European Union 35, 99
Charter of Human Rights and Principles on the Internet, Draft 51, 93
civil society 19, 43–9, 82–3, 89, 151–2, 170
Civil Society Advisory Committee (CSISAC) 47, 48
code of conduct 57–8
commons 124, 131–2
communication model 21–2, 116
Communication Rights in the Information Society (CRIS) 44, 46, 90
communication technology 17, 43, 54, 90, 145
community 123, 127–8, 134
Convention on the Elimination of All Forms of Racial Discrimination 35
Convention on the Rights of the Child 35
content regulation 113–17
contextual integrity 39
Council of Europe (CoE) 35, 49, 53–6, 74, 96, 105, 117–18
Creative Commons (CC) 138–9, 183, 210
cultural transmission 126, 134
culture, sharing 122, 129
cyberculture 122–4
cyber security *see* security
cyberspace 3, 7–8, 123, 128

Danish Institute for Human Rights 57
Danish blocking of content 115
data retention 102
data protection 38–9, 60, 76–7, 94, 100–3, 142
  data Protection, directive *see* EU Data Protection Directive
  Data Protection, Article 29 Working party 102, 142
Data Protection Agency (DPA) 119
Declaration of the Independence of Cyberspace 128
Deauville Declaration 2–3
democracy 19, 82, 85–6, 204, 222
digital divide 90
digital library *see* library
digital natives 122, 124
discrimination 14, 30, 35, 51

domain
domain, source 7–8
domain, target 6–8
domain, private 27, 39, 198
domain, public 27–9, 88–9, 96, 135, 139, 213
domain names 68–9, 71, 73, 76–9
domain name system (DNS) 68–71
Doubleclick 102–3

Electronic Frontier Foundation 28
Electronic Privacy Information Center (EPIC) 47
European Convention on Human Rights (ECHR) 35
European Court of Human Rights (ECtHR) 35, 54–5, 100
European Court of Justice 35, 99
European Digital Rights (EDRI) vii, 98–9
European Union (EU) 35, 99
EU Directive on Copyright 135
EU Directive on Data Protection 38
EU Directive on Data Retention 102
EU Directive on E-commerce 98, 100
EU Directive on Universal Service 92

Facebook 59, 95, 97, 140–1, 148
formation of identity 10, 19, 122, 125–6, 185
framing 6
Free and Open Source Software (FOSS) 129, 133
free culture 10, 128–9, 135, 138–9, 143
freedom of expression
freedom of expression, the right to 39–40
freedom of expression case law from ECtHR 55, 100
freedom of expression limitations 99
freedom of information 40–1, 96, 99, 100, 214

Garnham, N. 18, 82, 91, 116–17
gatekeepers 85, 93–5
global information highway 7, 79
Global Network Initiative 58
Google 58–9, 94–6, 100, 102–3

Habermas, J. 28, 34, 81–7

human rights
human rights activists 44, 102
human rights law 60, 74, 136–7
human rights protection 35, 59, 73–4, 216, 220
human rights standards 33, 36, 59, 61
human rights system 34–5
Human Rights Caucus 46, 50
Human Rights Watch 44, 97

ICANN 70–1, 73–6, 78
information age 112
information and communication technology (ICT)
ICT and development 52
ICT and capacity building 105, 164–5, 176–8
ICT and empowerment 147, 167
ICT and human rights 33, 37, 41–2, 47, 56, 60–2
ICT and public participation 86, 163
ICT policy 43, 45, 49–50, 53–4, 151
ICT sector 56, 58, 148, 222
information society 17–18, 23, 50, 53, 220
infrastructure, information 7–8, 17, 65
intellectual property rights 135–6
Inter-American Commission on Human Rights 36
International Bill of Human Rights 33–4, 50
International Covenant on Civil and Political Rights (ICCPR) 33, 37, 39–42, 99, 104
International Covenant on Economic, Social and Cultural Rights (ICESCR) 33, 136
International Telecommunication Union (ITU) 51, 66
internet
internet access 90–3, 168, 174
internet archive 118–19
internet blocking and filtering 97–9, 100, 114–16
internet censorship 44, 97, 102, 174
internet freedoms 3–4, 96–7, 174
internet governance 9, 50, 54, 66–7, 70
internet metaphor 6–10, 63, 224
internet policies 4, 116, 218, 222

Internet Governance Forum (IGF) 9, 51, 89, 105, 216

jurisdiction 54, 68, 71

Knowledge Ecology International 48

Lessig, L. 122, 128, 181
library 7, 92, 116, 119
liberal-economic model *see* public and private
Lisbon Treaty, 35
Luhmann, N. 20–4, 31, 91, 212

market 18, 27–8, 83, 93
market concentration 96
marketplace of ideas 7
media concentration 43
media evolution 108
medium 10, 23, 32, 107–9, 113, 117
metaphor 6–10, 63, 224
  metaphor, culture 122
  metaphor, infrastructure 66
  metaphor, medium 107
  metaphor, public sphere 82
multiple publics 87

national human rights institutions (NHRI) 36, 49, 222
net neutrality 75–6
new media 10, 107–9
New World Information and Communication Order (NWICO) 43

online collaboration 130–1, 176
online communities 123–5
open access (OA) 139
Organization for Economic Cooperation and Development (OECD)
  OECD Guidelines for Multinational Enterprise 57
  OECD Guidelines on the Protection of Privacy 77, 101

peer-production 124, 131–2
physical public spaces 29, 124
political community 27–8, 32, 85, 126, 131, 171
privacy
  privacy, informational 38–9
  privacy case law from ECtHR 55
  privacy, the right to 37–9, 61, 100–3, 118
Privacy International 101, 103, 141
privatized law enforcement 98
protection of children online 53, 113
public and private
  domains *see* domain
  distinction 25–6
  the feminist model 27, 30
  the liberal-economic model 27
  the republican model 27–8
  the sociability model 27–9
public as open 31–2, 112, 120
public debate 28, 40, 81, 87, 104–5, 175
public interest 25, 31–2, 42, 55
public life 25, 28, 32, 37, 83, 88
public participation 103–5
public sphere 81–6, 88, 94–5
public voice, the 47

republican model *see* public and private
right to communicate 46
right to freedom of association 41, 101, 104
right to freedom of peaceful assembly 41
right to take part in the conduct of public affairs 42, 104
rights-based approach 37, 49, 52
Ruggie, J. *see* UN Guiding Principles on Business and Human Rights
rule of law 74, 114

search engines 95–6
security 4, 9, 52, 54
self-regulation 98, 114–15, 134, 204
semi-private environment 29, 42, 118–19
semi-public environment 29, 42, 118–19
Seoul declaration 47
social change 6, 79, 84, 112, 142, 145
social life 29–30, 61, 141
social media 1–2, 112, 221–2

social network 19, 29, 118, 124, 126, 142
social systems 20–1, 176
soft law 35
Special Rapporteur *see* UN Special Rapporteurs
state administration 27, 35
surveillance 39, 55, 100–2

telecom sector 17, 52
Thompson, J.B. 31, 82, 110–11, 126
transparency 54, 75, 96, 103–4, 141

UN Special Rapporteurs 35, 42, 97
  La Rue, F. 52, 62, 92–3, 104
  Scheinin, M. 61, 101
UN Human Rights Council 35, 51, 57, 97, 216
Uganda case study
  collective bargaining 161, 166
  decision-making power 153, 171, 179
  fibre optic cable 168
  gender inequality 162, 171, 174
  knowledge fair 172, 178
  mailing list 151, 169, 170, 175
  political life 164
  rural women 151, 152, 173–4
  Women of Uganda Network (WOUGNET) 147, 149–51
United Nations Development Programme (UNDP) 51–2, 56, 72
United Nations Educational, Scientific and Cultural Organization (UNESCO) 43, 51–2, 105, 136
United Nations Guiding Principles on Business and Human Rights 57–8, 95, 222
Universal Declaration of Human Rights (UDHR) 33, 136

WHOIS database 76–7
Wikipedia case study
  German Wikipedia 181, 184, 186–8
  research on Wikipedia 183–4
  Wikipedia values 189–90
  Wikipedia editing system 198
  Wikipedia positions 208–9
  Wikipedia policies 207
  Wikipedia physical meetings 187, 211
  Wikipedia quality 184, 188, 190, 196, 201–2
World Summit on the Information Society (WSIS) 45–6
  WSIS, Geneva Declaration of Principles 50
  WSIS, Geneva Plan of Action 50